WATCH YOUR LANGUAGE!

WATCH YOUR LANGUAGE!

GRAMMAR, PUNCTUATION, SPELLING, VOCABULARY

Mary Ó Maolmhuire

GILL & MACMILLAN

Gill & Macmillan Ltd
Goldenbridge
Dublin 8
with associated companies throughout the world
www.gillmacmillan.ie

© Mary Ó Maolmhuire, 1999

0 7171 2824 5
Print origination in Ireland by Identikit

The paper used in this book is made from the wood pulp
of managed forests. For every tree felled, at least one tree is planted,
thereby renewing natural resources.

All rights reserved.
No part of this publication may be reproduced,
copied or transmitted in any form or by any means without written permission
of the publishers or else under the terms of any licence permitting limited copying issued
by the Irish Copyright Licensing Agency, The Writers' Centre,
Parnell Square, Dublin 1.

Contents

Introduction vii

UNIT 1	*Grappling with Grammar*	Nouns	1
	Punctuation Please!	Capital Letters and Full Stops	7
	How Do You Spell . . . ?	Spelling Rules OK! Plurals	13
	Words at Work	Word Formation	19

UNIT 2	*Grappling with Grammar*	Pronouns	24
	Punctuation Please!	Commas	30
	How Do You Spell . . . ?	Learning to Spell: Some Strategies	36
	Words at Work	Word Building	42

UNIT 3	*Grappling with Grammar*	Adjectives	49
	Punctuation Please!	Semi-colons and Colons	55
	How Do You Spell . . . ?	Decisions! Decisions! Spelling Traps	60
	Words at Work	Opposites Attract . . . Synonyms and Antonyms	65

UNIT 4	*Grappling with Grammar*	Adverbs	70
	Punctuation Please!	Question Marks and Exclamation Marks	75
	How Do You Spell . . . ?	Doubling Up: Double Letter Words 1	80
	Words at Work	Similes and Metaphors	85

UNIT 5	*Grappling with Grammar*	Verbs	90
	Punctuation Please!	Apostrophes	96
	How Do You Spell . . . ?	That Dumb Thumb! Silent Letter Words 1	102
	Words at Work	Colour Your Words: Idioms	107

CONTENTS

UNIT 6	Grappling with Grammar	The Past Tense 1	112
	Punctuation Please!	Quotation Marks	118
	How Do You Spell . . . ?	Prefixes and Suffixes	123
	Words at Work	Action Words	130
UNIT 7	Grappling with Grammar	The Past Tense 2	137
	Punctuation Please!	Dashes and Hyphens	142
	How Do You Spell . . . ?	Double Letter Words 2	148
	Words at Work	Words with Attitude	153
UNIT 8	Grappling with Grammar	Prepositions and Conjunctions	161
	Punctuation Please!	Brackets, Blobs and Dots	168
	How Do You Spell . . . ?	Silent Letter Words 2	174
	Words at Work	Words at Play: Puns, Proverbs and Quotable Quotes	180
UNIT 9	Grappling with Grammar	Reported Speech	187
	Punctuation Please!	All Of It: Challenge Time!	194
	How Do You Spell . . . ?	Confusing Words: Homonyms and Homophones	200
	Words at Work	Word Mix	206
UNIT 10	Bringing It All Together: Grammar, Spelling, Vocabulary		213

Introduction

'The limits of my language mean the limits of my world.'
LUDVIG WITTGENSTEIN

Correct and imaginative use of language is essential for good English. Yet many students experience difficulties in grammar, punctuation, spelling and vocabulary. They are generally very careless with punctuation, for example. They appear to know the rules but don't apply them in practice. Similarly, spelling is often a hit-or-miss affair, even though there are rules governing spelling, as there are for most things.

When our students write well, we say their language is 'colourful', 'vivid' or 'descriptive'. Yet, this kind of writing is rare, and as teachers we are constantly frustrated by our students' lack of vocabulary and needless and boring repetition. With grammar, too, we assume that our students are familiar with structures, tenses, parts of speech, etc. Yet, their written work often displays an ignorance of the basic rules and practices of good English.

This book comprises ten units, all of which (with the exception of Unit 10) contain four sections: grammar, punctuation, spelling and vocabulary. The book concentrates on the most important areas of language, and exercises them thoroughly. Actual explanations of grammatical elements, for example, are kept simple and to a minimum. The emphasis is on the word 'practice'. There are opportunities for oral class warm-ups and games, pair and groupwork activities, as well as lots of written work for the individual student. I have also provided a key for the teacher.

In grammar, punctuation and vocabulary, the exercises are progressive, in Stages 1 to 3. Students are encouraged to complete the exercises within a certain time limit. Stage 1 is broadly aimed at First and Second Year students. Stage 2 provides more challenging work, and Stage 3 exercises, although related directly to the Junior Cert. Higher and Ordinary Level exam, may also be used with a Transition Year group or Senior classes.

Each section within a unit is complete within itself, but may be used in conjunction with the other three. Personally, I feel that at least one period a week should be devoted to developing language skills. Alternatively, a module of language work, spanning a half-term, for example, could work well. However, even if time is a real constraint, this book contains many exercises that students may tackle themselves, without the direction of the teacher.

It is my firm belief that as students exercise their language skills, both orally and in writing, they will become aware, not only of how English works, but also of the practical benefits of expressing themselves clearly and precisely. At the same time, the 'Words at Work' sections, with their creative and functional writing exercises, will enlarge students' vocabulary, encourage them to explore words and their meanings, and exercise their imaginations.

Acquiring good language and communication skills will, of course, also provide a sound basis for Senior English work. Indeed, in the new English syllabus for Leaving Cert., the Department of Education and Science emphasises the importance of language skills:

> 'At both levels a competence in the accurate and appropriate use of language will be a fundamental requirement. **All students will be expected to be assiduous in their attention to paragraphing, syntax, spelling and punctuation.**'

I am convinced that exercising the language itself will result in a more confident and creative use of English by students. It will, of course, also enhance their performance in state exams. More importantly, however, they will be acquiring skills for life.

ACKNOWLEDGMENTS

For permission to reproduce copyright material grateful acknowledgment is made to the following:

Harper Collins Publishers for an extract from *Angela's Ashes* by Frank McCourt;

Minerva Press for an extract from *Paddy Clark Ha! Ha! Ha!* by Roddy Doyle;

The Harvill Press for 'What the Doctor Said' by Raymond Carver;

Faber and Faber Ltd for 'The Thickness of Ice' by Liz Loxley, an extract from *Dancing at Lughnasa* by Brian Friel and an extract from *The Power of Darkness* by John McGahern;

Colin Smythe Publishers for an extract from *The Whiteheaded Boy* by Lennox Robinson;

Jonathan Cape Ltd for 'Squaring Up' by Roger McGough;

James Kirkup for his poem 'The House at Night'.

Photos: Camera Press; Rex Features; Sporting Pictures (UK) Ltd.

UNIT 1

Grappling with Grammar

NOUNS

Question What is a noun?
Answer A noun is the name of:
- a person
- a thing
- a place
- a quality or emotion.

The word 'noun' comes from the Latin word 'nomen', meaning name. There are four kinds of nouns:

- common: student, burger, car, flower
- proper: Bart Simpson, Paris, Heinz Beans, August
- abstract: speed, energy, love, freedom
- collective: a **class** of students, a **flock** of sheep, a **bunch** of flowers, a **team** of footballers

Stage 1

Exercises

Classroom activities. Teacher directed. Oral and written.

A. **Common nouns** are 'common' to many persons, places and things. See examples given above.

1. Make a list of ten common noun objects in your classroom in under one minute. Start with the word 'chair'.

2. Compare your list with your neighbour's. Add to your own any of his/hers that you don't already have. Try to do this in under two minutes.
3. Ask the student beside you to tell you ten objects he/she has in his/her school **locker** in under one minute. Listen very carefully! Then, write down as many as you can remember in under one minute. He/she will time you and will check to see if you have them all.
4. Swop roles. This time you tell him/her ten objects you have in your **bedroom** at home. Your neighbour must write these down in under one minute as before. Then you check his/hers. The one who has remembered the most common noun objects wins!

B. **Proper nouns** name a particular person, place or thing. They are always written with a **capital letter**. See examples given above.
1. Write down the **first names only** of ten people in your class in 90 seconds.
2. Write down the names of ten towns or cities in Ireland in under 60 seconds. (Remember those capital letters!)
3. Ask your neighbour to name five brand name food or household items in under 30 seconds. You must write these down from memory in under 30 seconds also. Your neighbour will check to see if you have them all!
4. (Teacher): 'I will call out a **list of 20 common and proper nouns**. Listen carefully and write down only the **proper** nouns you hear.'

Now, swop copies with your neighbour and correct each other's work.

C. **Abstract nouns** are the names of qualities or emotions. These are things we cannot see or touch. See examples given above.
1. In pairs, write out a list of ten emotions in under three minutes. Your teacher will time you. Begin with the word 'love'.
2. Your teacher will now ask one student from each pair to call out their list. The other student pairs in the class will compare these with their own abstract nouns, and add to them any **new** ones they hear. At the end of this exercise you should have at least 20 abstract nouns each.
3. Underline the **abstract nouns only** in this list:
    happiness, restaurant, monster, guilt, humour, library, patience, beauty, stadium, scissors, disappointment, Germany, bicycle, sympathy, garden, friendship, wisdom, Tuesday, pride, youth

D. **Collective nouns** refer to a collection or group of people, animals or things. See examples given above.
1. Which collective noun would you use in the following phrases, instead of 'a lot'? The first letter of the word is given to you, as is the number of letters per word.

(a) a c____ of people (5)   (f) a l____ of pups (6)
(b) a f____ of ships (5)   (g) a b__ of musicians (4)
(c) a h__ of cattle (4)   (h) a f____ of birds (5)
(d) a s____ of beads (6)   (i) a h__ of bees (4)
(e) a g__ of thieves (4)   (j) a c_____ of stamps (10)

2. Match these collective nouns to the **common nouns** we usually associate with them.

   Example A pack of _____ : **wolves** or **cards**

   (a) a shoal of _____   (d) a clump of _____
   (b) a bunch of _____   (e) a set of _____
   (c) a plague of _____   (f) a board of _____

   Compare your answers with the student next to you. Remember there may be more than one common noun for each collective noun! Add any different ones to your own list.

3. Write five sentences of your own with the following collective nouns. Remember that you can use them with a number of different common nouns.

   Example pack: The story he told me was a pack of **lies**!
   or
   A pack of **hungry dogs** ran through a field of sheep.

   (a) bunch   (d) pack
   (b) litter   (e) collection
   (c) flock

Stage 2

Exercises

A. Common nouns

1. What is the common noun for someone who . . . ?
   (a) treats sick people   (f) designs buildings
   (b) writes for a newspaper   (g) studies the stars
   (c) investigates crime   (h) paints pictures
   (d) rides horses in a race   (i) cooks for a living
   (e) flies aeroplanes   (j) lends books

2. (a) Write two common nouns for each letter of the alphabet. Use your dictionary if you get stuck.

   Example A = apple, animal.

   Try to complete the exercise in under 25 minutes — 30 seconds per word!

   (b) Using at least 30 of the common nouns on your list, write a short continuous piece, in prose or dialogue, in which each word is used just once. (100–120 words)

3. (a) Study the pictures of 40 common household items (and pets!) on the next page for three minutes. Your teacher will time you.

WATCH YOUR LANGUAGE!

(b) Cover the page.

(c) Write out as many of the objects from memory as you can in under five minutes. (Remember to write them all with a **small** letter!) The student who remembers the most items wins!

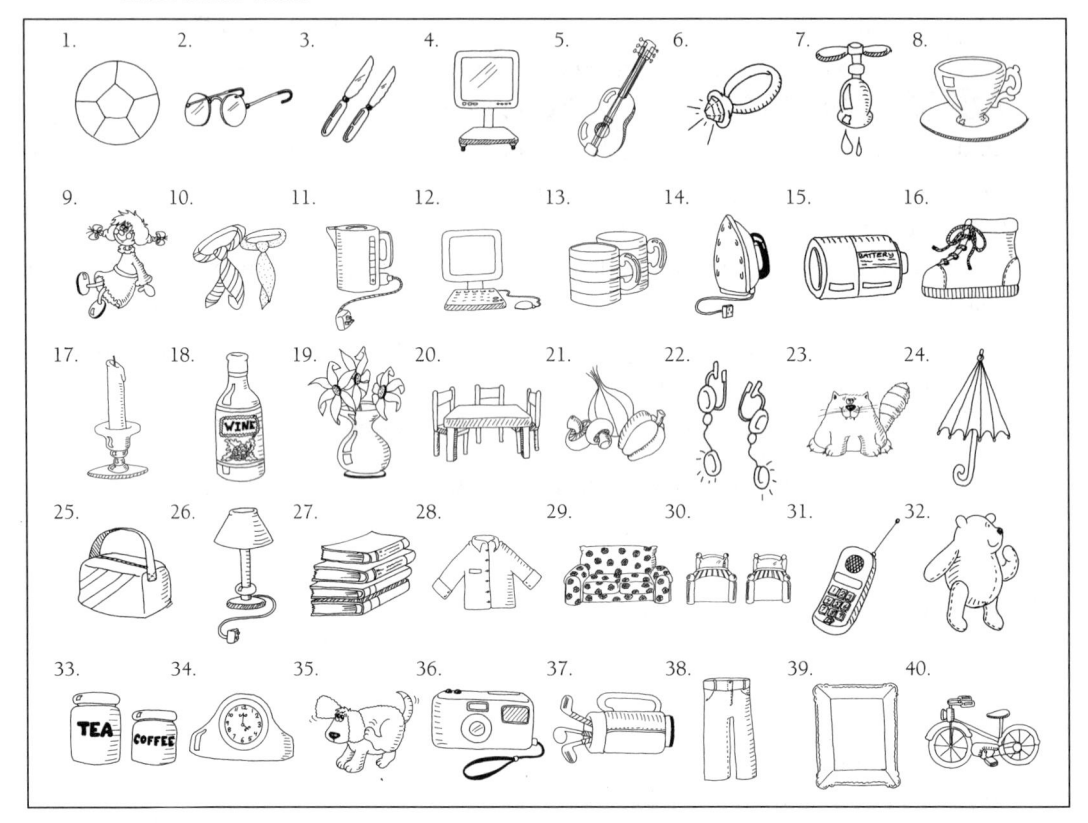

1.	2.	3.	4.	5.	6.	7.	8.
9.	10.	11.	12.	13.	14.	15.	16.
17.	18.	19.	20.	21.	22.	23.	24.
25.	26.	27.	28.	29.	30.	31.	32.
33.	34.	35.	36.	37.	38.	39.	40.

B. Proper nouns

1. Underline all the proper nouns in the following passage:

    Roddy Doyle was born in Dublin in 1958. He taught English and Geography at Greendale Community School, Kilbarrack, in north Dublin. His first play, *Brownbread*, was produced in Dublin in 1987. His first novel, *The Commitments*, was published in 1988, and made into a film by Alan Parker. His second novel, *The Snapper*, was published in 1990. *The Van* was shortlisted for the Booker Prize in 1991, and *Paddy Clarke Ha Ha Ha* actually won it in 1993.

2. Answer the following questions with proper nouns. (Don't forget those **capital** letters!)

    (a) Who is your favourite Irish league soccer team?

    (b) What is their home ground called?

    (c) Name three teams they have played this season?

    (d) What is the name of their manager?

    (e) Who is their best player?

    (f) Who is your favourite group or band?

GRAMMAR: NOUNS

   (g) What are the full names of the members of the group or band?
   (h) Where do they come from?
   (i) What countries have they played in?
   (j) What is the name of their biggest selling hit?
3. (a) Here are some faces from the world of TV, music and film. Who are they? You must give their **full** names.
   (b) Choose one star, and write a brief profile of his/her life and career, using as many proper nouns as possible. (100–120 words)

C. **Abstract nouns**
1. Give the abstract nouns corresponding to the following adjectives:

   Example   mad — madness

   (a) sane   (f) cruel
   (b) shy   (g) vain
   (c) gentle   (h) proud
   (d) exciting   (i) humble
   (e) wise   (j) true

2. Write one sentence for each of these ten abstract nouns which clearly illustrates its meaning.

   Example   It's madness to go out without a coat in that rain!

3. Fill in the gaps in the following passage with a suitable abstract noun from the box below. The number of letters is indicated in each case.

   humour, excitement, generosity, madness, patience, sanity, caution, guilt, truth, happiness

   Christmas is a time of unrivalled _____ (7) as far as shopping is concerned. In the _____ (10) of the days leading up to the big event, we all lose our _____ (6) and spend, spend, spend. No one seems to feel the least ____ (5) at the prospect of

WATCH YOUR LANGUAGE!

having an enormous overdraft in the New Year, and even the most crotchety neighbour appears to have a sense of _____ (6). 'It's all for the kids,' we say. The smiles on their faces when they open their presents on Christmas morning are worth every penny. We have no _____ (8) with those who say we should exercise _____ (7). The ____ (5) of the matter is, Christmas is the one time of the year when everyone, even the least fortunate, experiences a little _____ (9). And after Christmas, we can always rely on the _____ (10) of our friendly bank manager, can't we?

D. Collective nouns

1. Fill in the blanks in the following sentences with a suitable collective noun from the box below:

   nest, suite, hum, board, litter, bunch, swarm, ray,
   bouquet, hordes, block, chain, canteen, wad, pile

   (a) The _____ of directors decided to go ahead to build a 20 storey _____ of flats and a _____ of shops.
   (b) When Denis and Aileen got married, they got a ____ of tables from Gran, and a _____ of cutlery from Uncle John.
   (c) When really famous bands visit Dublin, they don't just book a room in a hotel, they book a ____ of rooms.
   (d) A ____ of sunlight lit up the corner of her drab room.
   (e) What a lovely _____ of puppies!
   (f) The film star took a ___ of notes from his wallet, and tipped the waiter £100.
   (g) It was easy to speak privately in the restaurant as the ___ of conversation from those around us completely drowned out our words.
   (h) _____ of tourists visit our town every year, especially Americans.
   (i) He was a romantic. He brought her a _____ of flowers, a ____ of grapes, and a huge ____ of magazines when she was ill.
   (j) She was badly stung by a ____ of bees while on holiday in Spain.

2. Write out these sentences, choosing the most suitable collective noun from those in brackets:
   (a) The bus slowed down behind a (party, herd, clump) of cattle.
   (b) On Valentine's Day, Tom bought a huge (packet, bunch, bundle) of flowers for his girlfriend.
   (c) Mum has bought a new (case, set, pack) of luggage for her holidays.
   (d) Gran says that she will leave me her antique (collection, group, chest) of drawers.
   (e) Sally, our dog, had her (pile, litter, stack) of pups in the garage.

3. Write a sentence of your own for each of the two words you rejected from the sentences in Exercise 2.

   Example (a) The soldier hid behind a **clump** of trees.

PUNCTUATION: CAPITAL LETTERS AND FULL STOPS

Stage 3

EXERCISES

The exam. Personal writing.

This photograph is taken from the 1997 Junior Cert. Higher Level Paper 1.

1. What emotions is the child experiencing in this picture? Make a short list of abstract nouns that might fit those emotions.
2. Put yourself inside the head of the little girl. Write a prose composition, which might begin with the question: 'Who do you think you're looking at, Mister?!' You are, of course, free to use your own starting sentence. Try to include as many different types of nouns as possible from this unit, also.

Punctuation Please!

CAPITAL LETTERS AND FULL STOPS

Question When do we use capital letters?

Answer
1. For **names** of:
    - people (Mary, Paul, Bono)
    - countries (Ireland, France, USA)
    - cities (Dublin, Cork, Paris)
    - rivers (Slaney, Liffey, Amazon)
    - months, days (March, Friday)
    - brand names (Cadbury's, Kelloggs, Nescafé)
    - books, films (*The Van*, *Star Wars*)
    - football teams (Manchester United, Shamrock Rovers).
2. For the **first** word in direct speech: '**G**et up now!' roared Mum.
3. At the **beginning** of a sentence: **W**e hate Monday mornings.

Question When do we use full stops?

Answer
1. When you want to mark the **end** of a **sentence**: 'Before you meet your handsome prince, you have to kiss a lot of frogs.'
2. After **initials**: M. C. Moore, P. J. Lynch.
3. After words that have been **abbreviated** (shortened): Mon. Feb. St. Dr.

WATCH YOUR LANGUAGE!

Question Why do we use full stops?
Answer
1. Full stops help the reader to **make sense** of what you are writing.
2. Full stops show that you have **finished** a point you have been making.
3. Full stops allow the reader to **pause** for a moment, in order to **think about** what you've just written.

Stage 1

Exercise 1
1. Write down the full names (first name and family name) of five film stars or sports heroes in under one minute. Swop copies with the student beside you. Correct each other's exercise, giving two marks per name — but **only** if capital letters are used for **both** names.
2. Write down the names of ten products advertised on TV in under one minute.
3. Write one sentence per product, describing what it is or does.

Exercise 2
1. **In pairs**, write one **amusing** sentence with a full stop at the end. (Time limit: 90 seconds)
2. One student from each pair then reads their sentence out loud to the whole class.
3. Students must write down all the sentences they hear, **highlighting** the full stop at the end in each case.
4. 'Today is Saturday. This is Sara's/Tom's favourite day. . . .' Continue the story for eight more sentences. Each sentence must begin with a capital letter and end with a full stop. It should also include **one** other capital letter word. Try to write a **completed** story (a mini-saga) within the ten-sentence exercise.

Exercise 3
Abbreviations
1. Write out the following with **full stops** and **capital letters**:

mr s t murphy	st anthony	dr b ryan
td	man united	usa
rte	gaa	merrion sq
park ave	o'connell st	ms g gibbs
taney rd	sr agnes	mrs p tancred
la law	o j simpson	b b king
madison ave	d j carey	

2. Write the following in **abbreviated** form:

County Galway	Reverend Smith	Lansdowne Road
Professor Martin	Parnell Square	County Cork
General Michael Collins	Automobile Association	Patrick Street
Mister Sean Browne	Federal Bureau of Investigation	

PUNCTUATION: CAPITAL LETTERS AND FULL STOPS

Doctor Sheila Conlon   General Post Office   County Cavan
Saint Brigid's Church   Prime Minister   Teachta Dála
Bachelor of Science   Bachelor of Commerce   Bachelor of Arts

Exercise 4
Odd Man Out! Remember! In each of the following groups, only **two** words should start with a capital letter. Write these down. Do not write down the other words.
1. thomas, woman, boy, jennifer, man
2. galway, country, australia, place, land
3. atlantic, sea, river, alps, mountain
4. hour, spring, october, month, april
5. irish, language, buddhism, religion, church
6. energy, peter, angry, woman, london
7. pupils, spain, cautious, austria, city
8. canada, pepper, liffey, science, week
9. mother, america, rupert, cheese, ocean
10. madrid, county, vegetable, bicycle, raleigh

Stage 2

Exercise 1
Rewrite the following sentences with **capital letters** where necessary and **full stops** at the end. Don't rush it! Write carefully.
1. the film starts at eight o'clock
2. my pen-friend lives in paris
3. i read an article about the spice girls in *bliss* magazine
4. the most common surname in the world is chang
5. birds sing
6. a young italian boy wrote 500 letters to his girlfriend but she married the postman
7. school is boring but so is the telly sometimes
8. when i really concentrate i can do this
9. i bet man united will win this weekend
10. friday is my favourite day of the week

Exercise 2
Classroom exercise, in pairs.
1. (a) Choose a partner.
   (b) Within a time limit of ten minutes, write nine sentences, beginning with a sentence of just two words, then one with three words, then four, and so on until you get to sentence number nine which, of course, should have ten words in it! Remember those **capital letters** at the beginning and **full stops** at the end of each sentence.
2. Exchange your sentences with another pair of students from the class, and **check** theirs for capital letters and **full stops**. Award two marks per sentence for correct punctuation, making a total of eighteen marks in all.

WATCH YOUR LANGUAGE!

Exercise 3
Your teacher will give you a time limit of ten minutes for stages 1–4 of this exercise.
1. Open your textbook at any page on which there is a **short story** or an extract from a **novel**.
2. Choose a passage of 5–6 lines (wherever a **sentence stops**).
3. Write the passage into your copybook, **leaving out** all the **full stops** and **capital letters**.
4. Make a note in the margins of your copy of the **page** of your textbook in which you found the passage.
5. Close your textbook.
6. Exchange copybooks with your neighbour.
7. **Replace** as many **full stops** and **capital letters** in your neighbour's passage as you feel are necessary. (Time limit: five minutes.)
8. Exchange copybooks again. You now have your **own** passage back **with** full stops and capital letters. But are they correct?
9. Now, open your textbook, and correct the passage. (Time limit: five minutes.)

Exercise 4
Capital letter quiz

Individual exercise for class or homework, or as a table quiz in the class, with a time limit set by the teacher of perhaps 20–25 minutes. Remember! All the answers must be written with a **capital letter**!

1. Write down the names of all six characters in the TV series *Friends*.
2. Which team won the English FA Cup Final in 1998?
3. What are the capital cities of France, Spain, Italy and Germany?
4. Name all the members of the Simpson family.
5. Which chocolate company sponsors *Coronation Street*?
6. Name five major supermarket chains in Ireland.
7. Write the titles of five books that have been made into films.
8. Which month has the fewest number of days?
9. Which county won the All Ireland Hurling Final in 1996?
10. Complete the following advertising slogans:
    (a) '_____ is good for you.'
    (b) 'A ____ a day helps you work, rest and play.'
    (c) 'Beanz _____ _____.'
11. Who won three gold medals for Ireland in the 1996 Olympics?
12. Which female singer starred in the film *The Bodyguard*?
13. Write the first names of all five members of the group Boyzone.
14. Name five brand labels of sports gear.

PUNCTUATION: CAPITAL LETTERS AND FULL STOPS

15. In which major cities would you find the following?
    (a) Eiffel Tower
    (b) Vatican
    (c) Empire State Building
    (d) Oxford Street
    (e) Old Trafford
16. Name five mountain ranges in Europe.
17. Complete each of the following statements with a word beginning with a capital letter:
    (a) '____ that door!'
    (b) '____ till your father gets home!'
    (c) '____ me up, Scottie.'
    (d) '____, Romeo, wherefore art thou, Romeo?'
    (e) '____ up, Doc?'
18. Name five TV series with a one-word title.
19. Name five animal characters from books, magazines, cartoons or films.
20. On which days of the week do you usually do the following?
    (a) Watch *Coronation Street*
    (b) Go to a disco
    (c) Go to church
    (d) Eat pancakes
    (e) Pig out!

Stage 3

Exercise 1

Rewrite the following passages, putting in all the necessary **full stops** and **capital letters**:

1. he sat back a sense of complete helplessness had descended upon him to begin with, he did not know with any certainty that this was 1984 it must be around that date, since he was fairly sure that his age was thirty-nine, and he believed that he had been born in 1944 or 1945; but it was never possible nowadays to pin down any date within a year or two
   (from *1984* by George Orwell)
2. the story was quickly told eight years before, johnny fontane had been extraordinarily successful he had been singing with a popular dance band he had become a top radio attraction unfortunately the band leader, a well-known show business personality named les halley, had signed johnny to a five-year personal services contract it was a common show business practice les halley could now loan johnny out and pocket most of the money
   (from *The Godfather* by Mario Puzo)
3. years later éamon and i were together with other irish representatives in st john's, newfoundland; he was telling his stories in a thronged hall in the university, i was lecturing on peig sayers and the blasket islands in the audience i noticed a group of young inuit or 'eskimos', surely the first of their race to attend university they were gazing up at the stage in wide-eyed wonder as if éamon has descended from outer space suddenly on a throwaway phrase or gesture on éamon's part the inuit group fell apart in uncontrolled laughter; probably some old inuit of their acquaintance resembled the character éamon was portraying the irish art of storytelling was seen to transcend the boundaries of tribe, time and space
   (from *The Master* by Bryan MacMahon)

WATCH YOUR LANGUAGE!

Exercise 2

1. Here are some 'Television Highlights' from *The Irish Times*. I have removed all the capital letters. Can you replace them?
   (a) the woman in white (bbc1, 8:50pm). two part adaptation of the novel by wilkie collins, starring tara fitzgerald and ian richardson. the appearance of a mysterious woman dressed in white sparks off a tale of crime, passion and intrigue. part two can be seen tomorrow.
   (b) fantasy schedule (c4, 8:00pm). this sunday evening of programmes voted for by viewers opens with the brookside episode in which jimmy and eddie make a grim discovery under mandy's patio. also included is a father ted episode and melvyn bragg's interview with the late dennis potter.
2. Can you write a 'Television Highlights' style article of your own? Include the following:
   (a) The name of the programme, channel and time of transmission.
   (b) The actor(s)/presenter(s) involved in the programme.
   (c) A brief summary of what it's about. (50–70 words)
   (d) The reason(s) why you, the critic, would recommend this programme to the viewer. (50–70 words)

Exercise 3

The exam. (1996 Junior Cert. Higher Level, Paper 2, Section 3, Fiction)
Here is the opening extract from this section. I have removed all the full stops and capital letters, but all the other punctuation is correct.

1. Write the extract into your copy (without looking at the exam paper, of course!), putting in full stops and capital letters where necessary.
2. Having completed this task, consult the exam paper (or ask your teacher), in order to check how correct your punctuation is.

> she was waiting for them as soon as they opened the door
> her face was tragic it was drawn and pale and the eyes were staring from her head she just got up from the stool and riveted her eyes on her son tommy and stood there and then came forward and took him into her arms the room door above the fireplace opened and micil, their father, came down wearing a shirt and trousers and his big feet bare, and you could see the very white of his skin just below where the neck of his jersey ended it was like a pillow case left on a mahogany chest
> 'so yeer back!' that was big micil with a sigh at the end of it
> delia's hand had gone up to her son's forehead she started then and pushed him out from her to look into his eyes
> 'you're hot,' she said 'your forehead is hot what happened to ye? where were ye?'
> tommy didn't answer it was mico who answered standing exactly where he stood when he came in, the water dripping from his clothes and body, making pools of wet on the concrete floor he told the story in a few sentences she came away from her oldest

SPELLING: PLURALS

son then and she approached mico on her bare feet and her eyes blazing she raised her right hand and swung it high and she brought the back of it in a stinging crack against the good side of mico's face he had been expecting it and his eyes didn't blink, or his body move out of position, and she raised it again and she hit him again and she raised it a third time, but before it could fall big micil caught it in his fist and held it and threw it roughly away

'that's enough now,' he said 'that's enough now, i'll have no more'

How Do You Spell . . . ?

SPELLING RULES OK! PLURALS

Rule 1
Most words just add 's' to make the plural:

word — **words**   book — **books**
teacher — **teachers**   parent — **parents**

Exercise 1
Write the plurals of the following nouns:
1. friend _____
2. student _____
3. brother _____
4. sister _____
5. chocolate _____
6. burger _____
7. star _____
8. film _____
9. pet _____
10. dog _____

Exercise 2
Now write a short paragraph (50–70 words) **connecting** all of the above words in some way and using them in the plural only. Begin like this: 'John/Sheila Ryan had lots of **friends**. . . .'

Rule 2
Words ending in a vowel (a, e, i, o, u) **and** 'o' add 's' also:

radio — **radios**   video — **videos**   stereo — **stereos**

Exercise 1
Write one sentence for each of the above words, using the plural form of the word only in each case.

Exercise 2
'Why do people watch horror videos?' Write a paragraph of 100–120 words which attempts to answer this question, using the plural form of the word **at all times**.

WATCH YOUR LANGUAGE!

Rule 3
But! Words ending in a consonant (all other 21 letters of the alphabet — b, c, d, f, g . . .) **and** 'o' add '**es**' in the plural:

    hero — hero**es**   potato — potato**es**

Exercise 1
Here are six words ending in a consonant and 'o':

hero, echo, motto, potato, tomato, volcano

Fill in the blanks in the following sentences with the plural form of a word from the list above:
1. 'Don't worry. Be happy' and 'Smile and the world smiles with you' are good _____ for life.
2. The actor was so bad, the audience threw rotten _____ at him.
3. There are _____ of her childhood on every page.
4. _____ are common in Italy.
5. Hercules and Andromeda were _____ in ancient Greece.
6. Tommy Murphy eats a ton of _____ with his dinner!

Exceptions: Watch out for these!

    solo — solos   piano — pianos   halo — halos

Exercise 2
Write one **question-style** sentence for each of the words in Exercise 1 **and** the three exceptions, using the plural form of the word only.

Example   Do they really have two pianos in their house?
                Are there any volcanoes in Ireland?

Rule 4
Words ending in a consonant **and** 'y' change the 'y' to 'i' **and** add '**es**':

    baby — bab**ies**   lorry — lorr**ies**

Exercise 1
Write the following words in the plural:
1. country _____
2. secretary _____
3. hurry _____
4. study _____
5. try _____
6. spy _____
7. lady _____
8. ferry _____
9. opportunity _____
10. penny _____

Exercise 2
Write a short piece of **dialogue** (100–150 words) in which each of these words is used once only, in the **plural**. Begin like this:

    Tom: You want to visit other **countries**? Why?
    Mary: Because I . . .

SPELLING: PLURALS

Rule 5
Words ending in a vowel **and** 'y' **keep** the 'y' and add 's':
    play — plays   boy — boys

Exercise 1
Write the following words in the plural:
1. chimney _____
2. tray _____
3. holiday _____
4. day _____
5. key _____
6. valley _____
7. toy _____
8. trolley _____
9. monkey _____
10. storey _____

Exercise 2
Write one **negative** sentence for each of these words, using the plural form.
Example   I haven't seen Siobhan for **days**.

Rule 6
Most words ending in 'f' or 'fe' **drop** the 'f' or 'fe' and add 'ves':
    half — hal**ves**   wi**fe** — wi**ves**   loaf — loa**ves**

Exercise 1
Write the plurals of these words:
1. thief _____
2. yourself _____
3. calf _____
4. leaf _____
5. scarf _____
6. wolf _____
7. life _____

Exceptions: Watch out for the following words ending in 'f'. They add 's' in the plural:

chief	chief**s**
handkerchief	handkerchief**s**
cliff	cliff**s**
cuff	cuff**s**
belief	belief**s**

Learn these!

Exercise 2
Write six sentences in which **two** of the words from Exercise 1 or the exceptions are used in each sentence in the **plural** form only.
Example   The **thieves** stole a container of **scarves**, believing it to be full of expensive furs.

WATCH YOUR LANGUAGE!

Rule 7

Words ending in 's', 'x', 'z', 'ch', 'sh' or 'ss' add 'es' in the plural:

bus	bus**es**
fox	fox**es**
waltz	waltz**es**
ben**ch**	ben**ches**
brush	brush**es**
class	class**es**

Exercise 1

Write the following words in the plural:
1. dish _____
2. glass _____
3. six   _____
4. watch _____

Exercise 2

Answer the following questions with a complete sentence, using a suitable word from Rule 7 and Exercise 1 in the plural form only.
1. What sort of food do you like to cook?
2. Doesn't Tony wear contact lenses?
3. Are trains the only means of transport in your area?
4. Which dances were most popular at the turn of the century?
5. What did you buy for the garden?
6. Which numbers are difficult to throw on a dice?
7. What are the Swiss famous for?
8. Which animals and are often hunted for their tails?
9. What do artists and house painters have in common?
10. What do many schools run at night time during the winter?

Rule 8

Some words **do not change** at all in the plural:
- fish words — salmon, herring, trout, cod, ray
- the following — deer, sheep, aircraft, series, species, buffalo, giraffe, pheasant, swine

Exercise 1

Write one **negative** sentence for each of the fourteen words above, using the plural form only.

> Example   Some **species** of animals are still **not** respected by man.

Exercise 2

Choose ten of the fourteen words above and write a sentence for each that **disagrees** with the negative statement made in Exercise 1, as in a debate.

> Example   I believe that we have a healthy respect for all **species** of animals.

SPELLING: PLURALS

Rule 9
Some words have **no singular form**. They can only be used in the plural:

shorts	jeans
measles	scissors
police	cattle
belongings	dregs
outskirts	pliers

Exercise 1
Fill in the blanks in the following sentences with a word from the list above which is used only in its **plural** form. The first letter is given to you.
1. When cutting out a pattern, you need a sharp s_____.
2. Sheila knew she wouldn't get the nail out without a p____.
3. Tom will only wear Levi j____.
4. Uncle Peter looks really funny in s____, because his legs are so skinny.
5. She gathered up all her b_____ in a black sack, and trudged off down the street.
6. The p____ arrested him at six o'clock.
7. Mr. Ryan's c____ strayed onto the main road, and two were killed.
8. Poor Susan! She picked up the m_____ from her little brother.
9. The old man stared into the d____ of his drink, wishing the glass were full again.
10. There is a large graveyard on the o_____ of the village.

Exercise 2
'Teenagers are snobs. They will only buy designer jeans.'
You have been asked to debate this topic in the next issue of the school newsletter. Write about 200 words either for or against the motion, including words that can **only** be used in their **plural form**, where possible.

Rule 10
Some words **change quite a lot** in the plural. We call these **irregular** plurals. They don't appear to follow any rule, but you will be familiar with many of them already:

    foot — feet   man — men   mouse — mice

Exercise 1
Write the plural of the following words:
1. child   _____
2. tooth   _____
3. woman   _____
4. louse   _____
5. goose   _____
6. ox   _____

WATCH YOUR LANGUAGE!

Exercise 2

Dialogue

Pat: *What's wrong with those children at all?*

Mary: *Oh, that's right, blame me! — or your mother. If you ask me, nobody listens to the women in this house, anyway.*

Continue the dialogue between Pat and Mary, using the words given in Rule 10 and Exercise 1 just once each.

SUMMARY

Rule 1. Most words add 's' (student — students).
Rule 2. Words ending in a vowel **and** 'o' add 's' too (video — videos).
Rule 3. Words ending in a consonant **and** 'o' add 'es' (hero — heroes).
Rule 4. Words ending in a consonant **and** 'y' change the 'y' to 'i' and add 'es' (baby — babies).
Rule 5. Words ending in a vowel **and** 'y' keep the 'y' and add 's' (play — plays).
Rule 6. Most words ending in 'f' or 'fe' drop the 'f' or 'fe' and add 'ves' (wife — wives).
Rule 7. Words ending in 's', 'x', 'z', 'ch', 'sh' or 'ss' add 'es' (bus — buses, fox — foxes).
Rule 8. Some words don't change at all (salmon, deer, sheep).
Rule 9. Some words have no singular form (jeans, scissors).
Rule 10. Some words are totally irregular (foot — feet, man — men).

And finally . . . test yourself! A 'mixed bag' exercise.

Re-read and study **all the rules** before you attempt this last exercise, as your knowledge of the rules is being tested here. Your teacher will set a time limit of 20 minutes for this task. Good luck!

Write the plural of each of the following words:

1. loaf _____
2. piano _____
3. pony _____
4. pheasant _____
5. bus _____
6. giraffe _____
7. chief _____
8. valley _____
9. ox _____
10. potato _____
11. fact _____
12. baby _____
13. church _____
14. child _____
15. wife _____
16. light _____
17. factory _____
18. tax _____
19. buffalo _____
20. chocolate _____

21. holiday   _____   22. boss   _____
23. soprano   _____   24. mystery   _____
25. waltz   _____   26. salmon   _____
27. cuff   _____   28. country   _____
29. play   _____   30. radio   _____

Words at Work

WORD FORMATION

Stage 1

Let's begin by forming some **new** words from those you already know. For example, if we take the word 'ash', and add the word 'tray' to it, we get a new word — **ashtray**. These kinds of words are called **compounds**.

Exercise 1

Now you do it. Combine each word from list A with a suitable word from list B in order to form a new word. Write them out as a list, under C.

A	B	C
ash	tray	**ashtray**
book	ache	_____
door	box	_____
tape	room	_____
night	paper	_____
tooth	recorder	_____
match	step	_____
post	room	_____
dining	man	_____
wall	shop	_____
bed	club	_____

Exercise 2

Classroom activity; in pairs.

Here are some more words you both know, but this time you must think of your own 'partner' or **combining** words to add to them to make **one** new word. There may be more than one possibility in some cases. Your teacher will time you. Try to complete the exercise in fifteen minutes.

WATCH YOUR LANGUAGE!

1. pick
2. flash
3. hitch
4. house
5. dark
6. light
7. brief
8. gold
9. school
10. camera

Exercise 3

Now write one sentence of your own for **each** of the new compound words you've made in Exercises 1 and 2.

All of the examples in Exercises 1 and 2 are compound nouns, that is, made up of two nouns; for example, bedroom = two nouns, **bed** and **room**.

We can also make compound adjectives, for example curly-haired, long-playing, and compound verbs, for example break through, go ahead.

Compounds are sometimes written:
- as one word — bedroom,
- as two words — living room, or
- with a hyphen between — curly-haired.

If in doubt check it out in your dictionary! (See also exercises on hyphenated words in Unit 7 — Punctuation Please!)

Stage 2

Exercise 1

Combine the words in the following list with the words in the box below to make compound nouns and adjectives. Use your dictionary to check if the compound is one word, two words or hyphenated.

1. stark
2. science
3. driving
4. hot
5. broad
6. dog
7. good
8. head
9. flat
10. well
11. snack
12. self
13. spot
14. petrol
15. letter
16. dish
17. cross
18. prime
19. old
20. ice

footed, blooded, ache, minded, naked, cream, looking, tired, known, roads, fashioned, fiction, licence, service, bar, head, cloth, station, minister, light

Exercise 2

1. How many words can you think of that could combine with the following keywords to form a completely new word? Try to come up with at least four per keyword. Remember your related word might come **before** or **after** the keyword.

   Example sand; new words: quick**sand**, **sand**castle

VOCABULARY: WORD FORMATION

(a) sea
(b) wind
(c) sand
(d) water
(e) out
(f) post
(g) under
(h) up
(i) light
(j) back

2. Now practice using your new words by writing **two sentences** per keyword.

Exercise 3

Here are some examples of **compound verbs**. (These are also called phrasal verbs.) Note that each is a combination of a verb and a preposition, for example 'write' (verb) **and** 'off' (preposition).

1. to write off
2. to bring in
3. to give up
4. to break through
5. to get away
6. to go ahead
7. to take over
8. to get on
9. to look out
10. to send up
11. to tip off
12. to hold up
13. to turn up
14. to come across
15. to run off

Now, complete each of the following sentences with a suitable **compound verb** from the list above. Only ten are needed for this exercise. Make any necessary changes to the spelling.

1. John _____ _____ the car last weekend.
2. Mum is always promising to _____ _____ smoking.
3. Miss Ryan will _____ _____ from Mr. Murphy next month.
4. You have to _____ _____ for pickpockets in the city centre.
5. Poor Tom! His best friend _____ _____ with his girlfriend.
6. The storeman _____ _____ the police in return for a fat reward.
7. The council are _____ _____ with their plan to cut down the trees.
8. The thieves _____ _____ with £10,000 in banknotes.
9. Dad _____ _____ some very old books when he was clearing out the attic.
10. The school draw _____ _____ over £1,000 for charity.

Stage 3

Another useful way of forming new words is to start with a particular part of speech, for example a noun, and add to it its related adjectives, adverb and verb. These are often referred to as 'word families'.

Example	Noun	Adjective	Adverb	Verb
	student	studious	studiously	study

WATCH YOUR LANGUAGE!

Exercise 1

1. Complete the following table:

Noun	Adjective	Adverb	Verb
obedience	_____	_____	_____
_____	deceitful	_____	_____
_____	_____	_____	describe
success	_____	successfully	_____
_____	_____	_____	recognise
_____	thoughtful	_____	_____
laziness	_____	_____	_____
_____	punishing	_____	_____
_____	_____	_____	invent
care	_____	carefully	_____

2. Write sentences using:
   (a) 'success' as an **adjective**
   (b) 'describe' as a **noun**
   (c) 'punishing' as a **verb**
   (d) 'deceitful' as a **noun**
   (e) 'recognise' as an **adverb**

Exercise 2

The word in capitals can be used to form a word that fits suitably into the blank space in the following sentences. Fill each blank in this way.

Example	The manager's **signature** was at the bottom of the letter.	SIGN
	The chair looked hard, but in fact was very **comfortable**.	COMFORT

1. Only recently have people realised what a _____ situation the world is in. — DANGER
2. We have known for a long time that we live in a world where nuclear war is a _____. — POSSIBLE
3. Such a war could be started _____, just by someone pushing the wrong button. — ACCIDENT
4. But we are _____ by more immediate dangers. — THREAT
5. We have only recently realised that the world's resources, such as coal and oil, are _____. — EXHAUST
6. Population is increasing at a _____ rate, particularly in those countries that can support such populations least efficiently. — DRAMA
7. Millions face _____, but things will almost certainly get worse. — STARVE
8. We have hardly started to learn how to use the world's resources in an _____ way. — ECONOMIC
9. It is possible that we have realised the _____ of such products as coal and oil too late. — SCARCE

VOCABULARY: WORD FORMATION

10. Yet we still continue to be too _____ with our unnecessary   WASTE
    use of petrol, electricity and food, as if no danger existed.

Exercise 3

The exam. Functional writing. (1997 Junior Cert. Higher Level, Paper 1, Section 3, Question 2)
   'Imagine you are a newspaper reporter. Write a REPORT for your paper suggested by the photograph [below]. Your report should not be longer than [one A4 page].'

Write your report according to the above instructions, using words from this unit. Here are some more you might use:

an outbreak	crossroads	to look out
to break out	well known	a lookout
to break up	prime minister	to run off
to go ahead	cameraman	to come across
to go back	housewife/wives	to uphold
longsuffering	flashback	an uproar
hardworking	a breakthrough	watertight
hardhearted	doorstep	to break through
a write off	postpone	to outwit
prime time	to take over	outlook

Feel free to add any of your own choice, of course.

UNIT 2

Grappling with Grammar

PRONOUNS

Question What is a pronoun?

Answer A **pronoun** is a word which **replaces a noun** in a sentence. 'Pro' comes from the Latin word meaning 'for', so a pronoun **stands for**, or takes the place of, a noun. Without them, writing can be very repetitive.

Example Imagine your name is Siobhan Ryan, and you asked your mother for £5. If there were **no pronouns**, this is what would happen.

> Siobhan Ryan went to Siobhan Ryan's mother. Siobhan Ryan asked Siobhan Ryan's mother if Siobhan Ryan's mother could give Siobhan Ryan £5 for a school concert. Siobhan Ryan's mother sighed, took out Siobhan Ryan's mother's purse, opened Siobhan Ryan's mother's purse, then handed the £5 to Siobhan Ryan.

Phew! Here is the same situation, **with pronouns**.

> **I** went to Mum and asked **her** if **she** could give **me** £5 for a school concert. **She** sighed, took out **her** purse, opened **it**, then handed **me** £5.

Much better, isn't it?

In this unit, we will be exercising:

- ◆ personal pronouns (I, me, myself)
- ◆ possessive pronouns (mine, yours), and
- ◆ relative pronouns (who, which, that).

GRAMMAR: PRONOUNS

Stage 1

PERSONAL PRONOUNS

When a pronoun replaces a noun which names **a person or persons**, it is called a **personal pronoun**:

I	me	myself
you	you	yourself
he	him	himself
she	her	herself
it	it	itself
we	us	ourselves
you	you	yourselves
they	them	themselves

Exercise 1

Circle the pronouns in the sentences below:
1. Mary did her homework all by herself.
2. Peter was delighted when he won the cash.
3. Sheila didn't like the dress, so she gave it to Rita.
4. I got up late this morning.
5. Between you and me, I didn't understand a word.
6. Our aunt Jackie came to see us last summer.
7. 'The twins don't like them,' she said, referring to the mushy peas.
8. 'Do it yourself, you lazy lump!' he roared.
9. They never really liked us — just the money.
10. 'I don't fancy her!' he said. 'You fancy her yourself!'

Exercise 2

In the following sentences, which **nouns** do the **pronouns in bold** refer to?
1. Jack was carrying the vase into the living room. At the door, **he** dropped **it**.
2. 'Watch **yourself**, Tom. **You**'re going to get hurt,' shouted Peter.
3. When the cat saw Sarah with the milk, **it** purred, and followed **her** into the kitchen.
4. These flowers are from John, Teresa. **He** told me to give **them** to **you**.
5. Tracy and Orla are quite capable of doing this work by **themselves**.
6. The little boy ran away from his mum. We found **him** and brought **him** back to **her**.
7. My grandad bought me a pair of runners and **he** gave **them** to me for Christmas.
8. 'Yes, we are very proud of **ourselves**,' said Tom and Simon.
9. The old man walloped the thief with **his** umbrella, much to **his** surprise.
10. The teacher corrected Barbara's work, and praised **her** for it.

WATCH YOUR LANGUAGE!

Exercise 3

(a) Write ten sentences of your own, like those in Exercise 2, in which it is easy to identify the noun to which the **pronoun** refers.

(b) **Don't** underline the pronouns.

(c) Exchange your copy with your neighbour, and ask **him/her** to **underline all the pronouns** used, and to say which noun or nouns they refer to, in your sentences.

Stage 2

POSSESSIVE PRONOUNS

The possessive pronouns are:

mine, yours, his, hers, ours, yours, theirs

We use these to replace **a noun and a possessive adjective** in a sentence. In dialogue especially, it avoids boring repetition.

Example That's **my bag**. → That's **mine**.

Exercise 1

In the list below, replace the possessive adjective and noun in each case with a **possessive pronoun**, as shown in the first example.

That's **my bag**.	That's **mine**.
That's **your car**.	That's _____.
That's **his book**.	That's _____.
That's **her problem**.	That's _____.
That's **its bone**.	That's _____.*
That's **our secret**.	That's _____.
That's **your child**.	That's _____.
That's **their house**.	That's _____.

* If the **gender** of the owner of the bone is unknown, you may use either 'his' or 'hers'.

Exercise 2

Rewrite the following piece of dialogue by **replacing** the possessive adjectives and nouns in bold with a **possessive pronoun**.

Steven: Is that my shirt you're wearing?

Helen: No, of course not. It's **my shirt**. I never wear **your shirts**. You're always going on about them. It's boring.

Steven: Oh really?! And what about Stan's shirts then? You like **his shirts**, don't you? You're always borrowing them.

Helen: That's true, but **his shirts** are nicer than **your shirts**. That's why I wear **Stan's shirts**.

Steven: Right! Well, that's it then. I'll have to start wearing Tina's shirts then, won't I?! I'll have you know, I like **Tina's shirts**. They're very nice.

Helen: Fine. We'll all swap! **Our shirts** for **Stanley and Tina's shirts**. What do you think?
Steven: Oh, I don't know!! **Your shirts**! **My shirts**! **Tina's shirts**! **Stan's shirts**! It's all too ridiculous for words!
Helen: You started it.

Exercise 3

1. Write a description of yourself, in five sentences, using the pronouns **I**, **me** and **mine**.
2. Write a similar piece on any famous person — sports star, film star, singer, etc. — using the pronouns he, him, his **or** she, her, hers.
3. Discuss the good and bad points about some characters from your favourite TV soap, book or film, using the pronouns they, them and theirs. (100–150 words max.)

Stage 3

RELATIVE PRONOUNS

WHO, THAT, WHICH, WHOSE and WHERE are all relative pronouns. As the name suggests, they **relate** to a particular **noun** in a sentence.

1. WHO refers to **people only**, and to the **subject** of the sentence usually, that is, the **person** who is **doing the action**.
   Example The woman **who** won the car couldn't drive.
   In this sentence the woman is the **subject**. The pronoun relates to her.
2. THAT refers to both **people** and **things**, and to either the **subject** or the **object** in a sentence.
   Example She's the woman (subject) **that** won the car.
   or
   He's driving the car (object) **that** the woman won.
3. WHICH refers to **things only**, and to either the **subject** or the **object** in a sentence.
   Example This is a scheme (subject) **which** should work.
   or
   These are problems (object) **which** you must solve.
   Note: THAT can also be used for **things**, instead of WHICH.
   Example This is a scheme **that** should work.
4. WHOSE is a **possessive** relative pronoun. It refers to people, things and animals. It denotes possession or ownership.
   Example 1. She's the girl **whose** brother is a millionaire. ('Whose' refers to the girl.)
   2. **Whose** book is this? ('Whose' refers to the **owner** of the book.)
   3. That's the horse **whose** leg was broken. ('Whose' refers to the horse.)
5. WHERE is actually a relative adverb, used to talk about places.
   Example That's the town **where** I was born.

Note: You can **leave out** the relative pronouns WHICH, WHO and THAT when they relate to the **object** in the sentence.

> **Example** Those are problems (which) you have to solve. (In this sentence 'problems' is the object, 'you' is the subject and 'solve' is the verb.)
> or
> She's the woman (whom) I met last week. ('Whom' is the objective case of 'who', referring to the woman, the object of the sentence.)
> or
> She's the woman (that) I met last week.

Now let's practise using these various types of relative pronouns.

Exercise 1

Combine the following **pairs of sentences** to form **one sentence**, by replacing the word in bold with a suitable relative pronoun.

> **Example** I'd like to buy runners. **They** will match my new jeans.
> I'd like to buy runners **which/that** will match my new jeans.

1. This is my brother. **He** lives in Cork.
2. I went to see the house. They lived in **it** when they were first married.
3. This is the boss. **He** founded the company.
4. What we really need is a canteen. **It** would cater for all our students.
5. That's the hospital. She was born **there**.
6. The writer is Bryan MacMahon. **He** wrote *The Master*.
7. *Friends* is a TV series about six young people. **They** live in New York.
8. John knows the family. **Their** house was burnt down.
9. Did you lose the ring? I gave **it** to you on your birthday!
10. That's the guy! **His** brother stole my car.

Exercise 2

Fill in the blanks in the following piece of dialogue, with a suitable relative pronoun in each case.

Denis: It's like a ghost town these days _____ everyone sleeps and nothing much happens.

Mary: It wasn't always like this, though, was it? Do you remember that guy _____ came home from the States and started a shirt factory on Patrick's Street?

Denis: Oh yeh! He was the fella _____ was going to make us all rich, _____ shirts were going to be worn all over the known world, from Passage East to Timbuctoo! Yeh. I remember him. It didn't last, but.

Mary: Yeh. Two years in _____ we all had loads of money and blew it on holidays, _____ at least the sun was guaranteed, not like here.

Denis: Yeh. And do you remember when there was that raffle for a Merc, and Paddy Redmond (_____ son was a right waster) crashed it into the front wall of his house the very first week _____ he had it!

GRAMMAR: PRONOUNS

Mary: *Right enough, he did! But sure, who in their right mind would give a car like that to a fella _____ couldn't drive?! _____ fault was that, I wonder?*

Denis: *Don't ask me. I only know that Paddy was the one _____ won it. The son drove it back to the garage _____ it had been bought, and the front wing (_____ had been badly dented) cost about a thousand to repair! Can you believe it? A thousand pounds! . . .*

Now **continue** the dialogue between Denis and Mary for another ten lines, using each of the relative pronouns 'who', 'that', 'which', 'whose' and 'where', **twice** each.

Exercise 3

The exam. Personal writing.

Read the following passage carefully and underline or highlight **all the pronouns**.

On Sunday mornings you see them everywhere. They seem to come out of nowhere. Sometimes, in twos and threes, sometimes in groups, with a leader. They always wear bright gaudy colours and seem to advertise themselves. You almost expect them to run over to you promoting some new product for washing. They run on footpaths, on roads, on grass, in parks, on concrete, anywhere. They even dodge in and out and between cars, risking life and limb. They are . . . yes, the joggers!

Some are tall and athletic and have a suntan no matter what season of the year it is. Some are short and stumpy and not just a little overweight. Their faces always look the same — convulsed. A dangerous shade of red flashes like a neon light behind the permanently trickling drops of sweat. Inside the body their hearts are pounding, possibly at a dangerous rate. Do they ever look joyous? No, they look as if they are in constant agony.

When they reach a traffic light they are at their most curious. They are frustrated because their rhythm has been interrupted, so they stamp up and down as if throwing a tantrum, and glare at the cars and drivers speeding by. Sometimes I smile out at them but this is a risky business. They stamp even faster and breathe more furiously. On cold mornings their breathing is for all the world like a dragon breathing fire and hatred.

Once the light changes they hop, skip and jump a little before 'taking off' horizontally once more. And off they go, pounding the earth with their rubber soles and short socks. Do they ever feel as ridiculous as they look? And where in God's name are they going in such a hurry? Usually round and round in circles!

Imagine creatures from another world gazing at this spectacle. What conclusions could they draw but that these people belong to a special species — humanoid but at a different stage of development from the rest of us. Recognisable because of their uniform and strange facial gestures. Classifiable as 'the questers after youth'. Their main rule — self-punishment.   (300 words approx.)

Now, write a similar piece (of the same length approximately) on **one** of the following topics:
- Sunday drivers
- Football fanatics
- Sales fever

WATCH YOUR LANGUAGE!

Use the three different types of pronoun (personal, possessive and relative) as far as possible, in order to avoid the kind of **repetition** outlined in the introduction to this unit.

And finally . . . a problem pronoun!
Should you say 'Sarah and **I**' or 'Sarah and **me**'?
Look at these two sentences.

(a) Sarah and **I** ate six doughnuts each.

In this sentence, **Sarah and I** are the **subject** of the sentence. They are performing the action (ate). **I** is correct in this case.

(b) Sean gave the £5 to Sarah and **me**, to share.

In this sentence, **Sean** is the subject, performing the action (gave), and **Sarah and me** are the **objects**. Therefore, **me** is correct in this case.

So . . . **I** for **subject**, and
 me for **object**, is the rule.

Exercise 4

Fill in the correct word — **I** or **me** — in the following sentences, according to which is correct in the situation. Remember, **I** for subject, **me** for object.

1. Tom and ___ went to the cinema.
2. Philip and ___ bought popcorn.
3. Donna gave Tom and ___ two tickets for the disco.
4. Mum and ___ went shopping for jeans.
5. Dad gave ___ some money.
6. My friends and ___ went to Paris on a school trip last Easter.
7. The coach driver told Tom and ___ to sit down and stop singing.
8. Brian sent a Valentine card to both Trudy and ___ .
9. Trudy and ___ hate Brian. He's a nerd.
10. The class and ___ are getting really good at this 'pronoun' business!

Punctuation Please!

COMMAS

Question When do we use commas?

Answer 1. When we wish to **pause** in a sentence, to **separate** the different parts of it.

Example When we got to the top of the hill we paused for a moment, took our bearings, and admired the view.

The comma before 'and' is correct here because we are pausing, but it isn't correct before the last item in a **list** — see 2 below.

PUNCTUATION: COMMAS

2. When we want to separate items in a **list** of things or people.

    Example   Brian ate three burgers, two bags of chips, a portion of onion rings, a doughnut and two Mars bars.

    When writing a list of items, the **second last** item is **not** followed by a comma, because the word 'and' signals the **last** item in the list and **takes the place** of a comma.

3. When we want to separate a **direct quotation** from the rest of the sentence.

    Example   'I hate the Simpsons,' Tracy said.

As with full stops, commas help the reader to make **sense** of what you write.
The comma is a **short pause** but an important one, particularly in a long sentence.
Commas are **sharper** and **clearer** in a sentence than a succession of 'ands'!

Stage 1

Exercise 1

Classroom exercise. Oral. Teacher directed.

(a) Within a time limit of thirty seconds, you will be asked to call out a list of **five items**, under one of the following headings:
- Food
- Book titles
- Sports
- Pet hates
- Careers
- Favourite music groups
- TV programmes
- Weekend activities
- Films
- Holiday destinations

(b) Your teacher will select students at random, and will also choose the topic.

(c) If selected, you must call out the word 'comma' between each of the items, except for the last two, where you must call out the word 'and'.

   Example   Films: Last year I saw *Titanic* comma *First Contact* comma *Romeo and Juliet* comma *Men in Black* and *Mars Attack*.

If a student fails to say 'comma', he/she is out! If he/she says comma between the last two items, he/she is out! (This exercise may also be done **in pairs**. First Student A selects the topic and Student B responds. Then they **switch roles** after thirty seconds, and Student B selects the topic.)

Exercise 2

Rewrite these sentences, putting in the necessary commas. All the other punctuation is correct.

1. The semi-finalists were Wexford Cork Limerick and Tipperary.
2. Mrs. Ryan arrived looked at the house phoned the auctioneers and bought it on the spot.
3. Michael tripped grazed his knee cut his hand cried a bit and then told his mum.
4. On holidays we bought postcards sombreros three donkeys a flamenco doll and indigestion tablets.

WATCH YOUR LANGUAGE!

5. Sam hopped skipped and jumped his way through the dancing competition.
6. 'I'd like an answer today please Jane' Miss Furlong sighed.
7. My friend who is tall handsome intelligent and rich is taking me to Eurodisney at Easter.
8. 'I'm going home now' said James grabbing his teddy bear.
9. Sandra loves *Eastenders Coronation Street Brookside Baywatch* and *Friends*.
10. Shamrock Rovers Finn Harps Bohemians and Cork City are all Irish soccer teams.

Exercise 3

Terry is very excited. He has just been picked for the school football team, and he has written a letter to his friend, Dave, in Cork, telling him all about it. However, in his haste, he has forgotten to put in any full stops, capital letters or commas! Can you **rewrite** this letter, so that it is clearer and makes more **sense**?

---

35 meadow avenue
thurles
co tipp
20 january 1999

hi dave

guess what? i finally did it got picked for the first team it's brilliant it's what i've always wanted i trained every monday wednesday saturday and sunday all last term during the christmas holidays too i can't believe they picked me and not loopy les from 3b he's a real headcase cheeks the teachers fakes absence notes chats up every babe in the school who'll listen to him he's sick i tell you i can't wait to try on the new team kit it's cool red black gray with a yellow stripe the women love it anne carroll says she'll come and see me play bring a few mates can't wait god! is that the time? have to go mate must train do sit-ups press-ups laps around the field you name it o'neill can do it!
see you at the finals in naas
take care be cool
terry

Stage 2

Look at this sentence:

   Mr. Gorman, the principal, is sick today.

We use a comma between **nouns in apposition**, that is, where there are **two nouns** in a sentence, and they both refer to the **same person** or the **same thing**. The second one simply tells us **more** about the first one. In the above sentence, 'Mr. Gorman' is a noun, and 'principal' is a noun; 'principal' tells us more about 'Mr. Gorman'.

PUNCTUATION: COMMAS

Here are some more examples:
1. **Michelle Smith**, the Olympic gold **medallist**, is Irish.
2. I was talking to my **neighbour**, Mrs. Feeney, about her dog.
3. **Dublin**, the **capital** of Ireland, is a popular European destination.

Exercise 1
Now, you do it, with the following sentences. Insert commas where they are needed.
1. Brigid's class went to Paris with their teacher Miss Greene.
2. John McDonald my sister's boyfriend buys her chocolates every weekend.
3. Doing homework even when it's necessary is a real pain.
4. Charlotte who was very nervous never said a word to him.
5. Two girls who were smoking in the loos got us all into trouble.
6. Man. United are happy with their manager Alex Ferguson.
7. A football kicked by Donna Graham struck a tree in Mr. Lyons's garden bounced off the cat and smashed his living-room window.
8. The plane took off rose a few hundred feet in the air and then nose-dived into the ground.
9. The film *Titanic* which cost $200 million to make has been a huge success at the box office.
10. Commas when used properly make our writing much easier to read.

Exercise 2
Can you **complete** the following sentences using your **own** nouns in apposition and inserting commas in the correct places? The first comma is supplied for you.

Example   Tom Jones, . . . could be: Tom Jones, the Welsh singer, performs on the track 'Perfect Day'.

1. Madonna, . . .
2. Limerick, . . .
3. George Clooney, . . .
4. William Butler Yeats, . . .
5. William Shakespeare, . . .
6. Galway City, . . .
7. The Simpsons, . . .
8. Jack Charlton, . . .
9. Daniel O'Connell, . . .
10. Arnold Schwarzenegger, . . .

Exercise 3
Read the following sentence:
   'We're going to Wicklow,' said Tom.

This is an example of the use of the comma when we want to separate **direct speech**, or **quotation**, from the rest of the sentence.

Can you fill in the **blanks** in the following sentences with a word of your own choice? And remember to put in the **comma**, as in the example above.
1. 'I would love to go to _____' said Gemma.
2. 'We are going on holiday in ____' said Mary.
3. 'The new shopping centre is _____' said Sean.

WATCH YOUR LANGUAGE!

4. 'I love my teddy bear and my teddy bear loves ____' said Garfield.
5. 'I always have to do the ____' grumbled Eric.
6. 'Make sure you're wearing your ____' warned the policeman.
7. 'Eat your ____' said Gran.
8. 'I have found the ideal ____' announced Jane.
9. 'That's it. I'm nearly ____' said Bob.
10. 'I'm getting really good at ____' said Peter.

Stage 3

Exercise 1

Here is an extract from a newspaper article about the cast of the award-winning TV series *Friends*. I have removed all the **commas** and **full stops**. Can you **replace** them? Use a red biro for clarity. Try to complete this task in under ten minutes.

THEY OWN six of the most recognised and best marketed faces in the world Every week 30 million viewers tune in to see what their television *Friends* are doing while millions more buy the T-shirts calendars cappuccino mugs and even cook books

But although Jennifer Aniston David Schwimmer Matthew Perry Matt LeBlanc Lisa Kudrow and Courteney Cox discover in every episode that a friend in need is a friend indeed a *Friend* in the movies has proved a different ball game altogether

Translating their television stardom into box office success has proved problematic and at times almost embarrassing — note LeBlanc playing straightman sidekick to a chimp in his first movie outing *Ed*

Now Jennifer Aniston she of the infamous hairdo has made her first attempt at actually carrying a movie on her name and her name alone

Having chosen to start small with supporting roles in *She's The One* and *'Til There Was You* Aniston opted for *Picture Perfect* a romantic comedy which hopes to match the surprise hit factor of *While You Were Sleeping*

Carrying it on her shoulders — with or without the much copied Rachel 'do' resting on them — is a brave move Her leading man is the little known Jake Mohn and she is even taking the risk of moving away from her kooky screen persona of the dizzy waitress to play a hard-nosed ambitious girl so intent upon success she invents a fiancée to enhance her career chances

She is aware however that her *Friends* success isn't a cast-iron guarantee to big screen fame

'Every movie I have done except for *Picture Perfect* I have had to audition for' she points out 'It's not as easy as "Oh you're a big star do this"'
(*Ireland on Sunday*, 11 January 1998)

PUNCTUATION: COMMAS

Exercise 2
(a) Select a piece of writing of about 300–350 words from one of the following sources:
- a book
- a newspaper
- a magazine
- a textbook

(b) Read it carefully, **circling** or **highlighting** every comma.

(c) Write a **summary** of the passage in about one-third of its length (100–110 words), using commas correctly, but **sparingly**, i.e. **one** in a short sentence, and no more than **two** in a longer sentence — unless you are required to **list** items, of course!

Read the rules and examples again before attempting this exercise.

Exercise 3
The exam. Reading comprehension.

The following is an extract from the 1995 Junior Cert. Higher Level paper, Section 1, Reading. Read it carefully. All the commas have been removed. Can you replace them? You should have 28. (Note: In paragraph 3, line 4, after the word 'irresponsibility', I have deleted a comma as it is before 'and' at the end of a list.)

> For a short time I was a waitress in a diners' club. The average age of the staff was 19 that of the clientele about 40. We the staff used to watch amused and slightly disgusted as overweight middle-aged swingers who in the light of day would claim that discos are a load of teenage nonsense jerked violently around to the latest hits — as they say. (They were either dancing or having heart attacks — I couldn't quite tell.) If in the eyes of adults 'teenage culture' is such a contemptible thing why given the opportunity do they throw themselves into it with so much enthusiasm and a lot less style?
>
> I may be cynical but I think it is partly due to jealousy. Some adults patronise teenagers because they are envious of their youth and because the respect they don't get from their peers they demand from their juniors. Even on the lofty level of our local tennis club this type of jealousy rears its head or rather swings its racket. If we were to put forward our strongest women's team it would consist entirely of teenage girls. Of course this never happens. The elder women play by virtue of their age not skill. After all teenage girls don't count as women.
>
> If there is such a thing as a teenager it refers to a state of mind and not a particular age range. At 20 you don't automatically become an adult because you've dropped the 'teen' in your age. Unfortunately 'teenager' has come to connote things like selfishness irresponsibility and arrogance. This means there are a lot of adults around who are still teenage. Equally if maturity is measured by attributes such as compassion and tolerance and not merely the number of years you've totted up then there are lots of adult teenagers around.
>
> I would like the word 'teenager' to be banned but I suppose that will never happen as a lot of people would stop making a lot of money.

Correct your work from your own set of exam papers — or ask your teacher (nicely) and he/she may do it for you.

And finally . . .
> *'I was working on the proof of one of my poems all the morning, and took out a comma. In the afternoon I put it back again.'*   OSCAR WILDE

How Do You Spell . . . ?

LEARNING TO SPELL: SOME STRATEGIES

'I'm no good at spelling.' Some students find spelling genuinely difficult. Others make spelling mistakes simply because they are careless or lazy. In this unit, we will look at ways in which you can become a better speller. But . . . be warned! There are no miracle cures. You will have to **work** at it!

Strategy 1 Sound patterns in spelling

Sounding out words before you spell them heightens your awareness of **sound patterns**. Two or more letters can combine to make one sound.

> **Example**   'er' in talk**er**, walk**er**, jump**er**

Associating the sound with the letters will therefore help with the **spelling** of the word. Here are some more examples of common sound patterns:

    'ing' in sing**ing**, danc**ing**, laugh**ing**
    'tion' in sta**tion**, men**tion**, por**tion** (pronounced 'shun')
    'ious' in env**ious**, grac**ious**, delic**ious** (pronounced 'y-us')
    'ence' in pati**ence**, lic**ence**, sci**ence**
    'ive' in effect**ive**, expens**ive**, detect**ive**

Exercise 1

(a) Read the example words out loud several times. In this way you will learn to link a particular **sound** to a particular **ending**.

(b) Your teacher will now call out the words from the examples and ask you to write them down, **first** the ending, and then the complete word.

> **Example**
> 1. Teacher calls out 'mention'.
> 2. You **hear** the ending 'shun'.
> 3. You **write** 'tion'.
> 4. You write 'mention' — breaking it up into two parts if you wish.

Now you can see that certain words have a **sound pattern**, and that these **patterns** have the same **spelling**.

SPELLING: SOME STRATEGIES

Exercise 2
Write five more words for **each** of these sound patterns. Consult your dictionary if you get stuck. Time limit: ten minutes.
1. 'ing'
2. 'tion'
3. 'ious'
4. 'ence'
5. 'ive'

Swop copies with your neighbour. Add his/her words to your own list, making sure the **spelling** is correct in each case.

Exercise 3
Does it **look** right?
Find the **correct** spelling of the word in each line, and **circle** it.

1. begining	beginning	bigining
2. position	posision	pozishon
3. discriptive	descriptive	diskriptive
4. furreous	furious	fureus
5. konveenience	convinience	convenience
6. emagenation	imagination	imagenation
7. giggling	gigling	geegleng
8. atractive	attractive	attraktive
9. industrious	indushtreous	industrous
10. skience	sieence	science

Strategy 2 'Spell it well' — words that rhyme
It is much easier to learn the spelling of words that rhyme.

Exercise 1
Write four more words which rhyme and end with the same patterns as the words listed below. It helps if you work through the alphabet — i.e. baking, c,d,e, faking!

Example baking, faking, making, raking, waking

1. ditch
2. fight
3. hopping
4. able
5. taste
6. hatch
7. cane
8. bold
9. tumble
10. mapped

37

WATCH YOUR LANGUAGE!

Exercise 2
Select **one or two** words from **each** of your sets and write a paragraph in which you use the words once only. Mind the spelling! (100–120 words)

Exercise 3
For each of the following 'ie' words add **one** other word which rhymes with it, and ends with the same two letters:

Example   relief: belief

1. die: _____
2. achieve: _____
3. pie: _____
4. niece: _____
5. belief: _____
6. field: _____
7. flies: _____

Add one other 'ei' word which rhymes with these (the first letter is your clue):

8. receive: d_____
9. receipt: d_____
10. eight: w_____
11. either: n_____

Strategy 3 'Cloze' it!
A cloze-style exercise involves **filling in** a missing letter or letters in a word, in **stages**. The aim is to learn the spelling by **working through** it in stages, becoming **familiar** with each part or syllable of the word as you work.

Example   Let's use the word hospital as an example. It can be broken up into five stages. **Cover up** each stage as you complete it, before you attempt the next stage, that is, cover 1 before you attempt 2, and so on. By the time you get to stage 5, you should be thoroughly familiar with the word, and confident in your spelling of it.

1. ___pital
2. hos__al
3. hospi__
4. ___tal
5. hospital

Remember that you are concentrating on **one part** of the word only at each stage, and learning **that** part. Students often believe they are bad spellers because many words are marked as spelt wrongly in their copies. However, if you examine these words carefully and look them up in your dictionary, you will find that you have usually only misspelt one or two letters in each word. The rest of the spelling may be absolutely correct! So, become aware of how words break down into parts (syllables), and follow a certain pattern, or where parts of the word are quite simply broken up into more easily learned segments, for example mag-az-ine.

Exercise 1
Here are some more words for you to complete and learn. Remember to follow the guidelines for 'hospital'.

SPELLING: SOME STRATEGIES

(a) microphone:
1. ___crophone
2. mic___one
3. micro___
4. microph___
5. ___

(b) magazine
1. ___azine
2. mag___ine
3. magaz___
4. ___ine
5. ___

(c) character
1. ___racter
2. char___er
3. charac___
4. ___ter
5. ___

(d) symbolise
1. ___bolise
2. sym___ise
3. symbol___
4. ___ise
5. ___

(e) disappointment
1. ___appointment
2. disap___ment
3. disappoint___
4. ___ment
5. ___

(f) development
1. ___velopment
2. de___ment
3. develop___
4. ___ment
5. ___

Exercise 2
Here are some more words that are commonly misspelt. Create your **own** stages 1–5, following the examples in Exercise 1.

1. accommodation
2. beautiful
3. disappear
4. literature
5. necessary
6. embarrass
7. government
8. prejudice
9. appearance
10. humorous
11. advertisement
12. athletics
13. believable
14. calendar
15. criticism
16. definite
17. description
18. immediately
19. laboratory
20. livelihood

Strategy 4
1. Look
2. Cover
3. Write
4. Check

Do you remember this way of learning your spellings in primary school? It is still a very good method, but again you must follow the stages 1–4 in learning the word, as outlined above.

Example   Here is the word 'marriage', from a spelling list of ten words. It is often misspelt. Learn to spell this word in the following way:
1. **Look** at the word, and try to learn the spelling.
2. **Cover** the word, and say it to yourself a few times — trying to **visualise** it, in your head.
3. **Write** the word, as you remember it.

WATCH YOUR LANGUAGE!

> 4. Uncover the word and **check** your spelling.
> 5. If **correct**, continue to the next word in the list.
> 6. If **incorrect**, (a) **Look** at the word again,
> (b) **Say** the word slowly, tracing it with your finger.
> (c) **Cover** the word.
> (d) **Write** the word.
> (e) Uncover the word and **check** the spelling.

You will almost certainly get it right the second time round. Be **patient**! Good spelling needs **care** and **work**.

Exercise 1

Here is a list of ten words, beginning with 'marriage'. You will see that they all have the same ending — 'age'. So you don't have to learn this bit of the word — patterns again! Learn these spellings using Strategy 4.

1. marriage
2. average
3. language
4. postage
5. teenage
6. manage
7. courage
8. message
9. wreckage
10. advantage

Exercise 2

Test yourself

Here are some definitions of words that have been used so far in this unit. The **first letter** of each word is given to you, and the number of letters. Write out each word, spelled **correctly** of course! Revise the spellings (using Strategy 4) **before** attempting the exercise.

1. Singers use one to make themselves heard at a large venue.　m_____ (10)
2. Every country has one of these. They are the ruling power.　g_____ (10)
3. The feeling we experience when we look forward to something and it doesn't happen.　d_____ (14)
4. We read a lot of this in school!　l_____ (10)
5. Hotels and guesthouses provide this.　a_____ (13)
6. What is left after a major car, plane or train crash.　w_____ (8)
7. An adjective meaning funny.　h_____ (8)
8. You have a favourite one which you will buy and read each week.　m_____ (8)
9. A strongly held belief in favour of or against a particular idea, or race of people.　p_____ (9)
10. The legal union of a man and woman.　m_____ (8)

Swop copies with your neighbour and correct each other's spellings.

SPELLING: SOME STRATEGIES

Strategy 5 Words within words

Another useful way of learning spellings is to spot words within words. Look at the word 'assignment'. There is another word **within** this word, that is, 'sign'.

Exercise 1

Here are some more examples. Can you find the word **within** the word? Underline or highlight it, when you do.

1. advantage
2. important
3. canteen
4. satisfactory
5. directory
6. continental
7. textbook
8. microphone
9. orchestra
10. secondary

Exercise 2

Put the words in the box below into their correct spaces to make 20 more 'words within words'.

Example   dis**appoint**ment

1. dis_____ment
2. _____rel
3. pheas_____
4. sur_____
5. qu_____er
6. re_____
7. hair_____er
8. mis_____stood
9. re_____ment
10. _____ly
11. sp_____
12. trum_____
13. dis_____ion
14. th_____
15. pass_____
16. _____th
17. un_____ful
18. h_____ed
19. ex_____ive
20. _____able

connect, appoint, success, fresh, face, pet, port, live, ant, arrow, bar, aunt, row, art, ear, dress, pens, too, reason, under

Exercise 3

(a) Working in pairs, or in teams of three, construct 20 of your own 'words within words'. You may use a dictionary. Put them into an exercise like the one above. Time limit: 20 minutes.
(b) At a signal from your teacher, exchange your exercise with another pair or team of students. You then have ten minutes to complete their exercise. The pair/team who finishes first — wins!

Strategy 6 DIY spelling

As its name suggests, this is the 'Do It Yourself' spelling strategy! If you **really** want to be a better speller, you have to take **control** of it. One very good way of doing this is to create your **own** spelling book or dictionary.

WATCH YOUR LANGUAGE!

Suggestions for use:
1. An **address** or **index book** will make a good personal dictionary.
2. **Collect** words from your exercises and your textbooks once a week and file them **alphabetically** into your 'dictionary of spelling'.
3. Decide on a **number** of words per week that you can realistically learn. Ten would be a good start, for example. Too many will discourage you, and defeat the purpose.
4. In **choosing** words, be sure to include those words which you **use** most frequently, and those which you **misspell** frequently also.
5. Leave a space of a few lines at the end of each index page for **sentence practice** using the words on that page.
6. Consult your **exam papers**, and include words that regularly appear in questions. For example, in **English**, the following words are often used: author, character, poet, scene, extract, text.
7. Set some time aside once a month to **revise** your 'dictionary', that is, **to re-learn** the words you've written in there. There is no point in simply collecting words and never looking at them again.

Remember your aim — to be a better speller. Stick with it! It will work.

Also, in the following units you will be doing lots of spelling practice, all of which will give you confidence. Practice really does make perfect.

Words at Work

WORD BUILDING

As you saw in Unit 1, it is possible to form new words from those you already know. In this way, we start **building** a vocabulary that is **more varied** and **less repetitive**. In this unit, we will be looking at words that relate to, or are associated with, a particular 'keyword', and also at how a thesaurus can help you to extend your vocabulary, thus increasing your word power.

Stage 1

Exercise 1

The keyword 'beverage' may refer to any number of different drinks, for example tea, coffee, water, juice.

Here are some more keywords. How many words can you think of that are associated with each of them?

1. Food
2. Travel
3. Cinema
4. Occupations
5. Art
6. Television
7. Space
8. Photography
9. Literature
10. Music

VOCABULARY: WORD BUILDING

Your teacher may allow you to work in pairs on this exercise, with a time limit of 10–15 minutes, or you may do it as an individual challenge.

Exercise 2
Now compare your lists of related words with others in your class.
(a) Add any you haven't thought of to your own.
(b) Choose one keyword and write a descriptive paragraph on that topic in which each related word is used once only. (100–120 words)

Exercise 3
(a) Here are 30 nouns. They can be divided up into six groups of five words each. The keyword for each group is given to you. You must place each word under its appropriate heading.

beach, oil, saucepans, microwave, cell, priest, luggage, reception, proposal, sink, exam, engagement, crime, computer, pupil, petrol, fridge, book, judge, hotel, fine, driver, service, tyre, dishwasher, ticket, honeymoon, study, sun, station

	Police	Garage	Kitchen	School	Holiday	Wedding
1.						
2.						
3.						
4.						
5.						

(b) Now write a piece of **dialogue**, between two people, which features **two** of the word groups and connects them in some way, for example 'holiday' and 'wedding' or 'garage' and 'police'. Try to use each related word within a group once only. (150–200 words)

Stage 2

Exercise 1
Find the missing link
Study the first pair of words below, and then complete the second pair, having worked out the 'link' between them.

Example Ireland, **island**. Asia, _____.
             Ireland, island. Asia, **continent**.

1. Eric Cantona, football. Ken Doherty, _____.
2. England, Prime Minister. Ireland, _____.
3. O'Casey, plays. Yeats, _____.
4. Cartoon, pictures. Dictionary, _____.
5. Evita, musical. Swan Lake, _____.
6. Apple, tree. Grape, _____.
7. Othello, tragedy. As You Like It, _____.

8. Numbers, maths. Notes,_____.
9. Country, rural. City,_____.
10. January, month. Autumn,_____.

Exercise 2

Having completed Exercise 1, add as many **related** words as possible to each link word.

Example snooker: cue, ball, player, round, tournament, champion, cup, etc.

Suggestion: Your teacher may choose to make this a competitive exercise, as in a table quiz situation, in class.
- In a class of 30 students, there could be six teams of five.
- Each team confers on the list of related words.
- The team which comes up with the most words for each link word, wins!
- Your teacher decides which starter word he/she will call out, and a time limit of three minutes per word is imposed. Your teacher chooses eight words in all.
- Good luck!

Exercise 3

Read the poem 'Squaring Up' by Roger McGough, and answer the following questions:
(a) Which 'key' or 'topic' word does the phrase 'Squaring Up' refer to?
(b) Underline all the nouns, verbs and adjectives that relate to this topic; for example, boxing-gloves (noun); bob (verb); gloveless (adjective).
(c) Write them all out in a **list** under these headings:
   Noun   Verb   Adjective
(d) Write a short article for the school magazine in which you express your opinions on this topic, **referring to this poem** to support your points. Use as many of your list words from (c) as possible.

Squaring Up

When I was thirteen and crimping my first quiff
Dad bought me a pair of boxing-gloves
In the hope that I would aspire to the Noble Art.

But I knew my limitations from the start:
Myopia, cowardice and the will to come second.
But I feigned enthusiasm for his sake.

Straight after tea, every night for a week
We would go a few rounds in the yard.
Sleeves rolled up, collarless and gloveless.

He would bob and weave and leave me helpless.
Uppercuts would tap me on the chin
Left hooks muss my hair, haymakers tickle my ear.

Without glasses, only one thing was clear:
The fact that I was hopeless. He had a son
Who couldn't square up. So we came to blows.

Losing patience, he caught me on the nose.
I bled obligingly. A sop. A sacrifice.
Mum threw in the towel and I quit the ring.

But when the bell goes each birthday I still feel the sting
Not of pain, but of regret. You said sorry
And you were. I didn't. And I wasn't.
ROGER MCGOUGH

Stage 3

USING A THESAURUS

In 1805, a man called Peter Mark Roget began to compile a catalogue of words, classed together in sections. Under each topic, he placed many words that are associated with each other. Forty-seven years later (in 1852) the book was published and entitled *Thesaurus*, meaning a 'treasury of words'.

Unlike a dictionary, a thesaurus doesn't explain the meaning of a word, but rather gives you a number of alternatives for the word itself. Here is a page from the *Webster Pocket Thesaurus*. You will notice that although the layout is similar to a dictionary, the actual content and emphasis are quite different. Using a thesaurus helps you to find the correct or **precise** word for the idea you want to express. It will also help you to avoid repetition and find an alternative word for one that has been overused.

---

go *v.* **LEAVE**: withdraw, depart, vacate, flee, fly, run, escape; **PROCEED**: advance, progress, move; **FUNCTION**: run, perform, operate; **SUIT**: conform, accord, harmonize, agree, fit; **EXTEND**: stretch, cover, reach; **ELAPSE**: transpire, pass; **DIE**: depart, succumb
goad *v.* prod, urge, prompt, spur, drive, press, push, impel, force, stimulate, provoke, encourage
goal *n.* aim, ambition, object, intent, end, purpose
go-between *n.* middleman, referee, mediator, agent
god *n.* deity, divinity, spirit
godly *adj.* righteous, devout, pious, holy
gone *adj.* moved, withdrawn, retired, departed, dissolved, decayed, extinct
good *adj.* **MORAL**: upright, honest, respectable, noble, ethical, fair, pure, decent, honorable; **KIND**: considerate, tolerant, generous; **RELIABLE**: trustworthy, dependable, loyal; **SOUND**: safe, solid, stable, reliable; **PLEASANT**: agreeable, satisfying, enjoyable; **HEALTHY**: sound,

WATCH YOUR LANGUAGE!

> normal, vigorous; **OBEDIENT**: dutiful, tractable, well-behaved; **GENUINE**: valid, real, sound; **DELICIOUS**: tasty, flavorful, tasteful
> **good-for-nothing** n. loafer, vagabond, bum, vagrant
> **good-looking** adj. clean-cut, attractive, impressive, beautiful, handsome
> **good-natured** adj. cordial, kindly, amiable, friendly
> **goodness** n. decency, morality, honesty, virtue
> **goof** v. err, flub, fail
> **gorge** n. chasm, abyss, crevasse, ravine
> **gorge** v. glut, surfeit, stuff, eat, fill
> **gorgeous** adj. beautiful, dazzling, superb, sumptuous, impressive, grand
> **gory** adj. blood-soaked, bloodstained, offensive
> **gossip** n. **RUMOR**: scandal, meddling, hearsay, slander, defamation; **TALEBEARER**: snoop, meddler, tattler, scandalmonger, muckraker, backbiter

Exercise 1

Examine the following three headwords on your thesaurus page: go, good, gossip.

Now fill in the blanks in the following sentences with a word chosen from one of the context words given with each headword.

> **Example**   Headword: go; Context words: leave, proceed, function, etc.
>   You must _____ the building immediately. The basement is on fire.

The obvious choice here is 'vacate', as the context is 'leave'. Your intelligence will tell you this, of course, once you have examined all the context words and eliminated those which do not apply. Clearly the context word 'function' and the words listed under it would be wrong for this sentence! So, the thesaurus challenges you to study words, and to be **precise** in your usage of them. Fill in the blanks in the following sentences, with words chosen from the thesaurus entries above.

1. I'm not sure this climate ____ with you, Mark.
2. Rita is a very dependable person and extremely ____ to her friends.
3. Barry is not just a harmless gossip. He is a _____ in other people's affairs.
4. Before I _____ this world, I really must change that wallpaper.
5. Her _____ in life is to be an astronaut.
6. I wouldn't believe a word of it. It's only _____.
7. Con is making real _____ in his relationship with Rachel.
8. That Mexican dish was very _____.
9. Bill has a nasty tongue. He's a notorious _____.
10. I'm not sure if the rope will _____ that far, Jan.

Exercise 2

Here are some more entries from the *Webster Pocket Thesaurus*. The words 'great' and 'nice', for example, along with 'good', are much overused.

VOCABULARY: WORD BUILDING

funny adj. **COMIC**: laughable, comical, whimsical, amusing, entertaining, diverting, humorous, witty, jocular, droll; **SUSPICIOUS**: curious, unusual, odd

futile adj. useless, vain, fruitless, hopeless, impractical, unsuccessful, purposeless, ineffective, ineffectual, unproductive, empty, hollow

glum adj. sullen, moody, morose, sad

gnaw v. tear, crunch, champ, masticate, bite, chew

great adj. **LARGE**: numerous, big, commanding, vast; **EXCELLENT**: exceptional, surpassing, transcendent; **EMINENT**: grand, majestic, exalted, famous, renowned, celebrated, distinguished, noted

nervous adj. **EXCITABLE**: impatient, restless, uneasy, unstable; **EXCITED**: fidgety, jittery, agitated, bothered

nice adj. likable, pleasant, agreeable, amiable

noise n. sound, clamor, racket, fracas, din, uproar

good adj. **MORAL**: upright, honest, respectable, noble, ethical, fair, pure, decent, honorable; **KIND**: considerate, tolerant, generous; **RELIABLE**: trustworthy, dependable, loyal; **SOUND**: safe, solid, stable, reliable; **PLEASANT**: agreeable, satisfying, enjoyable; **HEALTHY**: sound, normal, vigorous; **OBEDIENT**: dutiful, tractable, well-behaved; **GENUINE**: valid, real, sound; **DELICIOUS**: tasty, flavorful, tasteful

Read the following description of a school tour and **replace** each of the words in bold with a word of similar meaning from the above entries.

Arriving at Eurodisney at 10.00 a.m. on a sunny spring morning was **great**. We'd all had a good night's rest and were feeling **great**. Tommo had bought a **great** camera in the duty free and we all wanted to use it.

'Ah, go on, Tommo. Give us a go!' Shirley Lambert begged. 'I'd get **great** shots of the parade with that. I won't break it, I promise!' But much as Tommo thought Shirley was really **nice** he wasn't daft enough to lend her his **good** camera.

Everyone was really **excited** going through the gate. Tommo was **comical**, taking mock shots, and posing. Decco was his usual **glum** self, **gnawing** away at a chunk of rock he'd bought at the Eiffel Tower.

Mr. Barrett checked them all through the ticket desk.

'**Nice** camera, Tommo,' he said. 'You should get some **good** shots of the parade with that.'

'Yeh, Sir,' said Billy Sullivan. 'That's what Shirley said — 'specially of Tommo and Mickey Mouse. They can compare their **great** ears, can't they, Sir?'

'Now, now, Billy. That's not very **nice**,' said Mr. Barrett. 'Behave yourself. You know, I realise it's **futile** to expect you to be **great** friends but it would be really **good** if you and Tommo could get on, for even five minutes, instead of always sniping at each other. Really, it's not **amusing**.'

'No worries, Sir,' Billy grinned. 'I'll be really **nice** to him, I promise. Honest Sir. You won't recognise me, I'll be that good.'

'That's what worries me, Billy,' sighed Mr. Barrett. 'You and the word "good" just don't go together! Now, go on, the lot of you. Have a **great** time and try not to make too much of a **racket**. I'll see you back here at three.'

Exercise 3

The exam. Functional writing.
1. Ballet
2. Comedy
3. Cinema
4. Classical or Pop Music
5. Photography

Choose one of the above art forms and write a documentary-style article on it for the school magazine, in which you:
(a) Give a **brief** outline of its origins and history. (75–100 words)
(b) Define the various forms and areas of performance. (100–150 words)
(c) Discuss some modern-day examples of it, for example performers, style, venues. (100–150 words)

Use as many related words from a thesaurus as possible, in order to avoid the repetition of overused words like 'good' and 'great'.

UNIT 3

Grappling with Grammar

ADJECTIVES

Question What is an adjective?

Answer An adjective is a word that describes a noun. It tells us more about people, places, things, animals and feelings.

Adjectives make our writing more interesting, more colourful and more informative. Charles Dickens, for example, uses adjectives to wonderful effect in his books. Here is an example from *Hard Times*: 'Mrs. Gradgrind, a little, thin, white, pink-eyed bundle of shawls.'

Look at these two sentences:
- The street ran down to the factory.
- The **dusty, bustling** street ran down to a **black, foul-smelling** factory.

The adjectives 'dusty' and 'bustling' tell us more about the street, and 'black' and 'foul-smelling' appeal to our senses. We can visualise the scene because of the adjectives. They 'paint' it for us.

Stage 1

Exercise 1

In pairs.

The box below contains fifteen adjectives and fifteen nouns, all jumbled up together. Can you pair them off, as in the following example?

Example	Adjective	Noun
a	busy	office

WATCH YOUR LANGUAGE!

Your teacher will time you (five minutes), and the first pair of students to complete the task, wins!

beautiful, sky, interesting, castle, strong, programme, fresh, lovely, car, view, fast, glue, chest, golden, worm, girl, loaf, golden, black, duckling, tooth, hairy, rotten, rude, hole, wound, comedian, deep, wriggly, ugly

Exercise 2
In pairs, or as individuals, think of a good and interesting adjective for each of the nouns below.

Example   **Adjective**   **Noun**
             an   amusing   visitor

1. _____ boy   6. _____ driver
2. _____ film   7. _____ friend
3. _____ day   8. _____ drug
4. _____ dinner   9. _____ experience
5. _____ teacher 10. _____ game

Exercise 3
(a) Write one interesting adjective for each letter of the alphabet. Think hard and only consult your dictionary when you are really stuck — as in adjectives beginning with 'x', 'y' or 'z'! Give yourself a time limit of fifteen minutes for this exercise.

(b) **Combine** your list of **adjectives** with 26 **nouns** beginning with the same letter.

Example   an adventurous ant
              a beautiful bowl
              a cheerful chap

Try to create some funny or unusual combinations, if you can. Time limit: 20 minutes.

Stage 2
TYPES OF ADJECTIVES

1. **Descriptive.** This type of adjective includes a broad range of words including those that appeal to the **senses**.
   Example foul-smelling, dark, ugly, sharp, rude, sarcastic, looming, scorching, damaged, optimistic, delicious, deadly

2. **Possessive.** These adjectives show **ownership** or **possession**.
   Example **my** car, **your** book, **his** problem, **her** friend, **our** school, **your** teacher, **their** pitch

3. **Demonstrative.** These adjectives **point out** or **refer to** a **specific** object or person.
   Example **this** page, **that** man, **these** flowers, **those** students

4. **Proper.** These adjectives come from **proper nouns** and are always written with a **capital letter**.
   Example the **Celtic** tiger, our **Irish** heritage, the **French** language, the **Atlantic** Ocean

GRAMMAR: ADJECTIVES

Exercise 1

(a) **Locate and underline** each of the adjectives in the following sentences.
(b) Indicate which **type** of adjective it is by writing the letter 'D' over a **descriptive** adjective, 'P' over a **possessive** adjective, 'DM' over a **demonstrative** adjective and 'PR' over a **proper** adjective.

1. You can get a really tasty curry in the local Indian restaurant.
2. This pink ticket has some interesting but illegible writing on it.
3. Did you see those amazing pictures that Tom took of that French vineyard?
4. Scorching weather, long cold drinks, intelligent attractive company. What more could you want on a Mediterranean holiday?
5. The African continent is beautiful, but there are fierce and angry conflicts between its various tribes.
6. An industrious, good-humoured student is optimistic about the future and confident in terms of the exam.
7. 'What an appetising smell! Your lasagne is as delicious as you are beautiful, my darling,' the oily charmer said.
8. This room is freezing! I have never been so cold. My hands and feet are numb.
9. John is very intelligent and studious, but he panics before an exam and is petrified he will fail.
10. In the soft light of morning, the worn gravestones looked less sinister, less frightening than the night before.

Exercise 2

(a) Write the corresponding adjective for each of the following nouns.

Example	Noun	Adjective
	monster	monstrous

Noun	Adjective	Noun	Adjective
1. bitterness	_____	11. energy	_____
2. courage	_____	12. nation	_____
3. justice	_____	13. vanity	_____
4. sympathy	_____	14. truth	_____
5. patience	_____	15. certainty	_____
6. sense	_____	16. artist	_____
7. length	_____	17. suspicion	_____
8. apology	_____	18. mystery	_____
9. silence	_____	19. effect	_____
10. strength	_____	20. doubt	_____

(b) Now choose ten adjectives from the list and write a sentence for each one, remembering that adjectives describe nouns. Make them as interesting as possible, and vary the type of sentence, i.e. question, negative, exclamation.

Exercise 3

Here are two lists of adjectives that describe feelings and qualities, both good and bad. There are forty in all.

Good		Bad	
amazed	amused	afraid	angry
calm	confident	anxious	awful
cool	delighted	bored	depressed
enthusiastic	excited	disappointed	frightened
fascinated	friendly	frustrated	guilty
happy	interested	helpless	hurt
loving	optimistic	impatient	jealous
pleasant	proud	lonely	mean
quiet	sensitive	sad	uncomfortable
surprised	warm	upset	worried

Using words from these lists, write the **opening paragraph** (100–120 words) of a prose composition on **two** of the following topics:

1. What my family (or a member of it) means to me. (1997 Junior Cert. Higher Level paper)
2. A troublesome visitor. (1997 Junior Cert. Higher Level paper)
3. People who get on my nerves. (1996 Junior Cert. Higher Level paper)
4. 'The true perfection of a person lies not in what a person has but in what a person is.' Discuss this statement.

Stage 3

COMPARATIVE AND SUPERLATIVE OF ADJECTIVES

Rules:
1. Most adjectives simply add 'er' for the comparative and 'est' for the superlative.
   Example tall, tall**er**, tall**est**
2. If the adjective **ends in 'y'**, the **'y' changes to 'i'** before adding 'er' or 'est'.
   Example happy, happ**ier**, happ**iest**
3. If an adjective ends in a **consonant** and the **letter before** the last one is a **vowel**, then the **consonant letter** is **doubled** before adding 'er' or 'est'.
   Example big, bigger, biggest
4. Adjectives of **two or more syllables** usually add '**more**' for the comparative and '**most**' for the superlative.
   Example useful, **more** useful, **most** useful
5. Finally! There are some **irregular adjectives** which change **completely** in the comparative and superlative. You just have to learn these.

GRAMMAR: ADJECTIVES

Example
good	better	best
little	less	least
many	more	most
bad	worse	worst

'Worser' is **not** good English!

Exercise 1
Write the comparative and superlative forms of the following adjectives:

	Adjective	Comparative	Superlative
1.	smooth		
2.	wise		
3.	sunny		
4.	fat		
5.	foolish		
6.	dangerous		
7.	bad		
8.	noisy		
9.	truthful		
10.	beautiful		
11.	safe		
12.	long		
13.	strong		
14.	bitter		
15.	soft		
16.	slim		
17.	delicious		
18.	efficient		
19.	good		
20.	cool		

Exercise 2
Look at the following sentence in which the **comparative** form of the adjective is used.

Example   The **more** I run, the **fitter** I feel.   more \ run \ fit \ feel

Using the above sentence as an example, write ten more sentences according to this pattern, from the following words and phrases. Begin each sentence with 'The'.

1. warm \ weather \ happy \ are
2. more \ earn \ more \ spend
3. long \ wait \ impatient \ become
4. more \ see her \ less \ like her
5. big \ car \ more petrol \ use

6. more \ eat \ fat \ get
7. soon \ leave \ better
8. more \ merry
9. more \ work \ more \ builds up
10. less \ say \ better

Exercise 3

(a) Look at this sentence which uses the **superlative** form of the adjective:

> **Example** The **happiest** day of my life was when our team won the Leinster Cup.

Write **one complete sentence** in answer to each of the following questions. Then choose **one** of them and write a little more about the experience in the form of a **paragraph** (100–120 words), a **poem** or a **piece of dialogue**. Use as many interesting adjectives from this unit as you can.

1. What was the **happiest** day of your life?
2. What was the **worst** day?
3. What was the **most embarrassing** experience you've ever had?
4. What was the **most shocking** experience?
5. What was the **most exciting** moment?

(b) The exam. (1994 Junior Cert. Ordinary Level paper, Section 1, Media Studies)

Here is an advertisement for a stage production of Roald Dahl's *The Witches*.

1. Read the description of the show. **Circle** all the **adjectives** used in the text.
2. This piece of writing is designed to **persuade** people to go to this show. Would you be persuaded to go? Give **3 reasons** for your answer, using as many **adjectives from the advertisement and this unit** as you can.

A MAGNIFICENT AWARD WINNING BOOK.
A MAJOR HOLLYWOOD MOVIE.
NOW, LIVE ON STAGE

THE
WITCHES

What do you imagine when you think of witches? Broomsticks? Black cats? Cloaks and pointed hats? No, that's the stuff of fairy-tales and this first ever stage production of **Roald Dahl's** classic book is definitely no fairy-tale.

This is a fast-moving adventure story of a boy and his grandmother battling against REAL WITCHES: easily the most dangerous of all the living creatures on earth.

Sensational secrets will be revealed. You'll witness an extraordinary play of spine-tingling and spectacular events. There will be magical moments that you'll never forget and you'll gasp in disbelief at the astonishing goings-on. But, this action-packed drama, full of superb music, amazing illusions and a great deal of warmth and humour is designed for all the family.

THE WITCHES PROMISES TO BE THE CHRISTMAS ENTERTAINMENT OF THE DECADE

PUNCTUATION: SEMI-COLONS AND COLONS

Punctuation Please!

SEMI-COLONS AND COLONS

Stage 1

SEMI-COLONS

Question: When do we use semi-colons?

Answer:
1. When we want to mark a **longer** or more **important** break in a sentence than is served by a comma.

   Example 'Love is like the measles; we all have to go through it.'
   (Jerome K. Jerome)

   In this sentence a comma wouldn't have been sufficient. A full stop, however, would have been too much! So, the **semi-colon** was just right. It's job lies **between** a comma and a full stop.

   Example 'To lose one parent, Mr Worthing, may be regarded as a misfortune; to lose both looks like carelessness.' (Oscar Wilde)

2. When we want to separate complicated things in a list of connected items.

   Example Mum loaded up the trolley with delicious food for the party: barbecued chickens coated in crisp golden breadcrumbs; a whole ham glazed with pineapple and honey; fresh bread rolls swimming in garlic butter; chocolate chip and toffee crunch ice-cream.

3. When we want to separate statements that are connected, in a comparative sense.

   Example All the guys are posing; all the girls are bored.
   All the male tigers are spotted; all the females striped.

4. When two ideas are connected by one of the following words: however, therefore, indeed, besides, nevertheless, consequently.

   Example I waited for over an hour; **however**, she never arrived.

Exercise 1

Class exercise. Oral

Your teacher will call out the following:

'The members of the committee are: Peter Ryan, teacher; Sheila Fox, dentist; . . .'

The teacher will then ask each person in your class to add a person and his/her profession to the list. Your teacher will allow you **30 seconds** to come up with both. You must also **say** the word '**semi-colon**' after his/her job description.

Example 'Tom Murphy, builder — **semi-colon**.'

55

WATCH YOUR LANGUAGE!

Exercise 2
Divide into pairs and **write down** as many of the people's names and their jobs as you can remember from Exercise 1. There may be as many as 30, if your class has 30 students. The two students who write down the most names and professions **with semi-colons** are the winners! Time limit: fifteen minutes.

Exercise 3
Complete the following sentences with an idea **connected** to the first part by the words in bold.
1. The guest speaker never arrived; **therefore**, _____.
2. Tim's father approved of his plans; **indeed**, _____.
3. Shauna didn't really believe in ghosts; **nevertheless**, _____.
4. He practised hard for his driving test; **however**, _____.
5. You can't leave at this hour of the night; **besides**, _____.

Exercise 4
Complete the following sentences. Remember, there should be some **connection** between the first and second half of the sentence.

> **Example**   The rain fell in sheets; _____.
> The rain fell in sheets; it soaked me through to the bone.

1. The first thing Tom did was to turn on the telly; _____.
2. Everyone had to eat some of Sarah's curry; _____.
3. Some students travel by bus; _____.
4. Joe's teacher approved of his plans; _____.
5. I love the summer holidays; _____.

Here is an extract from *Oliver Twist* by Charles Dickens. Read it, carefully noting the use he makes of the **semi-colon** in his description of the children, the man and the old woman.

> There was no fire in the room; but a man was crouching, mechanically, over the empty stove. An old woman, too, had drawn a low stool to the cold hearth, and was sitting beside him. There were some ragged children in another corner; and in a small recess, opposite the door, there lay upon the ground something covered with an old blanket. Oliver shuddered as he cast his eye towards the place, and crept involuntarily close to his master; for though it was covered up, the boy felt that it was a corpse.
>
> The man's face was thin and very pale; his hair and beard were grizzly; and his eyes were bloodshot. The old woman's face was wrinkled; her two remaining teeth protruded over her under lip; and her eyes were bright and piercing. Oliver was afraid to look at either her or the man. They seemed so like the rats he had seen outside.

Exercise 5
Here is another extract from *Oliver Twist*, from which I have **removed eight semi-colons**. Write it out into your copybook, replacing these semi-colons where you feel they are appropriate.

PUNCTUATION: SEMI-COLONS AND COLONS

(Look at No. 2 in the list of uses of the semi-colon at the start of this unit, and read the above extract again before you begin.) Note how the **comma** is also skilfully used in this extract.

'Stop thief! Stop thief!' There is magic in the sound. The tradesman leaves his counter and the carman his waggon the butcher throws down his tray the baker his basket the milkman his pail the errand-boy his parcels the schoolboy his marbles the child his toys. Away they run, pell-mell, helter-skelter, slap-dash tearing, yelling and screaming knocking down passengers as they turn round corners, and rousing up the dogs. The streets and squares re-echo with the sound.

Exercise 6

Now choose a **character** from a short story, novel or play you have read, and write a brief description of that character using **semi-colons** to balance your sentences, in the way that Dickens does in the extracts above.

Stage 2

COLONS

Question When do we use colons?

Answer When we want to make a **stronger** punctuation mark than a semi-colon. It is very useful for:

1. introducing a **list** or a note, and after expressions like 'for example' and 'the following'.
   Example Students going on the Paris trip should bring the following: their passport, comfortable shoes, one bag or suitcase and an umbrella.
2. introducing a **title** or **quotation**.
   Example The first line of the poem is: 'I wandered lonely as a cloud.'
3. introducing **direct speech**.
   Example Dad looked up from his paper and said: 'Are you going somewhere, Susan?'
4. separating different parts of a sentence where the idea or thought is connected. In this situation a colon is used in the same way as a dash.
   Example No excuses this time: your work must improve.
   I like work: it fascinates me. I can sit and look at it for hours.
   In these examples the **colon** pulls us up sharp, forcing us to make a significant pause before continuing.
5. introducing the main **theme** or **subject matter** of a piece.
   Example Drug abuse: the menace of the nineties
   Ireland: the best address on Earth

57

6. moving a thought from its **premise** (introduction) to its **conclusion** (summary of the point).

> Example Punctuation is important (premise): it helps the reader to make sense of what you write (conclusion).

Two points to note:
1. Don't add a dash after a colon when introducing a list.
2. Don't put a capital letter after a colon in the same sentence.

Exercise 1
Oral. Teacher directed.

Your teacher will call out a situation which requires a list of items, and will then select students at random to supply one item each.

> Example Teacher: Give me a list of items you would need if you were planning a trip to a **jungle** in Central America.
> Student A: I would need a rucksack
> Student B: and insect repellent
> Student C: and . . .

The teacher continues on round the class until there are ten items. At the same time as the items are being called out, each student must try to write them all down. The one who lists the **most** items wins!

Remember! Each list must be **introduced** by a **colon**, and **commas** must be put after each item, **except** between the last two — where you will write 'and'.

Exercise 2
Write out these sentences, inserting a colon where you feel it should be placed in each case:
1. Sugar a sweet source of tooth decay.
2. Smoking a serious hazard to your health.
3. School can be OK it's here we make friends for life.
4. Homework a necessary evil.
5. To make a sickeningly delicious dessert, you'll need five tins of golden syrup, two lbs of butter, two lbs of brown sugar. *Et voilà!* Toffee fudge sauce for the whole class!
6. The weather continued as it had for several days hot and humid with storms at night.
7. The dogs began to bark they must have sensed an intruder.
8. There was a wonderful surprise waiting at home my new car had been delivered.
9. I don't watch soaps they're too predictable.
10. I was very late for work there was a pile-up on the M50.

Exercise 3
Place a colon after each of the following **titles**, and write a short statement about each of them:

> Example *Coronation Street*: the longest-running 'soap' in television history.

PUNCTUATION: SEMI-COLONS AND COLONS

1. *Eastenders*
2. *Titanic*
3. *Match of the Day*
4. *The Full Monty*
5. *Romeo and Juliet*

Exercise 4

Now choose ten titles of your own. They may be the names of books, films, TV programmes, CDs, magazines or comics. Write a statement about each one, as you did for Exercise 3. Remember to **begin** with the title followed by a **colon**.

Stage 3

THE EXAM: MEDIA STUDIES

Exercise 1

Write out the following sentences, placing a colon, semi-colons and commas in each one, as required:

1. The line-out is John O'Leary back Tom Murphy wing forward Sean Duignan scrum half Barry O'Neill hooker. Everyone else as was.
2. The film crew consists of Stan Carey camera operator Mary Slevin assistant to the producer Paul Thornton best boy Brian Nutley clapper loader Laura Ryan scenic artist Tom Shanahan carpenter.
3. Miss Streisand requests the following for her concert tour John Lyle piano tuner Stacey Grant masseuse Stanley Moorehead stress counsellor Michael Sullivan stage manager Irene Coates choreographer.
4. When in Paris, please contact the following people Michel Dumont chef 'Café de Paris' Odette Brumard couturier Marcus Ryan restaurateur Yves Montand movie star Jeanne Auban cabaret artiste.
5. The cast is as follows Eugene McRoarty caretaker Maura Tancred landlady Tom Shaw salesman Denise Schneider German visitor Sean Lyons barrister.

Exercise 2

Go colon hunting!
Search through a **newspaper** or **magazine** and cut out the sentences you can find that use a colon. **Headlines** are a good place to start.

Stick these sentences into a single page of your copybook. Think of a suitable **title**, which includes a colon, for your page; for example, Colossal Colon Hunt: The Search Starts Here.

WATCH YOUR LANGUAGE!

How Do You Spell . . . ?

DECISIONS! DECISIONS! SPELLING TRAPS

- 'ie' or 'ei'?
- 'able' or 'ible'?
- 'ful' or 'full'?
- 'e' or no 'e'?
- 'ce' or 'se'?

Decisions, decisions! Which do we use? It's often difficult to decide in spelling, but there are some rules that govern the above 'traps'. Let's look at some examples, and then exercise them.

Trap 1 'ie' or 'ei'?

Rule: 1. Usually the 'i' comes **before** the 'e'.
> Example   priest, believe, niece, grief

2. But 'e' comes before 'i' after 'c'.
> Example   ceiling, receipt, deceive

3. Exceptions (weird ones!). These must be learned, as the rule simply doesn't apply.
> Example   weird, seize, foreign, either, neither, protein, leisure, neighbour, weight, Sheila, Keith, Neil

Exercise 1

Fill in the blanks in the following sentences with suitable words from the box below.
1. My _____ is always baking cakes. Her _____ is constantly in use!
2. There were only _____ of them left on the _____, battling it out for the cup.
3. Our _____, Sheila, _____ all day at her son's wedding.
4. No matter how hard he _____, he simply couldn't find the _____ for his suit.
5. The _____ was covered in scenes from the _____ of Pope Gregory.

> eight, niece, field, sieve, reign, receipt, cried, neighbour, tried, ceiling

Exercise 2

Write a paragraph (100–120 words) in the form of a story which uses all of the **exceptions** listed under Rule 3 **once** only. You might, for instance, begin with this sentence: 'Keith didn't look foreign, but Neil did.' You may, of course, compose your own opening sentence.

Trap 2 'ful' or 'full'?

Rule: When you want to add 'full' to another word, drop the final 'l'.

> Example   joy plus **full** becomes **joyful**
> use plus **full** becomes **useful**

So, the rule is very simple. A word **cannot** end in 'full' — it must end in 'ful'.

60

SPELLING: SPELLING TRAPS

Exercise 1
Fill in the blanks in the following sentences with suitable words from the box below.
1. He was my _____ friend for many years, kind and _____.
2. Granny was _____. Even when times were hard she was always _____.
3. Tom is _____ never to make mistakes in his spelling, because he hopes to become a _____ journalist.
4. Karen's love life is _____ at the moment. She's just too _____ around boys.
5. 'How could Brian be so _____? I think he's _____!', Sarah muttered.

bashful, deceitful, uneventful, thoughtful, successful, wonderful, awful, cheerful, careful, faithful

Exercise 2
Write a short paragraph (70–100 words) which connects each of these five words in some way:

1. painful
2. beautiful
3. doubtful
4. disgraceful
5. spiteful

Trap 3 'ce' or 'se'?
Rule: 1. The word with 'c' is a **noun** (**the/a** practice).

> **Example** Selling alcohol to underage teenagers is a widespread **practice**.

2. The word with 's' is a **verb** (**to** practise).

> **Example** Barry **practises** the guitar for three hours every day.

Exercise 1
In the following sentences, decide which of the words in brackets is **correct**, in terms of the meaning of the sentence.
1. 'That's good _____ (advice/advise),' the man said. 'I'll speak to my solicitor tomorrow.'
2. A publican is _____d (licence/license) to sell alcohol.
3. Inventors _____ (device/devise) new ways of doing things.
4. _____ (practice/practise) makes perfect.
5. 'I _____ (advice/advise) you to watch out for pickpockets in this street,' said the guide.
6. 'If you _____ (practice/practise) hard, you really will succeed,' her piano teacher said.
7. The man lost his _____ (licence/license) when he was found drunk at the wheel of his car for the third time.
8. What is it? It's a _____ (device/devise) for extracting salt from water.

Exercise 2
Practise the above words in sentences of your own — using each of the words once only, both as a **noun** and as a **verb**.

WATCH YOUR LANGUAGE!

Trap 4 'able' or 'ible'?
Rule: Although it's difficult to remember whether a word ends in 'able' or 'ible', the fact is that **most** words end in 'able'. Here are ten commonly used 'able' words.

1. acceptable
2. reasonable
3. accountable
4. biddable
5. capable
6. considerable
7. comfortable
8. fashionable
9. miserable
10. reliable

Exercise 1

In the following piece of dialogue, fill in the blanks with a suitable 'able' adjective from the list above. (One word has been used twice.)

Dad: Really, Tina, it is not _____ to your mother and me that you come home at this hour!
Tina: Chill out, Dad. I'm quite _____ of taking care of myself. I am fourteen, you know.
Dad: Yes, but not very _____, it seems! You promised to be home by eleven.
Tina: But it's only ten past twelve. Everyone in Sarah's house was still up. We were just getting _____ in fact, when I had to leave.
Dad: Oh were you now?! Listen to me, young lady, this is the second time you've been late this week. What's wrong with you? You used to be so _____, so trustworthy.
Tina: That's not fair, Dad! I am trustworthy. If you and Mum were just a little bit more _____, you'd know that it's just not _____ for teenagers to behave exactly as you 'oldies' want us to any more. This is 1999, Dad, not 1899!
Dad: _____ or not, young lady, we're not talking about clothes here, we're talking about behaviour! Your mother and I have gone to _____ trouble to bring you up properly.
Tina: And to make my life _____, you mean! It's not fair. You're always on my back.
Dad: No, Tina. That is not true. We just want you to be _____ for your actions, that's all.

The 'ible' ending **sounds** like a suffix to the word: sens**ible**, terr**ible**. Saying the word **aloud** may help.

Exercise 2

Now fill in the blanks in the following sentences with 'ible' words from the box below.
1. 'Who's _____ for the mess in here?' roared the Head.
2. What an _____ story! Did you make that up?
3. 'Is that cheese _____?' she asked, wondering about the grey fuzzy bits on one side.
4. 'Correcting your homework would be a lot easier if your handwriting were _____, John,' sighed Miss Cronin.
5. Sarah's very _____. She always does the right thing.
6. 'I can be a little _____ about your hours of work, if that helps,' the Manager said.
7. That's _____ news. I'm really sorry.

62

SPELLING: SPELLING TRAPS

8. You're so _____, Peter! You believe everything she tells you.
9. He's the most _____ bachelor in Kerry.
10. What a _____ day! It hasn't stopped raining since 7 a.m.

flexible, responsible, horrible, legible, gullible, sensible, incredible, terrible, edible, eligible

Trap 5 'e' or no 'e'?
Words ending in 'e' can cause problems, when we wish to add a new ending (suffix). What do we do? Keep the 'e' or drop it? Here is the rule.

Rule
1. When the suffix begins with a **vowel**, or a 'y' is added, we **drop** the 'e'.

   Example   dive   div**ing**   div**ed**
                 bone   bon**y**

2. When the suffix begins with a **consonant**, we **keep** the 'e'.

   Example   bare   bare**ly**
                 face   face**less**
                 refine   refine**ment**

3. There are some exceptions. Learn these, as they are often spelled incorrectly:

argue	argument
true	truly
due	duly
whole	wholly
humble	humbly
courage	courageous
notice	noticeable
like	likeable **or** likable

Exercise 1

Add 'ing' and 'ed' to these words, **dropping the 'e'** according to Rule 1. The first one is done for you.

1. hate — hating — hated
2. cycle — _____ — _____
3. starve — _____ — _____
4. save — _____ — _____
5. rave — _____ — _____
6. bake — _____ — _____
7. declare — _____ — _____
8. hope — _____ — _____
9. love — _____ — _____
10. live — _____ — _____

WATCH YOUR LANGUAGE!

Exercise 2

Add 'ly', 'less' or 'ment' to the following words, **keeping the 'e'**, as in Rule 2. But **you** must decide which suffix you can add to the word given! The first one is done for you.

	ly	less	ment
1. advance			advancement
2. care			
3. refine			
4. late			
5. nice			
6. face			
7. definite			
8. hope			
9. require			
10. precise			

Exercise 3

Write out the following paragraph with the correct spelling of the words **in brackets**, according to the rules you have studied, and to their use and meaning within the passage.

Margaret was (hope) for a miracle. She couldn't believe that Kevin actually (hate) her. Claire was (rave) surely? After all, Margaret (love) him and they were (save) for a house, weren't they? He was (definite) in line for (advance) at work, and her mother had already (bake) the wedding cake, for heaven's sake! She had even sold her car in order to save money and was now (cycle) to work every day. (Late), however, she had noticed that Kevin was getting (care) about time, and wasn't quite as (love) as he'd been. Perhaps Claire was right. Kevin hadn't actually (declare) his intention to marry her, but he had said he'd always wanted to marry a woman of (refine) and taste — like her.

'To hell with him!' she thought. 'I have (starve) myself for that man! How dare he hate me?'

'(Precise)!' a little voice inside her said. 'You're better off without him, Margaret. Off you go and find some nice, (name), (face) bureaucrat with lots of money instead.'

'Too true!' said Margaret to the teddy on her desk. 'That'll do me (nice)! I'll be (live) it up this weekend, Kevin Ryan, but without you. Hasta la vista, baby! — as Arnold would say.'

VOCABULARY: SYNONYMS AND ANTONYMS

Words at Work

OPPOSITES ATTRACT ... SYNONYMS AND ANTONYMS

Question What is a synonym?
Answer A synonym is a word which is very **close in meaning** to another word.
  Example **Student** is a synonym of **pupil**.
  When you use synonyms you avoid needless repetition and your writing becomes more interesting as a result. A **thesaurus** is a book with an alphabetical list of words and their synonyms. It is a very useful tool in your writing.
Question What is an antonym?
Answer An antonym is a word which is **opposite in meaning** to another word.
  Example **Happy** is an antonym of **sad**.

Exam questions often ask you to **compare** and **contrast** things, for example images, characters, plots and styles of writing. Having a variety of **synonyms** for **comparison**, and **antonyms** for **contrast**, will help you to write better answers to these kinds of questions.
  Let's practise.

Stage 1

Exercise 1
Sort out these words into ten pairs of synonyms:
  Example large — big
  small, expensive, neat, shut, reply, difficult, tidy, closed, right, large, dear, ill, answer, despise, tiny, correct, big, hate, hard, sick

Remember that very few words have **exactly** the same meaning. But some words are **almost** the same, i.e. **synonyms**!

Exercise 2
Match each of the words in bold in the following sentences to a synonym from the box below.
1. Golf takes up almost all of my **spare** time. _____
2. You can get a lot of **fun** out of solving puzzles. _____
3. Tom is an enthusiastic member of his local drama **club**. _____
4. I find Maths **difficult**. _____
5. Miss Hurley is very nice but she can be a bit **cutting** at times. _____
6. That film was really **dull**! _____
7. It's **icy** out there. _____

8. Sarah actually **likes** housework. _____
9. Richard Branson is extremely **wealthy**. _____
10. Dad discovered an **old** sword in the attic. _____

> pleasure, leisure, affluent, antique, society,
> tedious, glacial, enjoys, scathing, arduous

Exercise 3

Sort out these words into ten pairs of antonyms:

Example appear — vanish

relaxed, intolerant, fresh, understanding, strict, majority, pessimistic, friendly, vanish, wrong, minority, nervous, optimistic, appear, tense, easygoing, hostile, right, calm, stale

Exercise 4

Write the antonyms of these words. The first letter is given to you, as a clue.

	Antonym				Antonym	
1. absence	p_____		11. war	p_____
2. cheap	e_____		12. sense	n_____
3. failure	s_____		13. difficult	e_____
4. innocent	g_____		14. honest	d_____
5. kind	u_____		15. pleasant	u_____
6. careful	c_____		16. selfish	u_____
7. obey	d_____		17. capable	i_____
8. trust	d_____		18. approval	d_____
9. true	f_____		19. mature	i_____
10. vague	d_____		20. encourage	d_____

Stage 2

MORE ABOUT SYNONYMS

Because synonyms are close in meaning to another word, but not exactly the same, we must be careful which synonym of a word we use in a particular context. For example, if your Mum made you a cup of tea, and you appreciated it, you might say: 'Thanks, Mum. That was a **great** cup of tea.' But you would hardly say: 'That was a **momentous** or **magnificent** cup of tea.' These two words are synonyms of 'great', but would be inappropriate in this context. (Incidentally, *The Wordsworth Thesaurus for Home, Office and Study* has over 125 synonyms for 'great'!)

VOCABULARY: SYNONYMS AND ANTONYMS

Exercise 1
Fill in the blanks in the sentences below with the most **suitable** (appropriate) synonym from the four options given.
1. If you don't lift that saucepan carefully, you may _____ yourself.
   A. blister   B. sear   C. scald   D. singe
2. Mr. Murphy has been asked to _____ the next meeting of the Parents' Committee.
   A. present   B. preside   C. lead   D. chair
3. Miss Simpson was _____ of stealing money from the till.
   A. accused   B. alleged   C. charged   D. denounced
4. The deer in the Phoenix Park are quite _____.
   A. biddable   B. tame   C. broken in   D. domesticated
5. Margaret never bought anything for her friend's birthday. She was too _____.
   A. close   B. tight   C. mean   D. miserly
6. The President's personal _____ never left her side during the State Visit.
   A. defender   B. lifeguard   C. protector   D. bodyguard
7. She couldn't believe that he had bought her a _____ diamond ring.
   A. imitation   B. fake   C. artificial   D. false
8. There have been many changes in the _____ for Junior Certificate.
   A. plan   B. syllabus   C. agenda   D. programme
9. The sea was so _____ that many of the passengers were seasick.
   A. uneven   B. choppy   C. wavy   D. billowy
10. Mary buys most of the _____ she sees advertised on TV.
    A. goods   B. products   C. commodities   D. merchandise

Exercise 2
Below are five sets of words, each of which comprises a word and three synonyms for it, taken from the *Wordsworth Thesaurus*. Write one sentence for each synonym in each set. Your sentences should **clearly** show the difference in **usage** of each word, depending on the **context** in which it is used.

Example	bother	1. annoy:	That man annoys me!
		2. disturb:	I don't want to disturb you.
		3. upset:	I hope this won't upset you.

	Word	Synonyms
Set 1.	bother (verb)	annoy, disturb, upset
Set 2.	courtesy (noun)	consideration, kindness, politeness
Set 3.	deep (adjective)	bottomless, grave, mysterious
Set 4.	enterprise (noun)	activity, business, project
Set 5.	foreign (adjective)	alien, distant, strange

WATCH YOUR LANGUAGE!

More About Antonyms

You can also form antonyms by:

(a) adding a prefix to a word.

Example	happy	**un**happy
	correct	**in**correct
	obey	**dis**obey
	perfect	**im**perfect

(b) changing the prefix.

Example	**a**scend	**de**scend
	internal	**ex**ternal

(c) changing the suffix:

Example	care**ful**	care**less**
	use**ful**	use**less**

Exercise 3

Using prefixes and suffixes, make antonyms from the following words:

		Antonym			Antonym
1.	just	unjust	7.	selfish	_____
2.	convenient	_____	8.	sane	_____
3.	advantage	_____	9.	like	_____
4.	patient	_____	10.	possible	_____
5.	increase	_____	11.	encourage	_____
6.	hopeful	_____	12.	merciful	_____

Some other less common prefixes can also be used to make antonyms:

Example	ab	+	normal	=	**ab**normal
	il	+	legal	=	**il**legal
	non	+	sense	=	**non**sense
	ig	+	noble	=	**ig**noble

You will find a lot more examples and exercises on prefixes and suffixes in Unit 6 — How Do You Spell . . . ?

Exercise 4

Write a paragraph in the form of a story which uses each of the antonyms from Exercise 3 once only. Here is a starter sentence: 'George felt that it was very **unjust** to dismiss Shane, but the rest of the team felt it was **impossible** to work with him.' You may compose your own, of course.

VOCABULARY: SYNONYMS AND ANTONYMS

Stage 3

Exercise 1

The exam. Personal writing. (1997 Junior Cert. Higher Level paper)

'Write the conversation (in dialogue form) that might occur between a parent and a teenager after the parent comes home from a parent/teacher meeting.'

Imagine that the following is the first draft of the above personal writing exercise. You will notice that certain words are in bold, because they are **repeated**. Can you write a **second draft** using synonyms of your own for those words in bold? Use a thesaurus if you get stuck!

Dad: Well, Pat, that was a terrific parent/teacher meeting, really . . .

Pat: **Terrific**? That's great Dad, really **great**!

Dad: Will you let me finish?! I was about to say that I was **really** . . .

Pat: I know, I know, Dad, but there's no need to say it, like. I'm a **great** son, and that's all there is to it.

Dad: No! That is not all there is to it! I have never been so embarrassed in my entire life. Did you hear me? **Embarrassed**, dreadfully **embarrassed** for you, Pat. I . . .

Pat: Yeh. Yeh. I heard. You've never been so embarrassed in your **entire** life, etc., etc. So what's the problem? It's only the Mocks, right?

Dad: Only the Mocks?! Oh, well, that's all right then, Pat, isn't it? It's only three months to your exam. You'll have no **problem** there at all, will you? Not my brainy son, oh no!

Pat: Yeh, well, I am **brainy**. You just don't see it, that's all. You don't understand, do you? I'm under a lot of pressure, you know, a lot of **pressure**. You parents never **understand** that — **never**.

Dad: Oh, so I don't understand now. I know nothing about **pressure**, I suppose. I'm only your **parent**, right?!

Pat: Got it in one, Dad! It's not your fault entirely, of course. You are getting on a bit and the old grey matter doesn't work too well. Hey! No sweat. It happens.

Dad: Getting **on a bit**, am I? Listen, sunshine, I may be ancient in your eyes, but I still have all my **grey matter** intact, I can assure you! What's more, I'm still your Dad! Up those stairs this minute and get studying, or this **old** man, whose brain doesn't work too well, will ground you for a month!!

Exercise 2

Now, **continue the dialogue** and complete the personal writing exercise, using **synonyms** and **antonyms** where appropriate. Refer to words used throughout this unit, if you need some inspiration. (200–250 words)

And finally . . .

Teacher: Who can explain what a synonym is?

Peggy: I can, Miss! It's a word you use instead of the one you can't spell.

UNIT 4

Grappling with Grammar

ADVERBS

Question What is an adverb?
Answer An adverb is a word that tells us more about a **verb**.

Dealing with adverbs

1. Adverbs give us more **information** about verbs, about **how** something is done.
   Example The dinner was planned **precisely**,
   cooked **carefully**,
   and eaten **quickly**.
2. Adverbs can also tell us **when** something is done.
   Example She wrote home **immediately**.
3. Adverbs can also tell us **where** something happens.
   Example The match was played **away**.
4. There are levels of **comparison** for adverbs, as there are for adjectives.
   Example carefully   **more** carefully   **most** carefully
5. Lots of adverbs are **formed** very easily from **adjectives**. In most cases, you simply add '**ly**'.
   Example clever (adjective) → cleverly (adverb)
   Be careful, though, because some **adjectives** also end in 'ly'.
   Example friendly, lively, elderly, lonely, silly, lovely.
6. In some cases, there will be a slight change in the spelling when forming adverbs from adjectives.
   (a) When an adjective ends in 'y', in order to make the adverb, we drop the 'y' and put in 'i' before adding 'ly'.
   Example angry → angrily

GRAMMAR: ADVERBS

(b) When an adjective ends in 'e', and has two consonant letters before the 'e', we drop the 'e', before adding the 'ly' (or just 'y' if 'l' is the second last letter in the word).

Example gentle → gently.

(c) However, if an adjective ends in 'e' but has just one consonant letter immediately before the 'e' (and a vowel letter before that), then we keep the 'e' before adding 'ly'.

Example sincere → sincerely
wise → wisely
delicate → delicately

So you can see that dealing with adverbs needs a careful eye!

Stage 1

Exercise 1

(a) In pairs, decide who's A and B. Your teacher will **spell** out 20 adjectives. You must form **adverbs** from them.

(b) You must decide **how** the adverb will be spelt from the explanations at the beginning of this unit.

(c) There will be a time limit of **30 seconds** per example. A and B may consult on the spelling of the adverb. B must write both adjective and adverb into his/her copy.

(d) At the end, the teacher will ask you to **exchange** copies with another pair of students, and you will correct each others' work. Consult your dictionaries if in doubt about any of the spellings. The pair with the **most** correctly spelled adjectives and adverbs wins! (Time limit: ten minutes)

Exercise 2

Fill in the blanks in the sentences below with adverbs from Exercise 1.

1. She ate _____, taking tiny bites.
2. 'I don't frighten_____ ,' said Tom.
3. Mr. Riordan drives very _____, at a steady forty miles per hour.
4. 'You may speak _____, Simon,' the Principal said. 'I'm listening.'
5. The mother gazed _____ at her new baby.
6. Drinking _____ makes good sense.
7. 'To _____ go where no one has gone before.' (*Star Trek*).
8. _____, it won't be long before we can go home.
9. Rose has been behaving very _____ lately, don't you think?
10. They've been _____ married for over forty years.

WATCH YOUR LANGUAGE!

Exercise 3

(a) Write the **adverb** for each of the adjectives below. (Remember to check the spelling rules explained above.)

Adjective	Adverb	Adjective	Adverb
1. annual	_____	6. passionate	_____
2. beautiful	_____	7. quick	_____
3. definite	_____	8. reluctant	_____
4. gradual	_____	9. skilful	_____
5. menacing	_____	10. superb	_____

(b) Now write **two** sentences for each adjective/adverb combination.

> **Example** annual (adjective). He pays an **annual** visit to his Aunt Sarah in Cardiff.
> annually (adverb). His subscription to the *National Geographic* is paid **annually**.

Stage 2

TYPES OF ADVERBS

HOW?   WHERE?   WHEN?   HOW OFTEN?

1. **Adverbs of manner** answer the question **How**?
   > **Example** How did the old lady dress? She dressed **elegantly**.
2. **Adverbs of place** answer the question **Where**?
   > **Example** Where did he leave his coat? He left it **here**.
3. **Adverbs of time** answer the question **When**?
   > **Example** When did you last see Stephen? I saw him **yesterday**.
4. **Adverbs of frequency** answer the question **How often**?
   > **Example** How often do they eat out? They eat out at weekends, **usually**.

Exercise 1

Place each of the 24 adverbs from the box below under its correct heading in the following table:

Manner	Place	Time	Frequency
1. _____	_____	_____	_____
2. _____	_____	_____	_____
3. _____	_____	_____	_____
4. _____	_____	_____	_____
5. _____	_____	_____	_____
6. _____	_____	_____	_____

> never, eagerly, yesterday, seldom, now, outside, stubbornly, soon, kindly, early, usually, seriously, loudly, here, somewhere, sometimes, everywhere, tomorrow, always, there, today, painfully, often, anywhere

GRAMMAR: ADVERBS

Exercise 2
Now choose the most **suitable** adverb from Exercise 1 to complete the following sentences:
1. When May was ill, Tom treated her _____.
2. Brendan lives _____ else now.
3. 'Will I see you _____?' Karen asked.
4. 'How _____ do you see Paul?'
5. The children waited _____ for their Dad to bring home the new car.
6. Barry has concluded (however _____) that Susan doesn't fancy him.
7. You can see posters for *Godzilla* _____ these days.
8. 'I can't believe you're actually _____ for once!'
9. He's _____ very punctual.
10. Richard Branson is _____ rich!

Exercise 3
Using at least **three** of each type of adverb exercised so far (manner, place, time, frequency), write a 3–5 minute **scene** for a TV sitcom involving just **three** characters, entitled: *Never Too Late*. Keep it credible, and use as many adverbs from this unit as possible.

Stage 3

COMBINATIONS

Although we mainly use adverbs to describe **verbs**, there are times when we combine:
1. **adverbs** and **adjectives**
   Example   reasonably cheap
2. **adverbs** and **adverbs**!
   Example   incredibly quickly
3. **adverbs** and **past participles**
   Example   badly organised

Exercise 1
Choose **two** words, one from each box, to complete each of the sentences below.

Adverbs	Adjectives / past participles
absolutely, reasonably, badly, completely, seriously, fully, really, unusually, slightly, barely	cheap, huge, organised, changed, ill, quiet, damaged, insured, ready, sorry

1. Liam thought the restaurant was expensive, but I thought it was _____ _____.
2. Sean's mother is _____ _____ in hospital.
3. The fire destroyed our house, but fortunately we were _____ _____.
4. What a big ship! It's _____ _____.

WATCH YOUR LANGUAGE!

5. It wasn't a serious accident. The car was only _____ _____.
6. Lots of things went wrong because the trip was _____ _____.
7. The kids are usually very boisterous but they're _____ _____ today.
8. When Brian returned home after forty years in the States, everything had _____ _____.
9. I'm _____ _____ about losing your book. I'll buy you another one.
10. Denis was _____ _____ when the taxi arrived.

Exercise 2
Complete these sentences with a **second** adverb. Remember! It need not necessarily end in 'ly'. Look back at all the different types exercised so far.
1. The police were on the scene incredibly _____.
2. For such skilled technicians, they worked terribly _____.
3. We got home reasonably _____ from the match.
4. '4.30 a.m. is extremely _____, in my opinion, Gráinne!'
5. Everything went perfectly _____ on the day.
6. Bridget has behaved fairly _____ under the circumstances.
7. 'Do you come here _____?'
8. The garden is a mess! There are weeds absolutely _____.
9. 'How does she usually play?' 'Very _____!'
10. 'How will we approach the subject of the wedding?' 'Extremely _____!'

Exercise 3
The exam. Personal writing.
Adverbs of **manner** are used more frequently than any other type of adverb.
> Example   sleep **soundly**, eat **greedily**

(a) Match each of the following verbs to an adverb of manner from the box below.

1. feel   _____   6. speak   _____
2. argue   _____   7. behave   _____
3. whisper   _____   8. remember   _____
4. investigate   _____   9. listen   _____
5. react   _____   10. fall   _____

softly, frequently, angrily, clearly, deeply, attentively, thoroughly, stupidly, convincingly, continuously

(b) Now write a short narrative piece (100–120 words) in which you make an **imaginative connection** between the above verbs and adverbs. The situation might be one of conflict perhaps, **or** of reconciliation. Try not to **repeat** any of your verb/adverb combinations. Here is a possible starter for you: 'Although Donnacha tried to listen very attentively to what she was saying, his mind was really on the match.'

PUNCTUATION: QUESTION MARKS AND EXCLAMATION MARKS

> What does B.C. stand for?
> Before Calculators.

> What is a forum?
> Two-um plus two-um.

Punctuation Please!

QUESTION MARKS AND EXCLAMATION MARKS

1. Question marks

> Your son has the ability to go places – I wish he would!

Question When do we use question marks?
Answer Simple. We use them every time we ask a question.
  Example What's all this about then?
  But . . . (a) Do **not** put a **full stop** or a **comma** after a question mark.
  Example Who won the match?. Wrong!
  Who won the match? Right!
  And . . . (b) Do not use a question mark after an indirect question.
  Example **I asked him** who had won the match.

2. Exclamation marks
Question When do we use exclamation marks?
Answer Not so simple! We use them:
  (a) when giving an urgent message or order.
  Example Ambulance, please!
  Stop doing that! Sit down!
  (b) when expressing surprise or disbelief.
  Example A million pounds! I can't believe it!
  (c) in journalism. It suggests to the reader that what has been written is funny, exciting, dramatic or extraordinary in some way.
  Example Amazing triumph for home town team! Gazza Gazumped!
  It's snow joke! Blizzards in Bailieboro!
  (d) after exclamatory expressions (interjections).
  Example Wow! Gosh! You don't say! Well really! No way! Ouch!
  Help! Bah! Humbug!
  (e) to emphasise a strongly felt emotion, perhaps anger or joy.
  Example 'I hate you!' Jill screamed.
  'I'm so happy!' Hannah sighed.

WATCH YOUR LANGUAGE!

Stage 1

Exercise 1

In pairs. Oral and written.
(a) Decide who's A and B.
(b) Both A and B take **five minutes** to write out **five questions** on one or more of the topics from the box below. Do not let the other person see your questions!
(c) When the time is up, A asks B each of his/her five questions. B must answer with an **exclamation**-style sentence, which A must write down, with exclamation mark, under his/her own question.

> Example   A. Do you like the group 'Fab'?
>   B. Yeh! They're brilliant!

(d) Swop roles and repeat the exercise. This time, B must write down all the answers — with exclamation marks — to his/her own questions.
(e) Compare each other's work for correct use of exclamation marks **and** questions marks. (Time limit: 20 minutes)

> TV, groups, teams, holidays, food, subjects in school, films, friends, weekends

Exercise 2

Here are some answers to a quiz. Can you supply possible **questions**? Write them out. Remember those **question marks**. Time limit: 10 minutes.

1. Dublin
2. The Lee
3. Stratford-upon-Avon
4. *Romeo and Juliet* (film)
5. Wimbledon '98
6. Boyzone
7. Seamus Heaney
8. *Friends*
9. Mount Everest
10. Mary McAleese

Exercise 3

Write out the following sentences with **either** a question mark **or** a full stop at the end, depending on whether you understand the sentence to be a **direct** or an **indirect** question.

1. Can you tell me when the next train leaves
2. He asked me when the next train left
3. Why don't you ring her
4. Is that all you've written
5. She asked me if I could help her
6. Are you ever happy, Paula
7. What time is it
8. They asked for directions to the school
9. Do you know what you're saying
10. Hannah wanted to know if Jill was coming out to play

PUNCTUATION: QUESTION MARKS AND EXCLAMATION MARKS

Stage 2

When writing dialogue, we put question marks and exclamation marks **inside** the quotation marks.

Example   'Do you really hate me?' asked Paul.
'No, of course not!' snapped Diane.

Exercise 1

Punctuate the following piece of dialogue with question marks and exclamation marks where appropriate. Write it out into your copybook, with a new line for each character, as you see here.

Stephen:	Are you coming home
Tina:	What
Stephen:	Home. Are you coming home
Tina:	No. Not yet.
Stephen:	Why
Tina:	Why what
Stephen:	For God's sake, Tina Don't do this to me
Tina:	Don't shout at me
Stephen:	I'm not shouting. Sorry. I just want to know if you're coming home
Tina:	Yeh, Yeh OK. I know Just don't keep going on about it
Stephen:	But why aren't you coming home
Tina:	I told you I don't know Now, leave it, will you You're doing my head in
Stephen:	OK. OK. I'm sorry. I was only asking.
Tina:	Yeh, well, don't
Stephen:	Right I won't
Tina:	Good.
Stephen:	I'll see ye then. Next week. OK
Tina:	Yeh. Yeh. Whatever
Stephen:	Bye
Tina:	Yeh. Bye.

Exercise 2

Politely contradict these questions or statements using do/does/did and an exclamation mark.

Example   'Why didn't you finish it?'
'But I did finish it!'

1. I'm sorry you don't want to go out with me.
2. I am surprised that your mother doesn't drive.
3. Why don't you practise?
4. It's a pity Sarah doesn't like Maths.
5. Why didn't you tell me it was your birthday?

WATCH YOUR LANGUAGE!

6. I know you don't really love me.
7. It's a shame your brother doesn't like pizza.
8. I suppose they've cut off your phone because you didn't pay the bill.
9. You would play much better if you practised.
10. You would have passed if you'd studied hard.

Exercise 3

Look at this statement, followed by a question:

Example 'You can sing, **can't you**?'

Complete the following statements with a **question**. Don't forget the question mark!

1. You can dance,_____
2. He knows what he's doing,_____
3. They are coming with us,_____
4. You've got the tickets,_____
5. You haven't been fighting,_____
6. She's mad about me,_____
7. He's not totally daft,_____
8. We won't get in trouble,_____
9. It's over,_____
10. He can go as well,_____

Stage 3

Newspapers and magazines frequently use **exclamation marks** to:

1. promote a competition or offer.

WHAT A GOOD idea!
Ideas that are so good, we wonder why they weren't thought of before . . .

Win BoyZone!

Win Leonardo DiCaprio!

2. advertise a product or service.

exclamation **Dare!!**
COTY
PARIS · NEW YORK

3. highlight or emphasise a particular article.

Sugar scoop! *EastEnders'* Pat Evans, aka Pam St Clement, narrowly escaped a wild animal recently — and we don't mean Grant Mitchell! On safari in Africa, Pam was checking out some lion tracks when their owner emerged from the bushes to scoff her up! She made it to her jeep in the nick of time and word from the jungle is that her huge multi-coloured earrings frightened him off. Eek!

PAT IN HUNGRY LION HORROR!

PUNCTUATION: QUESTION MARKS AND EXCLAMATION MARKS

Question marks are used in the same way.

> What games are the GAA playing now?

> Was she trying to tell me something?

> Who'll look after them if you die?
> The Sun Life MoneyBack Plan will!

Exercise 1
(a) Look for some more examples of the use of question marks and exclamation marks in magazines and newspapers. Cut them out and paste them into a copybook/notebook under the headings 'Question Marks' and 'Exclamation Marks'.
(b) Choose **two** of each and write a brief comment on how effective the punctuation marks are in each case, in terms of persuading you to read the article or advertisement.
(c) Are there occasions where the **exclamation mark** seems overly dramatic or unnecessary? Comment on one of these instances.

Exercise 2
In the following articles, from *Sugar* magazine, two celebrities describe their most embarrassing moment. Note how the exclamation mark is used in each case. Is it appropriate, do you think, for the situation it describes? Comment briefly on both articles, then write an article of similar length (60–90 words) in which you describe your own most embarrassing moment. Try not to use more than three exclamation marks.

> **'A while ago,** as I left a club, I fell all the way down the stairs! When I got to the bottom I was faced with a crowd of people pointing at me — they recognised me from *Emmerdale*. The shame of it!'
> Paul Fox, Emmerdale

> **'I was once in the middle** of a dance routine when a fan threw a teddy bear on stage. As I went to do a tricky move, I slipped over on the bear and landed with a thump on my behind! I tried to adapt my fall into a funky dance move, but no one was fooled as I staggered back up in agony! Most of the audience and the band laughed their heads off as I hobbled around to finish the set. Arrrgh!' AJ, Backstreet Boys

Exercise 3
The exam. Media studies.
Using either question marks **or** exclamation marks, write a caption for each for these pictures, numbered 1 to 6.

WATCH YOUR LANGUAGE!

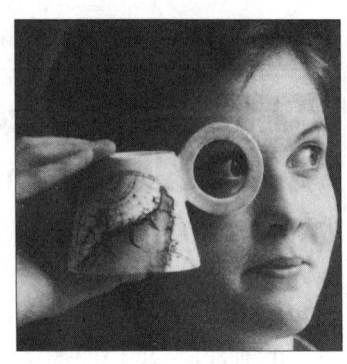

4. 5. 6.

How Do You Spell . . . ?

DOUBLING UP: DOUBLE LETTER WORDS 1

One of the most common errors made in spelling double letter words is to leave out one of the two letters.

| Example | hoby | wrong! | hobby | right! |
| | rubish | wrong! | rubbish | right! |

There are no hard and fast rules here. You just need to **learn** the correct spelling through **practice** and by **being careful**. In this unit, you will be exercising double letter words from double 'b' to double 'l'. So let's begin!

1. **Double 'b' words**

   Here are some of the most common ones:

abbreviate	rubber
flabby	rubbish
gobble	scribble
hobby	stubborn
robber	wobble

Exercise 1

(a) Study the ten words above for ten minutes in class. Remember it will be easier to learn these spellings because each word contains a **double 'b'** and they are written in **alphabetical** order.

(b) When the ten minutes are up, your teacher will call out each word in the order in which you have learned them. Write them out, one underneath the other, in a list, being very careful with those **double 'b's**!

(c) Exchange your copy with the person next to you. You will now correct his/hers, and he/she will do likewise with yours. Please refer to the **original spelling list** when correcting each word.

SPELLING: DOUBLE LETTER WORDS 1

(d) Give **one** mark for each word spelled correctly, and a total mark out of ten.
(e) If a word has been spelled **incorrectly**, cross it out and write the **correct** spelling of the word beside it, again checking from the original list.
(f) Take back your own copy and write out any words **you** have spelled incorrectly, **five times** each.

Exercise 2

Now look again at the ten double 'b' words listed above, this time for **meaning**. Then fill in the gaps in the following sentences with the most suitable word from the list.

1. Sometimes it's very handy to _____ a word, especially when writing notes.
2. 'Simon! Please don't _____ your food!'
3. Everyone should have a _____.
4. I know I write _____ at times, but I just can't help it!
5. Mum is always talking about her _____ thighs. Dad just ignores his.
6. The bank _____ got away with fifty thousand pounds and a box of the manager's cigars.
7. In drawing class, she's always borrowing my _____
8. 'I can't understand a word you've written, Paul! It's such a _____.'
9. Jelly _____ s.
10. 'Why are you so _____ ?!'

Exercise 3

Use your imagination and write a paragraph or a piece of dialogue in which all ten double 'b' words are used. There should be a sense of **story** or **narrative**, that is, some common idea/theme, linking all ten words. (100–120 words)

2. Double 'c' words

accent	account
accept	occasion
accident	occupation
accommodation	occur
according	succeed

Six of the list words begin with 'acc', three with 'occ' and one with 'succ'. This should make them easier to learn and remember.

Do you remember those spelling strategies from Unit 2? Look for **sound** patterns in the double 'c' list.

Example accommoda**tion**, occupa**tion**

You **hear** the ending 'shun'. You spell it 'tion'. (See Unit 2, Spelling Strategy 1, Exercise 1.)

Exercise 1

As for double 'b' words.

WATCH YOUR LANGUAGE!

Exercise 2

(a) Underline the ending of each of the double 'c' words.

   Example   accent, accept

   Say the words **out loud**, as you underline the endings, making the connection between the sound and the spelling. These same sounds will occur in other words, remember. Therefore, the same spelling will apply.

(b) Play 'What's the Word?' with the student next to you. It's a bit like charades, but you use words instead of gestures. This is how it works:
   1. Decide who's A and who's B.
   2. A selects five words from the list, but does not say what they are to B.
   3. A gives a **definition** of each word to B, and/or an explanation of its use, where one might find it, who might need it, etc.
   4. B has to try to guess what each word is, but **quickly, and then spell it**. There is a time limit of two minutes for all five words. The aim is for B to guess and spell all five words within the time, or he/she loses the game!
   5. Change roles, with B testing A this time with the five remaining words — which must be guessed **in the order** in which they are presented to A.

   Have fun!

Exercise 3

Write ten sentences of your own, each one using one double 'c' word from the list above. Write the following types of sentences:

- **Three question** style sentences
- **Three negative statement** style sentences
- **One exclamation** style sentence
- **Two statement** style sentences
- **One** type of your **own choice**

3. Double 'd' words

add	odd
address	puddle
fiddle	riddle
giddy	shudder
middle	suddenly

Notice the pattern in the **four** words that end in 'le'. Also notice that 'suddenly', which is often misspelt, does not contain a 't'.

Exercise 1

As for double 'b' words.

Exercise 2

Go back and read Spelling Strategy 3 in Unit 2.

SPELLING: DOUBLE LETTER WORDS 1

Here is another **cloze style** exercise; but **without** the word being given to you at the top of the staged exercise. **You** must supply the complete word, once you have studied the stages and filled in the gaps in each one.

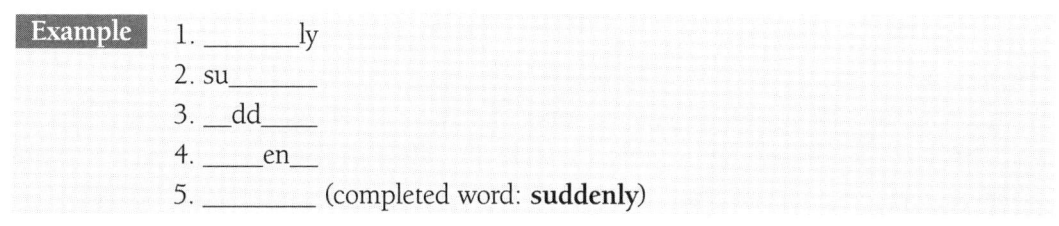

Example
1. _____ly
2. su_____
3. __dd____
4. ____en__
5. _____ (completed word: **suddenly**)

Remember! This is an exercise designed to help you to **spell** better. Therefore, it doesn't matter if you guess the whole word straight away. That's not the point. It's aim is to make you aware of how letters **combine** to form a complete word, and to learn to spell it **correctly**. Two-syllable words may be completed in only three or four stages.

(a) 1. ___ress
     2. add___
     3. _____

(b) 1. _____er
     2. __dd__
     3. shu_er
     4. _____

(c) 1. ___le
     2. ri__le
     3. ridd_
     4. _____

(d) 1. ___le
     2. mi__le
     3. midd_
     4. _____

(e) 1. _____le
     2. pu__le
     3. pudd_
     4. _____

Exercise 3

Consult your dictionary and see if you can find one double 'd' word for every letter of the alphabet.

Example 'a' for adder
             'b' for bidder
             and so on.

You may have a problem with some letters — but the **search** is the important thing. (What about 'yiddish' for 'y'?)

4. Double 'f' words

affair	efficient
affection	effort
afford	sufficient
coffee	toffee
daffodil	traffic

Did you notice how the double 'f' in all these words is followed by a **vowel**? This is also the norm with double 'c' words, for example accept, accident.

Exercise 1

As for double 'b' words.

83

WATCH YOUR LANGUAGE!

Exercise 2
Can you **unjumble** these words from your double 'f' list?
1. LODAFDIF _____
2. FOIATNFEC _____
3. TEFCINFEI _____
4. INSFUCFETI _____
5. CFTFAIR _____

Exercise 3
Write a nonsense poem, entitled 'Coffee Toffee' or 'The Daffodil Affair'. Use each double 'f' word from the list, repeating a particular word for effect perhaps, as in a refrain. Be as imaginative and crazy as you want. After all, Edward Lear got away with it, didn't he? (Read 'The Dong with the Luminous Nose'.)

5. Double 'l' words

cellar	excellent
challenge	illustration
collar	intelligent
collect	million
collision	villain

Again, notice how double 'l' is followed by a **vowel**. Notice too how some words have two **syllables** while others have three. If you break the words up into **syllables**, it may be easier to learn to spell them.

Example   cell-ar, ill-us-tra-tion

Exercise 1
As for double 'b' words.

Exercise 2
In pairs, play 'What's the Word?', as per instructions given in double 'c' words, Exercise 2.

Exercise 3
Now look again at the ten double 'l' words listed above, this time for **meaning**. Then fill in the gaps in the following sentences with a suitable word from the list.
1. 'What a wonderful_____!' she thought, admiring his drawing.
2. Uncle Colm has an impressive wine_____.
3. 'I_____ you to a duel, Sir!' the angry lover declared.
4. His car was in_____ with a lorry at the junction of Seahaven Road and Northbrook Avenue.
5. Everyone dreams of winning a_____ on the Lotto.
6. We're hoping for_____ results, as Marianne is a very_____ and hardworking student.
7. After the rugby match, Tom's_____ was not exactly white.
8. Sheila will_____ the photos on her way home.
9. He will never be any good. He's an out and out_____.

VOCABULARY: SIMILES AND METAPHORS

Words at Work

SIMILES AND METAPHORS

Question What is a simile?
Answer A simile is a **comparison** of two things or people **using** the words 'like' or 'as'.
  Example 1. He is **as** strong **as** an ox.
  2. She sings **like** an angel.

Question What is a metaphor?
Answer A metaphor is a **comparison** of two things or people **without using** the words 'like' or 'as'. The comparison is imaginative, but stronger than a simile.
  Example 1. He **is** an ox.
  2. She **is** an angel.
In sentence 2, for example, the girl is so wonderful that the one who admires her believes she is **actually** an angel.

Poets are especially fond of similes and metaphors.

Example simile   Like flames across the sky,
                       With wings all bristling,
                       Came the angel striding by.
                           from 'Tom's Angel' by Walter de la Mare
             metaphor The moon was a ghostly galleon tossed upon cloudy seas.
                           from 'The Highwayman' by Sir Henry Newbolt

Stage 1

SIMILES

Exercise 1

Your teacher will call out the first part of 20 well-known similes, with 'as', and you must supply the ending.

Example Question: He was as brave as_____?
            Answer: a lion.

You may work in pairs, writing your answers in your copybook. Your teacher will impose a time limit of 20 seconds per example. When all of the similes have been called out, you will be asked to swop your copy with another pair of students. Your teacher will then call out the endings and you will correct them. The pair of students with the highest number of correctly completed similes wins.

WATCH YOUR LANGUAGE!

Exercise 2
Complete the following well-known similes, in under five minutes:
1. as cold as _____
2. as mad as a _____
3. as light as a _____
4. as fresh as a _____
5. as sober as a _____
6. as bold as _____
7. as regular as _____
8. as weak as a _____
9. as blind as a _____
10. as busy as a _____

Exercise 3
Now write each of the above similes in a sentence of your own. Then extend the image into a **second** sentence which **explains** or **develops** the simile.

Example Aunt Jane was **as mad as a hatter**. She wore purple socks all year round and swore Elvis lived in her attic.

Stage 2

METAPHORS

Look at these examples of metaphors in use:
1. He **was** a **scarecrow** of a man.
2. The desert **was** a vast **sea of sand**.

Remember a metaphor is different from a simile, in that a simile says one thing is **like** another, whereas a metaphor says that one thing **is** another.

Exercise 1
Rewrite the following sentences, using a **metaphor** instead of the simile in each:

Example	Simile	His mind is like a vast library of facts.
	Metaphor	His mind is a vast library of facts.
	Simile 1.	The grass felt like a carpet underneath her feet.
	Metaphor 1.	_____
	Simile 2.	His tongue is as sharp as a blade.
	Metaphor 2.	_____
	Simile 3.	She is as immovable as a rock.
	Metaphor 3.	_____
	Simile 4.	A picture is like a poem without words.
	Metaphor 4.	_____
	Simile 5.	The pitch was like a battlefield.
	Metaphor 5.	_____
	Simile 6.	She is as busy as a bee.
	Metaphor 6.	_____
	Simile 7.	He is like a live wire.
	Metaphor 7.	_____

VOCABULARY: SIMILES AND METAPHORS

Simile 8.   The frozen lake was like a sheet of glass.
Metaphor 8.   _____
Simile 9.   He is like a giant in her eyes.
Metaphor 9.   _____
Simile 10.   Having no direction in his life, he is like a ship without a compass.
Metaphor 10. _____

Exercise 2

There is only **one metaphor** in each of the following sets of three sentences. Identify it by underlining it in each case.

1. He was like a devil.
   He was the devil incarnate.
   He was evil.
2. Her life was hell.
   She led a miserable life.
   She felt like she was living in hell.
3. All the world's a stage.
   The world is full of actors.
   The world is like a stage.
4. He was a great leader.
   He was a very tall man.
   He was a giant among men.
5. She was a rock of sense.
   She was very sensible.
   She was like a rock.

Exercise 3

Having practised with the metaphors in Exercises 1 and 2, choose ten of them, and write sentences **of your own** with these metaphors. Extend the image into a **second** sentence which **explains** or **develops** the metaphor.

> Example   Alan Shearer is a giant in their eyes. When he walks onto the pitch, every youngster wants to be him, to be a huge star.

Stage 3

THE EXAM: POETRY

Exercise 1

Do you remember the example of a metaphor from Sir Henry Newbolt's poem, 'The Highwayman'? Here is the verse from which it was taken:

> *The wind was a torrent of darkness among the gusty trees,*
> *The moon was a ghostly galleon tossed upon cloudy seas,*
> *The road was a ribbon of moonlight over the purple moor,*
> *And the highwayman came riding up to the old inn door.*

1. Identify three metaphors used in this verse.
2. Write a sentence for each one in which you **comment** on the comparison being made. For example, how **good** a metaphor is it? What **picture** is the poet painting for us?

WATCH YOUR LANGUAGE!

Exercise 2
1. Identify the metaphors in the following extracts from two poems — one by Norman Maccaig, one by Michael Hartnett.

   She was buckets
   and water flouncing into them.
   She was winds pouring wetly round house-ends.
   She was brown eggs, black skirts and a keeper of threepenny bits in a teapot.

   NORMAN MACCAIG

   She was a summer dance at the crossroads.
   She was a cardgame where a rose was broken.
   She was a song that nobody sings.
   She was a house ransacked by soldiers.
   She was a language seldom spoken.
   She was a child's purse, full of useless things.

   MICHAEL HARTNETT

2. Select five metaphors overall from these poems and write a sentence or two for each one, in which you comment on the comparisons being made between the woman and the object in each case. What is the poet saying about the woman? What qualities in her is he attempting to express through the metaphor?

Exercise 3
(1995 Junior Cert. Higher Level Paper 2, Section 2, Poetry)
Read the poem 'The Thickness of Ice' by Liz Loxley. It explores a relationship between the poet and another person by using an extended comparison or **metaphor**, with two skaters.

The Thickness of Ice

At first we will meet as friends
(Though secretly I'll be hoping
We'll become much more
And hoping that you're hoping that too).

At first we'll be like skaters
Testing the thickness of ice
(With each meeting
We'll skate nearer the centre of the lake).

Later we'll become less anxious to impress,
Less eager than the skater going for gold,
(The triple jumps and spins
Will become an old routine:
We will be content with simple movements).

VOCABULARY: SIMILES AND METAPHORS

Later we will not notice the steady thaw
The creeping cracks will be ignored,
(And one day when the ice gives way
We will scramble to save ourselves
And not each other).

Last of all we'll meet as acquaintances
(Though secretly we will be enemies,
Hurt by missing out on a medal,
Jealous of new partners).

Last of all we'll be like children
Having learnt the thinness of ice,
(Though secretly, perhaps, we may be hoping
To break the ice between us
And meet again as friends).

LIZ LOXLEY

1. Identify the **metaphors** which relate to the skaters.
2. There are also some **similes** in this poem (see verses 2, 5 and 6). Identify them.
3. Comment on **how** the metaphor of ice and skating is developed from verse 1 to verse 6.
4. What does the metaphor 'to break the ice' (in verse 6) mean, in the context of this poem?

Can you find other examples of similes and metaphors in the literature you are studying for Junior Cert.? Try to find at least **five examples of each**, and write them out into your copy. Try making up your own similes and metaphors. Your writing will appear more imaginative and interesting, as a result.

UNIT 5

Grappling with Grammar

VERBS

Question What is a verb?

Answer 1. A verb is a word that tells us what someone or something **does**. It is an **action** word and every sentence must have one.

> **Example** Birds **sing**. (Sing is the verb. It tells us what birds do.)
> Tom **works** in an office. (Works is the verb. It tells us what Tom does.)
> My computer **stores** information. (Stores is the verb. It tells us what my computer does.)

2. A verb can also tell us what someone or something **is**.

> **Example** Birds **are** beautiful.
> Tom **is** an accountant.
> My computer **is** very useful.

3. Verbs are also used in commands or orders.

> **Example** **Eat** your vegetables!   **Do** your homework!
> **Shut** that door!   **Do** these exercises!

Stage 1

Exercise 1

Alphaverb. Oral and written.
  (a) Your teacher will ask you to form **teams of three**.
  (b) You will be given a number: Team 1, Team 2, Team 3, etc. (In a class of 30, therefore, there will be ten teams.)

GRAMMAR: VERBS

(c) Your teacher will choose a team at random, and ask those three students to call out three verbs beginning with A, B and C, respectively. The team may confer — but must call out three verbs in under 30 seconds.
(d) One member from **each** of the ten teams writes down **all the verbs** that are called out by the other teams.
(e) Your teacher then continues to call out other teams at random, who must also think of three verbs, working their way through the alphabet. So, the second team chosen at random will call out three verbs beginning with D, E, F; the next team G, H, I; the next team J, K, L; and so on, to the end of the alphabet.
(f) A clue may be supplied for X and Z! (Teacher — see key.)
(g) Teams 9 and 10 may be asked to supply verbs for **any** three letters of the alphabet, chosen by the teacher. The team who has answered the **fastest**, and has a **clearly** written list of all the verbs called out, in alphabetical order, wins!

Exercise 2
Written. In pairs.
(a) Your teacher will call out the following instructions: 'I want five verbs associated with each of the following situations. You will have **30 seconds** to write down your **five verbs**, in each case. Are you ready? Here we go.'
   1. Five things you **do at home**.
   2. Five things you **do at the weekend**.
   3. Five things you **do at Christmas**.
   4. Five things you **do in the summer holidays**.
   5. Five things you **do when you're angry!**
(b) Compare your list of verbs with those of other pairs of students in the class. Add **five** more verbs to your own list, for each of the situations called out. You should now have **ten** verbs per situation.
(c) Individual exercise.
   Choose one of the five situations above, and write the opening paragraph of an essay (about 75 words) inspired by that situation. Use as many of the verbs you have written for Exercise 2 as possible. Try not to **repeat** a verb. Write your paragraph in the **present tense** and stay with this one tense throughout.

Exercise 3
Crossverb
(a) There are 37 verbs hidden in this Crossverb.
(b) In order to find them, write the **letter** in the space that is **the same as the number** in the box.
(c) You have been given seven of the letters.
(d) You must work out for yourself what the other nineteen letters are.
(e) The verbs are all in the **present tense**.

WATCH YOUR LANGUAGE!

(f) The verbs can go **across** or **down** only.
(g) Fill in the letters in the box also as you find them.
(h) In some cases one letter doubles as the last letter of one word **and** the first letter of another word.

Stage 2

Exercise 1
Listed below are five everyday words. What can we **do** with each one? Write out as many **verbs** (actions) as you can for each word.

Example	Cake: We can	bite it	bake it
		cut it	sell it
		eat it	buy it
		share it	long for it

Use your imagination. Extend the action a little, as with some of the following examples for 'cake':

Example	Cake: We can	fight for it	have it with tea
		give it to a friend	put it away for Sunday

Now you do it!
1. Copies   2. Pets   3. Friends   4. Money   5. Parents

GRAMMAR: VERBS

Exercise 2
Finding verbs
(a) Find the verbs in these sentences and **underline** them. Each sentence has **two** verbs.
1. Dad fried the eggs and burnt the chips.
2. You have to score the goal before you boast about it.
3. Claudia Schiffer is beautiful and has lots of money.
4. Mary sang, and cleared the hall in minutes.
5. The fire crackled and roared up the chimney.
6. Tina sulked all through class because she got detention.
7. Mrs. O'Neill fainted when she won the Lotto.
8. Mrs. O'Neill invited us all to swim in her pool in the Bahamas.
9. Tom Cryan buys six sports magazines every week and reads them on Sunday.
10. The class had good fun doing these exercises on verbs.

(b) Now write ten sentences of your own with two verbs in each sentence chosen from those in the box below:

played, is, ate, were, worked, ran, broke, jumped, was, seemed, lost, learned, rang, waiting, told, kicked, disappeared, cooked, left, travel

Exercise 3
In the following sentences, you must choose the verb which **best** completes the sentence in each case. Only **one** verb is correct. **Circle** the verb you choose, and write it into the space provided.
1. I lay on the beach and happily _____ in the heat of the sun.
   a) searched b) burnt c) basked d) bathed
2. A stone hit the windscreen and it instantly _____ into thousands of tiny pieces.
   a) shattered b) splattered c) cracked d) burst
3. The cost of buying a house has _____ considerably in the last few years.
   a) soared b) zoomed c) taken off d) risen
4. If you don't lift that saucepan carefully, it will spill and you may _____ yourself.
   a) skim b) peel c) scald d) singe
5. Sean is always _____ about how well he plays football.
   a) puffing b) boasting c) flaunting d) parading
6. The intruder was badly _____ by the guard dog at the factory.
   a) mauled b) damaged c) eaten d) torn
7. The thief _____ the flat in an attempt to find cash.
   a) looted b) ransacked c) pilfered d) invaded
8. Mrs. Ryan has just _____ the couch in her living-room.
   a) sewn b) dressed c) upholstered d) recovered
9. When it saw the dog by the water, the swan _____ its wings and rose into the air.
   a) flipped b) flicked c) flapped d) folded

WATCH YOUR LANGUAGE!

10. Sitting by the river, we could hear the _____ of the sheep in the field behind us.
    a) bawling b) braying c) barking d) bleating

Stage 3
VERBS AS NOUNS

Exercise 1

Verbs ending in 'ing' (participles) can also be used as **nouns**.

> **Example** The old lady was **walking** (verb) slowly, but she enjoyed **walking** (noun).

Complete the second sentence in each of the following with a **noun** made from the **verb** in bold in the first sentence:

1. Jane is **knitting** a jumper. She enjoys _____.
2. Tom **paints** every day. _____ is his hobby.
3. 'Don't **shout** at me! _____ is rude!'
4. Why don't you **smile** a bit more? _____ is good for your facial muscles.
5. Liz **shines** every object in the house. _____ things is her passion.
6. They **fight** all the time. _____ is second nature to them.
7. We all need to **cry**. Sometimes _____ really helps.
8. 'Please don't **whisper**! _____ in the library is forbidden.'
9. Aileen always **listens** to my problems. _____ is one of her best qualities.
10. Sheila **jogs** to work. She says _____ is excellent exercise.

Exercise 2

Here are ten sentences. The word in bold in each one is a **noun** that can also be used as a **verb**. Write ten sentences of your own, in the spaces provided, in which you use the word in bold as a verb. You may change the spelling of the word, for example 'fall' to 'fell', and the meaning and situation may change also.

> **Example** The Hobbit is a good **book**. (noun)
> Did the guard **book** you for speeding? (verb)

1. Sean had a nasty **cut** over his eye.
   _____

2. The enemy **attack** was fierce and merciless.
   _____

3. There was a **fall** in the price of oil last month.
   _____

4. 'There is a **charge** for that service, Madam,' the bank official said.
   _____

5. The Phoenix Park in Dublin is the largest inner city **park** in Europe.
   _____

GRAMMAR: VERBS

6. Matching up **paint and paper** takes time.

7. It's a long **walk** to the station from here.

8. Barbara won £500 in the **draw**.

9. Emma put on an **act**, but it didn't fool her mother.

10. The **departure** time is 9.30, for the train to London.

Exercise 3

Verbs and adjectives

Some words can be used as an **adjective** or a **verb**.

Example dry: It was a **dry** day. (adjective)
              Dry those clothes properly now! (verb)

The following words can be used as an adjective **or** a verb:

1. light
2. clean
3. clear
4. free
5. empty
6. tidy
7. idle
8. paint
9. stolen
10. broken

Can you write two sentences for each word, one in which the word is used as an **adjective**, and one in which the word is used as a **verb** — without changing the **spelling** of the verb?

Example light: adjective: Margaret wore a light suit for the Christening in June.
                    verb: You can't light a fire without matches.

Exercise 4

The exam. Personal writing.

Below is an extract from the Reading section of the 1994 Junior Cert. Ordinary Level paper.

1. Read it carefully, and underline all the **verbs**. You should find 36 (**excluding** auxiliary or helping verbs, like 'could', 'was' and 'didn't').
2. Write out the 36 verbs as a **list**.
3. Write a short composition on **one** of the following titles:
   (a) School isn't always easy (1994 Junior Cert. Ordinary Level paper)
   (b) A person I admire (1994 Junior Cert. Ordinary Level paper)
   (c) Learning to read
   (d) In my father's time . . .

Try to use as many of the **verbs** from the reading text as possible and also from the other exercises in the unit. Try not to **repeat** a verb.

WATCH YOUR LANGUAGE!

My father's hands were rough and exceedingly strong. He could gently prune a fruit-tree or firmly wrestle a stubborn mule into harness. He could mark and saw a piece of wood with speed and accuracy. But what I remember most is the special warmth from those hands as he would take me by the shoulder and point out the glittering swoop of a blue hawk, or a rabbit asleep in its lair. They were good hands that served him well and failed him in only one thing — they never learned to write.

When my father started school the punishment for a wrong answer was ten strokes of a ruler across a stretched palm. For some reason words and numbers just didn't make any sense to him. After several months he was taken out of school and put to work on the farm.

Years later, my mother, educated to the fourth year in primary school, often tried to teach him to read. Many years later still, I often grasped his big fist between my small hands and awkwardly helped him to trace the letters of his name. But he always grew restless. Fiddling with his fingers and flexing his hands he would declare that he had enough.

Then one night when he thought no one was looking he slipped away with my second-grade reader and laboured over the words. He pressed his forehead into the pages and wept. 'Not even a child's book,' he moaned. After that, no amount of persuasion could bring him to sit with a pen and paper.

Punctuation Please!

APOSTROPHES

Question When do we use an apostrophe?

Answer We use an apostrophe:
1. to show **possession**.
   > **Example** Laura's dog
   > Matthew's car
2. to **shorten** a word.
   > **Example** I have → I've
   > He is → he's

   This is also called **contraction**.

Rules
1. Students often use apostrophes wrongly, when writing the **plural of a noun**.
   > **Example** Shop's   Book's   Country's

   Sometimes shopkeepers, stall holders and restaurants get them wrong in their signs.
   > **Example** Hot Dog's for sale.
   > Tomato's, Carrot's and Potato's sold here.

   This is absolutely wrong and should be avoided.

PUNCTUATION: APOSTROPHES

2. 'Its' creates another problem. Students often put in an apostrophe (it's) when it's grammatically incorrect to do so.
   Example (a) 'The toy train is in **it's** original box.' (Wrong)
   (b) 'The toy train is in **its** original box.' (Right)
   Why? Because in (b), 'its' is a possessive adjective relating to the word 'box' (its box). 'Its' may only have an apostrophe when we want to shorten '**it is**' to '**it's**'. If in doubt, say the expression or sentence out loud. Can you say 'The toy train is in **it is** original box'? No. So you don't need an apostrophe.
3. The **possessive pronouns** (ours, yours, theirs, hers) **never** take an apostrophe.
   Example
our car	ours
your car	yours
their car	theirs
her car	hers

   Now that you know the rules, let's exercise them!

Stage 1

Exercise 1

(a) Study the following for five minutes:

I have	→ I've	I am	→ I'm	cannot	→ can't
you have	→ you've	you are	→ you're	could not	→ couldn't
he has/is	→ he's	we are	→ we're	will not	→ won't
she has/is	→ she's	they are	→ they're	would not	→ wouldn't
we have	→ we've			should not	→ shouldn't
they have	→ they've	I will	→ I'll	is not	→ isn't
		you will	→ you'll	was not	→ wasn't
		we will	→ we'll	were not	→ weren't
		they will	→ they'll	does not	→ doesn't

Note that with the **negatives**, the apostrophe replaces the 'o' in 'not'.

(b) Your teacher will select students at random, and call out an example from your list, for instance 'she has'. The student selected must:
   1. **call out** the shortened version ('she's')
   2. **spell** it out loud
   3. **write** it into his/her copy
   4. **show** it to the teacher.
   All within 20 seconds! Any student who fails to complete the task within this time is out!

(c) Play the game with each other, but this time the shortened verb must be extended into a **sentence**.

WATCH YOUR LANGUAGE!

> **Example** Student A calls out 'we are'.
> Student B: 1. says 'we're'
> 2. spells it out loud
> 3. writes it, **plus** another few words, to make a complete sentence. For example **'We're** playing a game with apostrophes.'

Time limit **30 seconds** per example this time, to allow for writing the sentence. Swop roles between each example.

Exercise 2

Imagine you are the teacher and correct the following piece of writing from a student who clearly isn't too familiar with the correct use of the apostrophe! Write out the corrected version as you go.

> My little brothers always getting into scrape's. If its not cutting the knee's off himself on the garden wall, its climbing the neighbours tree's or teasing his dog's. He has three and each has it's own kennel. Theyr'e very expensive pedigree dog's and Donnacha doesnt' understand that hes not supposed to go near them. Youll appreciate that its not easy being his sister when he brings all his friends' around to look over the wall at Mr Behans dogs'. They dont just look, you see. Theyre always whistling and shouting at them and then Mr Behan gets' mad and threatens' them with my Dad.
>
> Im thinking of emigrating. They're must be countrie's with no little brothers' **somewhere** on the planet.

Sometimes we have to decide whether to put an apostrophe **before** an 's' or **after** it. This is how it works.

> **Example** The Prince's spot cream is useless.

Here the cream **belongs** to the Prince so the apostrophe comes **before** the 's'. But what if the spot cream belongs to **two** (or more) Princes? What do we do then? We simply put the apostrophe **after** the 's'.

> **Example** The Princes' spot cream is useless.

So, the rule is, when the word which possesses something is **plural**, the apostrophe comes **after** the 's'.

Exercise 3

Now, insert the apostrophe in the correct place in the following sentences, depending on whether the **owner** is singular or plural. The word requiring the apostrophe is in bold.

1. The **girls** dresses were white.
2. The **ladies** day out was a disaster.
3. The **boys** heads nodded in agreement.
4. The **childs** foot slipped on the step.
5. The **mens** hands were freezing cold.
6. My two **sisters** boyfriends are total wimps.
7. His **friends** brother is a rock star.
8. All the **programmes** ratings fell by 10 per cent.
9. Both **parents** complaints were justified.
10. The **suns** rays are harmful.

98

PUNCTUATION: APOSTROPHES

Stage 2

Exercise 1
Rewrite the following shortened sentences in full.

Example   He hasn't fed the dog yet.
          He **has not** fed the dog yet.

1. They don't like Maths.
2. We can't see the telly.
3. She's always late.
4. We're never going to understand this.
5. It's really easy once you try.
6. They'll have a great time in Paris.
7. I couldn't contact him by phone.
8. They're late, as usual.
9. He doesn't listen to anyone.
10. You shouldn't have any difficulty with apostrophes — if you're careful!

Students often confuse **possessive adjectives** (its, your, their, whose) with **contractions** (it's, you're, they're, who's). Remember that contractions take apostrophes because the apostrophe is **replacing** a letter or letters in a word.

Example   it's = it is (the apostrophe is replacing the 'i' of 'is')
          they're = they are (the apostrophe is replacing the 'a' of 'are')

Exercise 2
Choose the correct form of the words in each of the following sentences and write them in the spaces provided.

1. (It's, Its) _____ a tragedy that the horse broke (its, it's) _____ leg during the big race.
2. (Your, You're) _____ not serious about (their, they're) _____ offer, are you?
3. (Whose, Who's) _____ car is it, anyway?
4. (Their, They're) _____ holiday was spoiled during (its, it's) _____ first week, by rain.
5. (Your, You're) _____ handwriting needs work.
6. (Whose, Who's) _____ the idiot who took my keys?
7. (Their, They're) _____ leaving the baby with (their, they're) _____ sister.

You can use apostrophes with **time words** (today, tomorrow, etc.).

Example   **Today's** meeting has been cancelled.
          Have you got **tomorrow's** schedule?

Exercise 3
Read the following sentences and write a new sentence for each, using 's' with the words in bold:

Example   The match **today** has been cancelled.
          Today's match has been cancelled.

1. The earthquake **last year** caused a lot of damage.

   _____

2. I have only **one week** of my holiday left.

   _____

WATCH YOUR LANGUAGE!

3. The *Irish Times* **last Saturday** carried that story.

4. You have to drive for about **an hour** to get to Bray.

5. They will show the big match on TV **this evening**.

Stage 3

THE EXAM: WRITING DIALOGUE

Exercise 1

The following is the Drama section from the 1994 Junior Cert. Higher Level paper. I have removed all the apostrophes from the dialogue. Can you **replace** them? (There are 31 in all.) Be **very careful** where you place the apostrophe in a word. Read back over the rules and examples from this unit, if in doubt.

Gerry: Im mad about you. You know I am. Ive always been mad about you.
Chris: When youre with me.
Gerry: Leave this house and come away with —
Chris: But youd walk out on me again. You wouldnt intend to but thats what would happen because thats your nature and you cant help yourself.
Gerry: Not this time, Chrissie. This time it will be —
Chris: Dont talk any more; no more words. Just dance me down the lane and then youll leave.
Gerry: This time the omens are terrific! The omens are unbelievable this time!
 (They dance off. After they have exited, the music from the radio set, which is in need of repair, continues for a few seconds, and then stops suddenly in mid-phrase. MAGGIE goes to the set, slaps it, turns it off. KATE moves away from the window.)
Kate: Theyre away. Dancing.
Maggie: **(Referring to the radio)** Whatevers wrong with it, thats all it seems to last — a few minutes at a time. Something to do with the way it heats up.
Kate: We probably wont see Mr. Evans for another year — until the humour suddenly takes him again.
Agnes: He has a Christian name.
Kate: And in the meantime its Christinas heart that gets crushed again. Thats what I mind. But what really infuriates me is that the creature has no sense of ordinary duty. Does he ever wonder how she clothes and feeds Michael? Does he ask her? Does he care?
 (Agnes rises and goes to the back door.)
Agnes: Going out to get my head cleared. Bit of a headache all day.

PUNCTUATION: APOSTROPHES

Kate: Seems to me the beasts of the field have more concern for their young than that creature has.

Agnes: Do you ever listen to yourself, Kate? You are such a damned righteous bitch! And his name is Gerry! — Gerry! — Gerry!

(Now on the point of tears, she runs off.)

Kate: And what was that all about?

Maggie: Whos to say?

Kate: Dont I know his name is Gerry? What am I calling him? — St. Patrick?

Maggie: Shes worried about Chris, too.

Kate: You see, thats what a creature like Mr. Evans does: appears out of nowhere and suddenly poisons the atmosphere in the whole house — God forgive him, the bastard! There! Thats what I mean! God forgive me!

(Maggie puts on her long-laced boots. As she does she sings quietly:)

Maggie: 'Twas in the Isle of Capri that he found her
    Beneath the shade of an old walnut tree.
    Oh, I can still see the flowers blooming round her,
    Where they met on the Isle of Capri.'

Kate: If you knew your prayers as well as you know the words of those aul pagan songs! . . . Shes right: I am a righteous bitch, amnt I?

Maggie: 'She was as sweet as a rose at the dawning
    But somehow fate hadnt meant it to be.
    And though he sailed with the tide in the morning,
    Still his hearts in the Isle of Capri.'

(Maggie now stands up and looks at her feet.)

Now, whos for a fox-trot?

Kate: You work hard at your job. You try to keep the home together. You perform your duties as best you can — because you believe in responsibilities and obligations and good order. And then suddenly, suddenly you realize that hair cracks are appearing everywhere; that control is slipping away; that the whole thing is so fragile it cant be held together much longer. Its all about to collapse, Maggie.

Maggie: **(Wearily)** Nothings about to collapse, Kate.

Exercise 2

Now **continue** the dialogue for another page, using apostrophes where **appropriate** in your writing.

WATCH YOUR LANGUAGE!

How Do You Spell . . . ?

THAT DUMB THUMB! SILENT LETTER WORDS 1

Silent letter words can be difficult to spell correctly, simply because we don't **pronounce** the 'silent' letters.

Example   dumb thumb

If you say these words out loud you will notice that the **sound** stops at the 'm'. So what we **hear** is 'dum' and 'thum'. When we come to **write** this type of word, therefore, we often misspell it.

In this unit we will be exercising silent letter words from silent 'b' to silent 'gh'. So let's begin.

1. **Silent 'b' words**

bomb	doubt
climb	dumb
comb	numb
crumb	plumbing
debt	thumb

Did you notice that **seven** of the list words **end** in 'mb', and that in 'debt' and 'doubt' the silent 'b' is the **second last** letter in the word? Plumbing is the only two-syllable word in the list. Before you learn the spellings, it would be a good idea to underline or highlight the silent 'b' in each word. That way, it will be **visible** and you are then more likely to **remember** to include the letter in your spelling of the word.

Exercise 1

(a) Study the ten words above for ten minutes in class. Remember it will be easier to learn these spellings because each word contains a silent 'b' and they are written in **alphabetical** order.

(b) When the ten minutes are up, your teacher will call out each word in the order in which you have learned them. Write them out, one underneath the other, in a list, being very careful with those **silent 'b's**!

(c) Exchange your copy with the person next to you. You will now correct his/hers, and he/she will do likewise with yours. Please refer to the **original spelling list** when correcting each word.

(d) Give **one** mark for each word spelled correctly, and a total mark out of ten.

(e) If a word has been spelled **incorrectly**, cross it out and write the **correct** spelling of the word beside it, again checking from the original list.

(f) Take back your own copy and write out any words **you** have spelled incorrectly, **five times** each.

SPELLING: SILENT LETTER WORDS 1

Exercise 2

(a) Which **five** words from the list are hidden in the boxes? Each word is in two parts. Spell out the completed word and write it into your copy.

DU	PLUMB
B	DOU
ING	T
BT	CRUM
DEB	MB

(b) Make your own boxes for the remaining five words from the list. Swop copies with your neighbour, and give yourself a time limit of one minute to figure out his/her words and **write them out**. The one who finishes first and whose words are **spelled correctly** wins!

Exercise 3

Write a complete sentence for each of the ten silent 'b' words on your list. **Vary** the type of sentence by writing:

- Two **statement** style sentences
- Two **question** style sentences
- Two **exclamation** style sentences
- Two **negative statement** style sentences
- Two types of your **own choice**

2. Silent 'c' words

scenario	sceptre
scene	scheme
scenery	school
scenic	science
scent	scissors

In many 'sc' words, the 'c' is silent, as in the above list. Read them out loud and you will not hear the 'c', so it is very easy to forget it. Circle the 'c' in each word. It will highlight the letter, and remind you to **keep it in**, when you are spelling the word. The list words are also in **alphabetical order** as found in the dictionary. Notice how the first six words begin with 'sce', the next two with 'sch' and the last two with 'sci'. This may also help.

Exercise 1

As for silent 'b' words.

Exercise 2

(a) Unjumble the following words from the list of silent 'c' words:
1. E N S C E I C
2. T S R C P E E
3. O N S A C E I R
4. E N S C E
5. S I R S C O S S

(b) Jumble up the remaining five words yourself. Swop yours with the person next to you. You must each unjumble the words in under one minute. The one who completes the task first — **with correct spelling** — wins. Remember to **check** the spellings with your **original** list.

Exercise 3

Write the opening paragraph (70–90 words) of a personal writing essay, entitled 'School scene'. Use each of the list words once only. You will need to think a little about how you can include the word 'sceptre', but it will be a good exercise for your imagination!

3. Silent 'e' words

awake	frame
brake	gate
complete	hate
disgrace	invite
explode	judge

Notice that the above silent 'e' words are in alphabetical order, one for each letter from A to J. **Underline** the silent 'e's before you learn them.

Exercise 1

As for silent 'b' words.

Exercise 2

(a) Go to your dictionary and find ten more silent 'e' words from the letters K to T. Write them out in a list, and underline the silent 'e' in each word.

(b) Play 'What's the Word?' with the student next to you. It's a bit like charades, but you use words instead of gestures. This is how it works:
   1. Decide who's A and who's B.
   2. A selects five words from his/her list, but does not say what they are to B.
   3. B must try to guess what each word is from A's description of its use or meaning.
   4. Have a time limit of **two minutes** for B to guess all five words and **write** them out, **spelling** them correctly!
   5. Swap roles. B now presents five words from his/her list, for A to guess.
   6. The one who guesses and correctly spells the most words within the time limit, wins!

Exercise 3

Using your **own** list of silent 'e' words from K to T, and the original list from A to J, write a complete sentence for each word, **underlining** the silent 'e' every time.

> **Example**   That boy's hair is a disgrace!

SPELLING: SILENT LETTER WORDS 1

4. Silent 'g' words

consignment	gnash
design	gnaw
designer	neigh
foreigner	resign
gnarled	sign

Notice that silent 'g's are usually followed by 'n' and the 'n' is sounded.

Example de**sign**, **sign**

It is useful to remember this when learning to spell the words. Circling the letter 'g' in each word will also help.

Exercise 1
As for silent 'b' words.

Exercise 2
Now look again at the silent 'g' words listed above, this time for **meaning**. Then fill in the gaps in the following sentences with the most suitable word from the list.
1. The President must_____ at once, before the scandal breaks.
2. We are expecting a_____ of Maxi Stor shelving this afternoon.
3. His hands were_____ and torn from hard physical work all his life.
4. 'Don't_____ anything, until you've read the small print, Pauline!'
5. I love to hear my horse_____ in greeting when I approach her.
6. Susan would prefer to_____ her own wedding dress.
7. They are suspicious of him because he is a_____.
8. 'There shall be weeping and_____ing of teeth.'
9. _____ clothes are expensive.
10. The puppy will_____ away at that bandage until it comes loose.

Exercise 3
Silent 'g' words quiz

This exercise is for fun — but will also enlarge your vocabulary. You will need your dictionary, preferably the *Concise Oxford Dictionary*, but any good-sized one should do. It may be done in class, with your teacher imposing a time limit of **20 minutes** — or for homework. (Clue: **all** the words **begin** with a silent 'g'.)
1. What is a small two-winged biting fly called? _____
2. What is an aboriginal waterhole called? _____
3. What is an Italian dish of small dumplings called? _____
4. This is a dwarfish legendary creature supposed to guard the earth's treasures underground (or your garden!). _____
5. What is the rod or pin on a sundial called? _____

WATCH YOUR LANGUAGE!

6. This is a coarse-grained metamorphic rock foliated by mineral layers, principally of feldspar, quartz and ferromagnesian mineral. _____
7. This is a type of antelope, native to South Africa, also called a wildebeest. _____
8. What is the knowledge of spiritual mysteries called? _____
9. This is the adjective of number 8, relating to knowledge, especially mystical knowledge. _____
10. This is an adjective — of or relating to the jaws. _____

5. Silent 'gh' words

although	eight
bought	fight
caught	high
cough	light
daughter	might

There are lots of silent 'gh' words! Did you notice how different the **sounds** are?

> **Example**
> although (-oh)
> bought (-aw-)
> cough (-off)

The 'gh' is silent though, and therefore often misspelt. So watch those spellings.

Exercise 1
As for silent 'b' words.

Exercise 2
(a) Which is the **correct** spelling of the following words from the list? **Underline** your choice, and **write** it into your copy.

1. Fite	Figte	Fight
2. Douhter	Daughter	Dauhter
3. Bought	Bouht	Bote
4. Cawte	Caught	Cauht
5. Alltough	Altdough	Although

(b) 1. What rhymes with 'high' and means a long sad breath? _____
    2. What rhymes with 'light' and is the opposite of 'wrong'? _____
    3. What rhymes with 'bought' and is the past tense of 'catch'? _____
    4. What rhymes with 'cough' and is a watering place for animals? _____
    5. What rhymes with 'fight' and is the opposite of 'loose'? _____

Exercise 3
Here are some more silent 'gh' words. Write five sentences with two of the words below in each sentence.

VOCABULARY: IDIOMS

1. enough
2. lighthouse
3. naughty
4. neighbour
5. night
6. nightmare
7. rough
8. sleigh
9. through
10. weigh

Example I think I weigh enough now.

Be as silly as you like!
Remember. The spelling's the thing!

Words at Work

COLOUR YOUR WORDS: IDIOMS

Question What is an **idiom**?

Answer An idiom is a group of words, in the form of a phrase or expression, that is in everyday use. An idiom is also known as a **colloquialism**. The interesting thing is that an idiom often means something quite different from the meaning of the **individual** words within it.

Example
1. **A piece of cake**. This describes something which is easy to do, but has nothing whatsoever to do with cake!
2. Similarly, we say: **in hot water**, meaning in trouble or disgrace.
3. Or **to let the cat out of the bag**, meaning to tell or reveal a secret — usually without meaning to!

All languages have their own idioms, and English is no exception. These phrases, when used wisely and imaginatively, will add colour and interest to your writing. In this unit, we will exercise a variety of idioms, under certain headings; for example, those that have to do with:

◆ families and/or friends (chip off the old block, thick as thieves)
◆ animals (look a gift horse in the mouth)
◆ parts of the body (to pull someone's leg).

So, let's begin.

Stage 1

Exercise 1

Oral and written. In pairs.
Your teacher will call out the first half of some commonly used idioms, and you must complete them.

WATCH YOUR LANGUAGE!

> **Example** Teacher: To look a gift horse . . .
> Student: in the mouth!

Working in pairs, you will have just **ten seconds** to answer. If you can't complete the idiom, it passes to the next two students, and so on. Your teacher will decide how long the game will last, and how many idioms to call out. One from each pair must write out **all** the idioms you hear! The pair of students who manage to get the most of them down, wins!

Exercise 2

Still in pairs, choose ten idioms from Exercise 1 — five each. Then talk to one another for **three minutes**, during which time you must use each of your chosen idioms at least once. The exercise must be completed in five minutes overall!

Exercise 3

Individual exercise for homework.
Write a short piece of dialogue **or** a descriptive paragraph in which all ten idioms from Exercise 2 are used just once. Be imaginative, but also make your writing exercise **credible**. The idioms must appear to the reader as natural elements of your story or dialogue. (150–200 words)

Stage 2

Exercise 1

(a) The following idioms can all be used when writing about families or friends. Match each idiom in Column A to its meaning in Column B. If you are not sure, check in your dictionary.

A	B
1. generation gap	1. family ties are stronger than friendship
2. chip off the old block	2. not a bit like one another
3. thick as thieves	3. difference in ideas and attitudes between old and young people
4. blood is thicker than water	4. person who looks or behaves like one of his/her parents
5. flesh and blood	5. extremely friendly with one another
6. different as chalk and cheese	6. member of the same family

(b) Write some fictional notes about a family called 'The Gogarty Gang', in which you use each of the six idioms above at least once. In addition, use the following idioms (which are also similes) to make comparisons about the **appearance** of people in the family:

1. as bald as a coot
2. as pretty as a picture
3. as blind as a bat
4. as fit as a fiddle
5. as deaf as a post

This exercise lends itself to humour, so have fun!

VOCABULARY: IDIOMS

Exercise 2
Here are some idioms using **parts of the body**.
1. to pull someone's **leg**
2. to keep an **eye** on something
3. to be a pain in the **neck**
4. to talk behind someone's **back**
5. to fall on one's **feet**

Write a sentence for each of these, which **clearly** shows the meaning and usage of the idiom.

Example   to be a pain in the neck
He's in such bad form these days, interfering all the time and being such a bore!
He's a **real pain in the neck**.

Some idioms are used to describe people's **attitudes** to life, the way they react to situations, whether they **conform** or not (join in or not join in). Here are some examples:

Idiom	Meaning
1. to live and let live	to be tolerant of others
2. it's no use crying over spilt milk	no point in regretting something that went wrong
3. to have your cake and eat it	to desire more than you can have
4. to have several irons in the fire	to have many plans and projects at one time
5. to keep up with the Joneses	to always do what your neighbours do
6. to go by the book	to do everything strictly according to the rules
7. to pay lip service to	to pretend to agree with an idea or belief
8. to stand out like a sore thumb	to be different, but in a bad way
9. to take the law into one's own hands	to act independently of the law; to do something illegal
10. to be like a fish out of water	not to feel at home or to be uncomfortable in a certain situation

Exercise 3
(a) Now, **replace** the words in bold in the following sentences with an **idiom** from the list above:
   1. When I was Treasurer of the drama group, I only **pretended to agree with** their ideas, for a quiet life.
   2. Siobhan is not very adventurous. She always **does everything according to the rules**.
   3. **Let people live as they want to**, that's what I say.
   4. With that bright pink hair and blackened teeth, Terry certainly **looks different**!
   5. There's no point in **regretting the past**. What's done is done.
(b) Write sentences of your own for the **remaining** five idioms.

WATCH YOUR LANGUAGE!

Exercise 4

Fill in the missing words in the following passage with an idiom **not** previously given to you. The word in bold in each sentence is the clue to the idiom you require. Check with your dictionary (or your teacher) if you get really stuck.

My Dad didn't ___ __ **eyelid** when I told him I wanted to travel to the Himalayas after school. In fact, instead of _____ ___ **roof** as I expected, and _____ ___ ___ **handle**, he was quite good about it. He even offered to pay my air fare. I couldn't _____ __ **ears**! He usually takes everything I suggest ____ _ _____ __ **salt**. This time, however, he said that he'd ____ ____ _ ___ **leaf**, in his attitude towards me, and that it was time for me to _____ __ __ ___ ___ **feet**. Of course, I wouldn't ___ __ **past** ___ to change his mind. I've always had to ___ ___ **line** up to now, haven't I?

Stage 3

Exercise 1

Here are ten adjective idioms:

    bone idle   bolt upright
    pitch black   soaking wet
    stark naked   stark raving mad
    dog tired   piping hot
    dead straight   stone cold sober

(a) Choose a suitable idiom from the list above to complete the following sentences:
1. Can you switch on the light? It's ____ ____ in here.
2. I can't believe it. He was ____ ____ ____ coming home from the pub last night.
3. Sheila is ____ ____. She's too lazy even to put her own sugar in her tea.
4. I love the smell of pizza when it comes _____ __ from the oven.
5. By the time we got to school, the rain was bucketing down and we were _____ __.
6. Give you £500 for a motorbike?! Are you ____ _____ __?!
7. The crowd whistled and cheered when Eugene ran ____ ____ on to the football pitch.
8. When we visited Gran in hospital, she was sitting ____ _____ in the bed, not a bother on her.
9. I won't wait up for the late film. I'm __ ____.
10. In Technical Graphics, Pat draws ____ _____ lines.

(b) Now try to write a **continuous** piece of prose in which all ten idioms are used just once. (100–150 words). Here's a 'starter' suggestion for you — but of course, feel free to choose your own.

Sean wondered how the hell he'd ended up standing **stark naked**, outside his own hall door

VOCABULARY: IDIOMS

Exercise 2

Idiom 'families'

Some words can be written in the form of:
- a **noun** idiom   you old **dog**!
- an **adjective** idiom   **dog** tired
- a **verb** idiom   to **dog** someone's footsteps

From each of the following families of idioms, see if you can make **one noun** idiom, **one adjective** idiom and **one verb** idiom — if possible! Use your dictionary if you get stuck!

Example   Animals   a dark **horse** (noun idiom)
                      a **catty** person (adjective idiom)
                      to **fish** for compliments (verb idiom)

1. Animals   (Clues: dog, cat, pig, horse, fish)
2. Body   (Clues: hand, leg, neck, finger, head, feet, stomach, heart, elbow)
3. Clothes   (Clues: hat, sock, boot, cuff, sleeve, trousers)
4. Food   (Clues: jam, pop, soup, goose, salt)
5. Colour   (Clues: white, blue, black, green, red)
6. Numbers   (Clues: one, two, three, nine)
7. Weather   (Clues: weather, cold, wet, wind)
8. Water   (Clues: swim, deep end, tide, canoe)
9. Sport   (Clues: line, game, cricket, belt)
10. Time   (Clues: clock, dot, wound up, chime)

Exercise 3

The exam. Media studies. Advertising.

1. Study these three advertisements, marked A, B and C. They each contain **an idiom**. Identify it, and write it out into your copy.
2. Now look at how the idioms are **used** in the three advertisements.
   (a) What is the **meaning** of the idiom in each case in relation to the **product** being advertised?
   (b) Do the idioms **work**, in terms of selling the products being advertised? Why? Give a reason for each one.
   (c) Which idiom is the most humorous? Give a reason for your choice.

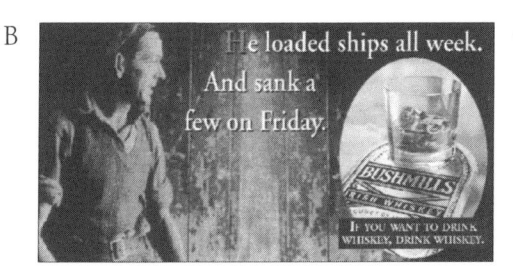

UNIT 6

Grappling with Grammar

THE PAST TENSE 1

When you change from the **present** tense to the **past** in your writing, the verb must change too.

> Example   I walk (present tense) → I walked (past simple)

Rules
1. Usually, you add 'ed' to the verb, to make it past, as in the example above.
2. However, some verbs do not change at all from present to past.
   > Example   I **read** textbooks every day. I **read** several yesterday, too.

   Can you think of any others like this one?
3. Verbs ending in 'y' in the present tense change the 'y' to 'ied' in the past.
   > Example   I **fry** everything. I **fried** everything last week, too.
4. Some verbs **double** their last letter before adding 'ed'.
   > Example   Prices **drop** all the time. Prices dro**pped** dramatically last year.
5. A large number of verbs are **irregular** and change quite a lot in the past.
   > Example   Jane **runs** everywhere. She **ran** to school yesterday.

   These are the ones you are most likely to speak and write incorrectly. So **watch** them!

Stage 1

Exercise 1

Oral. Teacher directed.
(a) Your teacher will select students at random from the class roll.
(b) He/she will call out a sentence in the present tense. You must change it to the past simple tense and add a **time** word.

GRAMMAR: THE PAST TENSE 1

> **Example** Teacher: Paul visits Canada every summer.
> Student: Paul visit**ed** Canada **last** summer, too.

Other time words are: ago, yesterday, last week/month/year, 1998, etc.

Exercise 2

Here are some more verbs in the present tense. Write a short sentence for each, in the past simple tense. Watch the **time** words — they're important.

attack, beg, come, direct, express, find, grow, hear, know, loan

THE PAST SIMPLE AND THE PRESENT PERFECT SIMPLE

Look at these two sentences:

> **Example**
> 1. Paul **wrote** to Linda last week. (past simple)
> 2. Paul **has written** to Linda three times already this week. (present perfect simple)

In Sentence 1, the action is **finished**, and took place at a specific **time** in the past. In Sentence 2, the action is still in the past ('has written') but with the strong possibility of it being **repeated** in the near future. There is always the suggestion or possibility of the action **continuing**, when we use the present perfect simple.

Words associated with the present perfect simple are: already, yet, just, now, up to now, so far, for ages/weeks/years.

Exercise 3

Now write the correct form of the verb in brackets (past simple or present perfect simple) in the following sentences, according to the **time** references at the end of each sentence:

1. Sally _____ (do) her Junior Cert. two months ago.
2. They _____ (drive) to France three times already.
3. Donna _____ (eat) six doughnuts yesterday afternoon.
4. The thief _____ (steal) five thousand pounds from the old lady's house last Christmas.
5. I haven't _____ (be) to that film yet.
6. Have you _____ (finish) it already?
7. John _____ (become) very angry and threatened to leave last night.
8. Sheila _____ (keep) all his letters for ages.
9. They _____ (emigrate) to America a long time ago.
10. Wexford _____ (commemorate) the 1798 rebellion in 1998.

Exercise 4

In pairs, or as an individual, can you complete the following table in under fifteen minutes? Consult your dictionary if you get stuck.

WATCH YOUR LANGUAGE!

	Present	Past simple	Present perfect simple
1.	I begin	I_____	I have_____
2.	I bring	I_____	I_____
3.	I buy	I_____	I_____
4.	I catch	I_____	I_____
5.	I do	I_____	I_____
6.	I drink	I_____	I_____
7.	I fall	I_____	I_____
8.	I fly	I_____	I_____
9.	I get	I_____	I_____
10.	I give	I_____	I_____
11.	I go	I_____	I_____
12.	I keep	I_____	I_____
13.	I know	I_____	I_____
14.	I mean	I_____	I_____
15.	I ride	I_____	I_____
16.	I ring	I_____	I_____
17.	I see	I_____	I_____
18.	I shake	I_____	I_____
19.	I sing	I_____	I_____
20.	I sleep	I_____	I_____
21.	I speak	I_____	I_____
22.	I stand	I_____	I_____
23.	I swear	I_____	I_____
24.	I take	I_____	I_____
25.	I teach	I_____	I_____
26.	I think	I_____	I_____
27.	I throw	I_____	I_____
28.	I understand	I_____	I_____
29.	I wake	I_____	I_____
30.	I wear	I_____	I_____

Exercise 5

Correct the verbs in bold in these sentences. Watch out for the time reference, to help you decide which **form** of the past to use, i.e. the past simple or present perfect simple.
1. I **throwed** the book away last week.
2. Tracy **run** to school yesterday.
3. Mr. Butler **rung** the bell late last Friday.
4. Donna has just **ate** six doughnuts!

GRAMMAR: THE PAST TENSE 1

5. My pigeon has **flew** over Mr. Ryan's wall twice this week.
6. The bank **rised** the interest rates last month.
7. The baby **begun** to bawl the minute Mam walked in.
8. Ralph has **blew** that trumpet until 2.00 a.m. every night this week.
9. I **seen** him kiss her at the disco last Saturday.
10. I already **done** lots of exercises in this unit!

Stage 2

THE PAST CONTINUOUS AND THE PAST SIMPLE

Look at this sentence:

Example   I **was doing** my homework when the phone **rang**.

'Was doing' is an example of the **past continuous** tense. As you can see, it is often combined with the **past simple** ('rang'). Writers frequently use the past continuous tense.

Example   'Mr. Gilmer was standing at the window talking to Mr. Underwood. Bert, the court reporter, was chain-smoking: he sat back with his feet on the table.'
(*To Kill a Mockingbird* by Harper Lee)

Uses

1. The form of the past continuous is 'was/were' plus the 'ing' ending on the verb. This tense refers to an action **in progress** in the past, but not **completed**. The action was **continuous**, going on for some time.

2. We use the past continuous for **two** actions in the past, happening **at the same time**.
   Example   'I **was minding** my brother while Mum **was making** the dinner.'
   The word 'while' is often used with this tense.

3. The past continuous is also used to describe the typical or habitual behaviour of people in the **past**.
   Example   Gordon **was always moaning** about work.
   Karen **was smoking** for three years before she gave it up.

Exercise 1

In the following passage, write the verbs in brackets in **either** the past continuous **or** the past simple tense. You must decide, from the **context**, which one is correct.

Last Thursday, Donna and her pal, Susan, _____ (walk) through the park on the way home from school. Two lads from Fifth Year _____ (stop) them. They _____ (look) for money and they _____ (ask) the girls. 'No way!' _____ (say) Donna. 'Get lost!' The two lads _____ (think) strongly of bullying the girls into giving them the money, when Mr. Macken, their Maths teacher, suddenly _____ (appear).

   'What's happening here?' he _____ (ask). 'I thought you two lads _____ (do) detention this week. You _____ (smoke) in the changing room, weren't you? Get back to school this minute, do you hear?!'

WATCH YOUR LANGUAGE!

Donna and Susan _____ (laugh) when the two lads _____ (turn) round and _____ (head) back in the direction of school. 'Thanks, Sir,' _____ (say) Susan. 'You were brilliant!'

'Now, now. No need for that,' Mr. Macken _____ (say). 'Off home with you now. See you tomorrow.'

'Did you notice he _____ (wear) the good suit?' _____ (say) Donna when he _____ (leave).

'Yeh! Must have a heavy date, wha!' _____ (grin) Susan. 'Still, he's O.K. old Mac.'

Stage 3

THE PRESENT PERFECT SIMPLE AND THE PRESENT PERFECT CONTINUOUS

So far in this unit, you have exercised:
1. the past simple (I ate)
2. the present perfect simple (I have eaten)
3. the past continuous (I was eating).

Now, look at this sentence:

> **Example**   Donna **has been eating** doughnuts all day.

This sentence is written in the **present perfect continuous** tense. The form is 'have/has been' plus 'ing' on the verb. We use this tense when we are talking about an action that **began** in the past, but is **not** completed. Donna is **still** eating doughnuts and is likely to eat even more before the day is out! There is always a strong suggestion or possibility of the action **continuing** into the future, with this tense.

Exercise 1

Let's exercise the **present perfect continuous** tense. Write ten complete sentences beginning with 'I have been (verb) + ing' in answer to each of the following questions:
1. What have you been doing since nine o'clock this morning?
2. What have you been learning about in this unit so far?
3. How long have you been living in your area?
4. How many hours study per night have you been doing this term?
5. How long have you been day dreaming about the holidays?
   (Use your **imagination** on the next five.)
6. Where have you been hiding all this time?
7. What have you been saying to him/her?!
8. Why have you been reading my diary?!
9. How have you been surviving without money?
10. Why have you been following me?

Students often leave out the have/has of the present perfect simple and continuous in their speech. So, when it comes to **writing**, the following type of error is common:

GRAMMAR: THE PAST TENSE 1

Example   I **seen** Tom twice this week. (Ouch!)
I **have** (or **I've**) seen Tom twice this week. (Right!)
But, since **writing** is a more formal exercise, we must really be more careful to avoid this mistake.

Exercise 2

Using the skeleton notes below, can you write out the **complete** sentence in each case, in **either** the present perfect simple **or** present perfect continuous, depending on the context. (If in doubt, go back over the explanations in this unit.)

Example   1. I/just/finish/homework
I **have** just finish**ed** my homework.
2. I/play/golf/Forrest Little/for years
I **have been** play**ing** golf in Forrest Little for years.

1. Sheila/not/sing/competition/yet
2. Peter/forget/my birthday/every year since/child
3. Have/wait/long?
4. I/not/understand/a word so far
5. Mary/bring me/magazines/for years
6. We/go/same resort/ten years now
7. 'You/drink!' she roared at her husband
8. I/not/sleep/since he left
9. Donna/eat/doughnuts/all day!
10. I/just/complete/exercise

Exercise 3

Read the following text carefully, correcting the verbs in bold as you go. Use **either** the **past simple, past continuous, present perfect simple** or **present perfect continuous**. Read the previous explanations and examples before you start!

Paul just **done** a really bad thing. He **is dating** Donna for six months now, but last Friday, while **he's going** to town on the bus, he **seen** Tracy, her pal, and **begun** to chat her up. They were **haven** a great time, until Paul looking out the window at the next stop **seen** Donna who **got** on the bus.

'**I just remembered** something, Tracy,' he said hurriedly. 'I have to get off here. See ya!' While Tracy **thinks** about this sudden change in Paul's behaviour, Donna **is paying** her fare. She **spots** Paul and **says**: 'How ya babe! **I just done** me homework. I **comin'** to see ya!' 'Yeh? Great!' Paul **is sweaten** bricks. 'I . . . eh . . . **I been thinking** about you, all day. I **didn't done** me Maths yet, and I **been** kind of hoping you might give us a hand — like.' 'I wish I could!' **laughs** Donna, 'but I **never been** much good at Maths. I **been studying** Calculus for three months now, and I still don't get it! Hey! There's Tracy! Hiya Tracy! Now, she **done** really well in Maths in the Mocks. Why don't you ask her to help you?'

Paul **smiles** weakly at Donna and at Tracy. Things were **got** complicated. 'Right. I will. But . . . eh . . . not now. O.K.? I'd much rather be with you. Let's get off here, and go for a burger, eh? I **been dying** to see you all week! What **was** you doin' anyway?' With that, the smarmy Paul **whisks** Donna off the bus, **winks** back at Tracy at the same time, and **steers** her off down the road to McDonald's at the rate of knots!

I tell ye, so far, that fella **had** the luck of the gods. Fair play to him!

WATCH YOUR LANGUAGE!

Exercise 4

The exam. Personal writing.

Write a scene with the three characters from Exercise 3 in it, perhaps set in a disco the following week or in school. Have come **confrontation** between them. Use all of the tenses you've been practising throughout this unit. (200–300 words)

Punctuation Please!

QUOTATION MARKS

Question When do we use quotation marks (also called inverted commas)?

Answer When we want to indicate:

1. direct speech:

   Example 'I love you,' he said. 'Do you?' she yawned.

2. quotations:

   Example 'She ran the whole gamut of emotions, from A to B.'
   (Dorothy Parker speaking about the actress Katherine Hepburn)

Uses

1. It's a matter of personal choice whether you use single or double quotation marks. Writers tend to prefer single marks, and magazines and newspapers double. However, if you are writing a quote within a quote, it might be wise to do it as follows:

   Example Tim said, 'Honestly, I can't believe that man! I have just spent two years completing this design and all he could ask was, "Does it come in yellow?" What a stupid question!'

   Note that the quote within the quote (from the 'stupid man') is written with **double** quotation marks, while the overall quotation (from Tim) is introduced and completed with **single** quotation marks.

2. All **other** punctuation marks **except** for colons and semi-colons are placed **inside** the quotation marks:

   Example Exception: (semi-colon) Laura said, 'Of course not'; and she meant it.

3. Sometimes quotation marks surround a single word that is used in an unusual way, or even invented:

   Example 'When he asked me to go "surfing" with him, I was thrilled, until I discovered he meant the Internet!'
   'I've been "teddy-sitting" with my niece's collection of bears.'

4. Always start the **first** word of direct speech with a capital letter, even if the speech starts **within** the sentence:

   Example The woman shouted hysterically, 'It's my son. They've killed him!'

PUNCTUATION: QUOTATION MARKS

5. If a sentence **continues** on after the speaker has been named, do **not** use a capital letter:
   Example 'In that case,' Colm said, 'wouldn't it be better to hire a car?'
6. If a **new** sentence starts after the speaker has been named, use a capital letter:
   Example 'We had a puncture,' Colm explained. 'We didn't get home until 2 a.m.'
7. Notice the **commas** in the following sentence interrupted by the unspoken words 'he said':
   Example 'Mole,' he said, 'you're the best of fellows!' (*The Wind in the Willows*)
8. Quotation marks are used for **titles** of poems, songs, episodes of TV and radio series, book series, words and phrases:
   Example Star Trek's 'The Borg'   Point Horror's 'Babysitter 11'
   'Don't Cry for me Argentina'   'Digging' by Seamus Heaney
   Helen had a cosy 'tête-à-tête' with Terry. Ben was thoroughly 'cheesed-off' with his job.

Stage 1

Exercise 1
(a) Decide who's A and B. Within a time limit of **two minutes** A asks B five questions about himself/herself, which B must answer, in **short** statements.
(b) After two minutes, the teacher says 'Stop!', and B must then write out the **questions** he/she has heard — from memory, and A must write out the **answers** — also from memory! Time limit of **two minutes** again. **Quotation marks** must be used in both cases.
(c) Now compare each other's work. A writes in the **questions** over his/her answers. B writes in the **answers** under his/her written questions. You may dispute the **content** of the questions or answers at this stage! (How well have you **listened** to each other, for example?) Watch those **quotation marks**!

Exercise 2
Write out the following sentences, inserting quotation marks where necessary:
1. I live in Galway, said Mary.
2. Did you have a good holiday? asked Jim.
3. I'm starving, said Donnacha. I hope there's something good for dinner.
4. I hope you realise, Dad said, that money doesn't grow on trees.
5. They missed the last bus, Sheila explained. That's why they're late.
6. Get out of my flower beds! Mr. Ryan roared.
7. Playing a battlement, no doubt. (Dorothy Parker, speaking about an elderly actress in *Camelot*.)
8. On hearing that President Calvin Coolidge had died, Dorothy Parker remarked: How could they tell?
9. Teacher: Who wrote To a Mouse?
    Gerry: I don't know, Miss, but I bet they didn't get an answer!
10. Teacher: How long can someone live without a brain?
    Gerry: How old are you, Sir?

WATCH YOUR LANGUAGE!

Stage 2

Students like to put dialogue in their essays, but sometimes it's handled pretty badly, and the page can end up looking as if it's been sprayed with quotation marks!

> **Example** 'I think someone, or something, is moving about in there,' Susan whispered. 'And I don't like it.' 'Should we not just go in and have a look?' 'Well, I'm certainly not putting a foot inside there! It's spooky.' 'Oh don't be such a wimp!' 'I just don't want to get my head blown off.' 'Don't be stupid. This is not *Exterminator 2* remember.' 'It could be, though, couldn't it?' 'You go in if you're so brave, but I'm staying right here.'

As you can see, the dialogue is lively, and starts off well in terms of punctuation. However, as it progresses, it becomes unclear who is saying what at any one time and the quotation marks, inserted back to back, are very confusing.

Exercise 1
Rewrite the above piece of dialogue, using **separate** lines for each character, as they speak. Give the name Peter to the other person in the conversation.

Exercise 2
Now continue the dialogue for a further ten to twelve lines, remembering to give each character a **new** line, each time they speak, even if it's only a short **interruption**.

> **Example** 'Susan?' Peter whispered.
> 'Yes, what?'
> 'Can you still see him?'
> 'Yes. I . . .'

Once you separate out the characters in this way, there is no need to keep repeating their names. The reader can figure out for himself/herself who is speaking at any one time. You will have noticed that this is how dialogue is written in novels and short stories.

Exercise 3
(a) Read the following extract from 'Louise', a short story by Somerset Maugham. You will see that I have removed all the quotation marks. Can you replace them?

> But one day the young man came to me in great distress and told me that his marriage was indefinitely postponed. Iris felt that she could not desert her mother. Of course it was really no business of mine, but I made the opportunity to go and see Louise. She was always glad to receive her friends at tea-time and now that she was older she cultivated the society of painters and writers.
>
> Well, I hear that Iris isn't going to be married, I said after a while.
>
> I don't know about that. She's not going to be married quite as soon as I could have wished. I've begged her on my bended knees not to consider me, but she absolutely refuses to leave me.

Don't you think it's rather hard on her?

Dreadfully. Of course it can only be for a few months, but I hate the thought of any one sacrificing themselves for me.

My dear Louise, you've buried two husbands. I can't see the least reason why you shouldn't bury at least two more.

Do you think that's funny? she asked me in a tone that she made as offensive as she could.

I suppose it's never struck you as strange that you're always strong enough to do anything you want to and that your weak heart only prevents you from doing things that bore you?

Oh, I know, I know what you've always thought of me. You've never believed that I had anything the matter with me, have you?

I looked at her full and square.

Never. I think you've carried out for twenty-five years a stupendous bluff. I think you're the most selfish and monstrous woman I have ever known. You ruined the lives of those two wretched men you married and now you're going to ruin the life of your daughter.

I should not have been surprised if Louise had had a heart attack then. I fully expected her to fly into a passion. She merely gave me a gentle smile.

My poor friend, one of these days you'll be so dreadfully sorry you said this to me.

Have you quite determined that Iris shall not marry this boy?

I've begged her to marry him. I know it'll kill me, but I don't mind. Nobody cares for me. I'm just a burden to everybody.

Did you tell her it would kill you?

She made me.

As if any one ever made you do anything that you were not yourself quite determined to do.

She can marry her young man tomorrow if she likes. If it kills me, it kills me.

Well, let's risk it, shall we?

Haven't you got any compassion for me?

One can't pity any one who amuses one as much as you amuse me, I answered.

A faint spot of colour appeared on Louise's pale cheeks and though she smiled still her eyes were hard and angry.

Iris shall marry in a month's time, she said, and if anything happens to me I hope you and she will be able to forgive yourselves.

(Extract from 'Louise' by Somerset Maugham)

WATCH YOUR LANGUAGE!

(b) Now imagine the dialogue that took place earlier between Louise and her daughter, Iris. The passage you've just punctuated gives you quite a bit of information about it. Write about 20 lines of an imaginary dialogue between Louise and her daughter, on that occasion. Mind those quotation marks!

Stage 3

THE EXAM: MEDIA STUDIES

Magazine and newspaper articles are written in short paragraphs. Each paragraph is set in a little from the left of the column, and quotations also. Read this article from the *Sunday Independent* (5 July 1998), in which Shirley Manson from the group 'Garbage' is being interviewed.

The current Garbage album, *Version 2.0*, entered the Irish charts at number four and now they're at the Copthorne Tara talking to a bunch of scribblers from Ireland, someone from Italy and someone from Iceland.

'Would you join the Spice Girls if you were asked?' you intelligently ask Shirley, who scrunches up her face in a look of mock horror before Duke volunteers 'I would!'

'How do you feel now, being in a band and doing press conferences?' someone else asks.

'We're going to split up!' Shirley announces. Everybody laughs, particularly her with her big foghorn of a hooting laugh.

Garbage have just returned from Paris. 'We were done over by British Customs last night. It was a good vibe being in Paris, then our vibe got crushed as we stepped into the UK,' says Shirley.

SOMEONE, naturally, asks about football, asks about the American viewpoint. 'They can't make money out of it so why should they be interested in it?' Shirley responds, with another big roar of a laugh.

Now Duke is saying: 'We'd all been in bands. All failed.' Another person is asking Shirley how does it feel to be the face of Garbage. 'Who else would you choose to be the face of the band? I'm the lead singer, I'm the loudest . . .'

And now Shirley is jumping around the Brixton Academy stage like a bantamweight boxer, singing: 'I can't use what I can't abuse.' Butch batters the drums, Steve punishes his bass, Duke makes shapes with his guitar. They sound great and they look like granddads on Viagra.

And out front, Shirley is belting out: 'I'm only happy when it rains, I'm only happy when it's complicated . . .'

Exercise 1

1. Write out the **questions** the interviewer asks her, using quotation marks each time.
2. Write out **all** of Shirley's responses to the interviewer's questions — with quotation marks, of course!
3. What does she have to say about her Paris experience?
4. When asked about football, what does she say is the American viewpoint?
5. What are the words of the song that Shirley is 'belting out' at the end of the article.

Exercise 2

Read this newspaper article about Tommy Wright, the Manchester City goalkeeper. Answer the following questions with quotations from Wright, using quotation marks, of course.

SPELLING: PREFIXES AND SUFFIXES

Tommy: I'll be Wright back

TOMMY Wright's latest video is not for the squeamish. It shows the keeper's right knee — with carbon implant — after seven serious operations.

To non-medical viewers it's like a multi-cracked, over-boiled egg.

'The hospital sent the video as a souvenir,' jokes the Manchester City man. 'But I hope there's never a sequel.'

Now Wright, 34, is starting yet another comeback. 'Joe Royle seems to want me around,' he says. 'The knee is fine and I'd love to give City fans something special in the last two years of my contract.'

'It was a horrible feeling being injured and useless when the club was sliding to relegation.

'I'd rather have been out there on one leg.'

Now Tommy contemplates 46 Cup Finals in Division Two. 'We are down among teams who never expected to be on the same pitch as City,' he points out. 'They will come to Maine Road as if it was Wembley.

'It starts with my old mate, Nigel Worthington, bringing Blackpool to our place on day one.'

Tommy insists City will bounce right back. 'We have very good players,' he argues. 'And the faith of our fans is unbelievable. Season tickets are selling as well as ever.'

The only cloud over Tommy is an ominous silence from Northern Ireland manager Lawrie McMenemy.

'I haven't heard a word since I pulled out of the squad against Slovakia,' he reveals. 'Maybe Lawrie is waiting to assess my fitness.'

Tommy's appalling medical record has cost a minimum of 25 caps. He hasn't figured in the team since the debacle against Albania which speeded the sacking of Bryan Hamilton.

Yet the keeper claims he will still regard himself as the country's No 1 if he resumes duty with City's first team.

'Alan Fettis has done well,' he acknowledges. 'But I have to believe in my own ability. It was injury that took away my international place, nothing else.'

1. What did he have to say about the video of his knee implant?
2. How does he feel about his knee now?
3. How did he feel when the club was heading for relegation?
4. How does he feel about the teams Manchester City will face in Division Two?
5. What does he say about Manchester City players and fans?
6. What is his reaction to the 'ominous silence' from Northern Ireland manager, Lawrie McMenemy?
7. What does he believe in at the moment?
8. What, according to Wright, deprived him of his international place?

How Do You Spell . . . ?

PREFIXES AND SUFFIXES

Students often make mistakes in spelling when adding a prefix or a suffix to a word.

Example	injoyable	instead of	enjoyable
	listend	instead of	listened

Quite often this is due to carelessness, but also to a lack of understanding of how words are constructed and what the prefix or suffix actually means. In this unit, you will find a broad range of prefixes and suffixes. Your task is to learn to spell and use them correctly.

WATCH YOUR LANGUAGE!

1. **Prefixes**: A prefix is a letter or group of letters placed at the **beginning** of a word to:
   (a) change or extend its meaning, or
   (b) form a new word.

Example	un	+	fair	=	unfair
	im	+	prove	=	improve

2. **Suffixes**: A suffix is a letter or group of letters placed at the **end** of a word to:
   (a) change or extend its meaning,
   (b) form a new word, or
   (c) form a plural, past tense, comparative, superlative, etc.

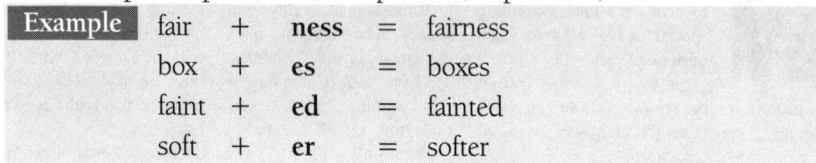

Example	fair	+	ness	=	fairness
	box	+	es	=	boxes
	faint	+	ed	=	fainted
	soft	+	er	=	softer

PREFIXES

Rules

1. There is usually **no change** in the spelling when you add a prefix to a word.

Example	un	+	safe	=	unsafe

   But — be careful when adding the prefixes '**un**', '**dis**' and '**mis**' to words which begin with 'n' or 's'. Remember to **keep** the double letter when you are spelling the new word.

Example	un	+	necessary	=	un**n**ecessary
	dis	+	satisfied	=	dis**s**atisfied
	mis	+	spell	=	mis**s**pell

2. Each prefix has it own meaning. The most common prefixes are:

re	meaning	(a) again	e.g. **re**appear
		(b) back	e.g. **re**turn
pre	meaning	before	e.g. **pre**paid
post	meaning	after	e.g. **post**graduate study
ex	meaning	(a) out of	e.g. **ex**port
		(b) former	e.g. **ex**-president
over	meaning	excessive	e.g. **over**rated
out	meaning	surpass	e.g. **out**do
un			e.g. **un**happy
dis		opposite in meaning	e.g. **dis**satisfied
mis			e.g. **mis**understanding
in			e.g. **in**ability

3. Many prefixes **change** the meaning of a word:
   (a) from the positive to the **negative**:

Example	happy	unhappy
	possible	impossible

SPELLING: PREFIXES AND SUFFIXES

(b) to its opposite:

Example en*courage*   *dis*courage
          *ex*terior   *in*terior

4. Some prefixes are **whole words** in themselves:
   (a) out   e.g. outline   (c) under   e.g. underground
   (b) over   e.g. overtake   (d) up   e.g. uproot

5. Lots of prefixes have to do with **numbers**:
   mono   meaning   one   e.g. monosyllable
   bi   meaning   two   e.g. bifocals
   tri   meaning   three   e.g. tripod

Let's exercise!

Exercise 1

(a) Match the prefixes in the box on the left to the words in the box on the right, in under **two minutes**:

   dis, re, in, over, bi, un, under

   paid, sensitive, lingual, rated appear, agree, decisive

(b) Now cover over your new words and see if you can write them from memory — **spelled correctly**, of course!

Exercise 2

(a) Put an appropriate prefix from the box below before the following words. The same prefix may be used for more than one word. Time limit: five minutes.

   un, im, in, dis, mis, ir

   ___active   ___appropriate   ___spell
   ___usual   ___understand   ___tasteful
   ___approve   ___responsible   ___patient
   ___detected   ___regular   ___movable

(b) Check your dictionary to see if your **spellings** are correct.

(c) Write one sentence for each word. Vary the type of sentence, i.e. three questions, three negative statements, two exclamation style sentences, two humorous sentences and two serious sentences. Watch the spelling!

Exercise 3

In pairs.

(a) Write down as many words as you can that start with the prefixes from Exercises 1 and 2. Time limit: ten minutes.

(b) Exchange copies with another pair of students, who will check the **spellings** of your words in a dictionary. Give **one mark** for each correctly spelt word. If a spelling is **incorrect**, please write it out correctly in the space beside it. Time limit: fifteen minutes.

(c) The pair of students with the **most** words correctly **spelt** win!

WATCH YOUR LANGUAGE!

Exercise 4

Here are some definitions of words beginning with:

out, over, under, up

Can you supply the words? Write them in the spaces provided:
1. a sudden explosion of anger: _____
2. to ask too high a price for something: _____
3. to draw a line under, to stress: _____
4. loud and noisy shouting from a crowd: _____
5. the edge of a town or village: _____
6. deceitful and sly; secretive: _____
7. liquid spilling over: _____
8. sophisticated and expensive: _____

And finally . . .

Here is a list of sixteen words with prefixes that come from Latin and Greek (like the number ones in Rule 5). These prefixes are common to many words, and once you have learned to spell them, you will have learned the hardest part of lots of related words. You will also have an important clue as to their meaning!

Prefix	Meaning of prefix	Word
ante	before	antenatal
anti	against	antisocial
auto	self	autobiography
bi	two	bicentennial
chrono	time	chronological
de	from	depart
fore	before	forewarn
inter	between	international
micro	small	microscope
mono	one, single	monorail
post	after	postscript
semi	half	semi-circle
tele	far	telephone
trans	across	transatlantic
uni	one, single	unilateral
vice	acting for	vice-principal

Exercise 5

(a) With the aid of your **dictionary**, find **one** other word for each of the prefixes in the above list.
(b) Write the words and their **meanings** into your copy.

SPELLING: PREFIXES AND SUFFIXES

Example | Prefix | Meaning of prefix | Word | Meaning of word
| --- | --- | --- | --- |
| ante | before | antenatal | before birth |

(c) Write one sentence for each new word.

SUFFIXES

Suffixes are extremely useful. If you understand them and how they are used, you can build up thousands of words and improve your spelling at the same time!

Rules

1. Adding a suffix to a word is usually quite simple:
   Example
   enjoy + able = enjoy**able**
   suburb + an = suburb**an**
   sing + ing = sing**ing**

2. When the root word ends in a silent 'e', you **drop** the 'e':
   Example
   tune + ing = tun**ing**
   hate + ed = hat**ed**

   Two important **exceptions** to this rule are:

   (a) Words ending in 'ce' or 'ge' **keep the 'e'** before the suffixes 'able' and 'ous':
   Example
   courage + ous = courage**ous**
   notice + able = notice**able**

   (b) When adding a suffix beginning with a **consonant**, you also keep the 'e' of the root word:
   Example
   care + full = care**ful**
   amaze + ment = amaze**ment**

3. When the root word ends in 'y', change it to 'i' before adding the suffix:
   Example happy + ly/ness = happ**ily**, happ**iness**

4. Words ending in 'l', 'm', 'n', 'p' and 't' usually **double** their last letter before adding the suffixes 'ed', 'er', 'in', 'est' and 'ing':
   Example
   patrol + ing/ed = patrol**ling**, patrol**led**
   begin + ing/er = begin**ning**, begin**ner**

5. By adding a suffix, you can make:

   (a) nouns from adjectives:
   Example good (adj.) + ness (suffix) = goodness (noun)

   (b) adjectives from nouns:
   Example mind (noun) + less (suffix) = mindless (adjective)

   (c) verbs from adjectives and nouns!
   Example
   damp (adj.) + en (suffix) = dampen (verb)
   terror (noun) + ise (suffix) = terrorise (verb)

6. Words ending in 'ic' add 'k' before a suffix:
   Example panic + ing/ed = panic**king**, panic**ked**

WATCH YOUR LANGUAGE!

Exercise 1
(a) Your teacher will select students at random and call out 20 words and suffixes. You must spell the word out loud **with** its suffix.

> **Example** Teacher calls out: '"Happy" plus "ness"'.
> You spell: 'H-a-p-p-i-n-e-s-s'.

(b) If you get it wrong, it passes to the next student and you must write the correct spelling out **five** times!

(c) **Everyone** in the class must write out all the words they hear.

(d) Exchange copies with your neighbour and **correct** each other's **spellings**. If in doubt, refer to the rules, or consult your teacher (who knows **all** things, of course!)

Exercise 2
(a) Match the suffixes in the box on the left to the words in the box on the right, in **two minutes**. Make any necessary **small spelling** changes.

able, ful, less, ship, ly, en, ing, ness, ous, ment	resent, rare, recognise, mind, harm, glory, strength, begin, good, friend

(b) Now cover over your new words and see if you can write them from memory — with the **correct spelling**, of course! — in **two minutes**.

Exercise 3
In pairs.
(a) Write down as many words as you can that end with the suffixes from Exercise 2. Time limit: ten minutes.

(b) Exchange copies with another pair of students who will check the **spellings** of your words in a dictionary. Give **one mark** for each correctly spelt word. If a spelling is incorrect, please write the correct version in the space beside it. Time limit: fifteen minutes.

(c) The pair of students with the **most** words correctly **spelt** win!

Exercise 4
(a) Make **adjectives** from these nouns using the suffixes in the box below. Watch the **spelling**!

y, ly, ish, like, ful

1. child   _____
2. truth   _____
3. fool   _____
4. prince _____
5. coward _____
6. hunger _____
7. life   _____
8. snob   _____
9. father _____
10. youth _____
11. plenty _____
12. skill _____
13. noise _____
14. leisure _____
15. fun   _____

SPELLING: PREFIXES AND SUFFIXES

(b) Now write a short descriptive paragraph beginning:
   'Thelma's family is really **snobbish** . . .'
   Use as many of the new adjectives you've formed as possible. (75–100 words)

Exercise 5

(a) Form **nouns** from these adjectives and verbs using the suffixes in the box below. Mind the spelling! Check the rules.

   ness, ment, er, ism

   1. swim _____
   2. govern _____
   3. kind _____
   4. real _____
   5. agree _____
   6. write _____
   7. improve _____
   8. cool _____
   9. win _____
   10. autistic _____

(b) Write one sentence for each new word.

Exercise 6

Prefixes and suffixes

(a) Make **adjectives** from these verbs using the suffix 'able'. Mind the spelling!

   1. value _____
   2. work _____
   3. advise _____
   4. forget _____
   5. transfer _____
   6. predict _____
   7. believe _____
   8. obtain _____
   9. recognise _____
   10. rely _____
   11. avoid _____
   12. vary _____
   13. repeat _____
   14. profit _____

(b) Form the **negative** of the new adjectives by adding the **prefix** 'un' or 'in' to each of them. Be careful! Which is the correct spelling: 'un' or 'in'? Check your dictionary if you're not sure.

And finally . . .

(a) Make two lists headed **Prefixes** and **Suffixes** from all the words that you have learned and exercised in this section.
(b) Include also those **new** words that you yourself have created.
(c) Write them out into your copy or folder in **alphabetical** order, as in a dictionary.
(d) Set aside a little time each week to learn the spellings of **ten** words from your lists.
(e) Refer to them when you are doing a homework assignment. Use them. Make them part of your speech and writing.

WATCH YOUR LANGUAGE!

Words at Work

ACTION WORDS

Question So what's an action word, then?
Answer It's a word that **leaps**, **soars**, **struts**, **flicks**, **screams**, **whispers**, **sighs**, **sprints** or **pounces**! It has life, movement and feeling in it. Every sentence must have a verb, but many students never move beyond the same dull, overused ones: see, show, say, tell, etc.

Let's exercise with more exciting ones!

Stage 1

'WALK THIS WAY!': VERBS OF MOVEMENT

The verb 'to walk' is in common use, but there are many different **ways** of walking. Here are just some of them:

amble	hobble	plod	strut
crawl	limp	shuffle	tiptoe
creep	march	stagger	trek
dash	meander	stride	trudge
dawdle	pace	stroll	wander

Exercise 1

(a) Your teacher will begin a story in this way with the verb 'amble':

'Pat was happy. He'd worked hard all week and now he'd decided to **amble** down to his favourite local for a pint and a game of snooker . . .'

(b) There are 20 verbs in alphabetical order in the above list. Your teacher will select nineteen students **at random** to **continue** the story, each one contributing **one sentence** which must contain the next verb on the list. Begin with 'crawl'. If an individual can't continue the story within 30 seconds, his/her turn goes to the next student selected. The game ends when your teacher gets to the verb 'wander'. You should aim to conclude the story with this verb. Your teacher may impose a time limit of ten to fifteen minutes for this story exercise. Have fun!

Exercise 2

Choose the **best** 'movement' verb from those in brackets in order to complete each of the following sentences:

1. When I struggled out of the ditch, I _____ (walked, slipped, staggered) up the hill to the nearest house.

VOCABULARY: ACTION WORDS

2. Sheila fell off the wall and had to _____ (walk, plod, hobble) home in great pain.
3. Rita _____ (dashed, dawdled, strolled) all the way to school.
4. The injured hurler _____ (ambled, marched, limped) off the pitch.
5. Mrs. Molloy _____ (walked, strode, trudged) wearily home, the heavy bags biting into her hands.

Exercise 3

Now select any **ten** movement verbs from your list, and write your own sentences for each one. Think about what kind of person might walk in a particular way, at what pace and in which situation. Create a **character**.

> **Example** Paul **struts** around the school yard like a peacock.
> 'For heaven's sake, Tina Roche, will you stop **shuffling** those feet and get a move on!' said Mrs. Ryan.

Stage 2

'SOUNDS INTERESTING!': SOUND VERBS

Exercise 1

Write out the 30 'sound' verbs in the box below into two lists of **quiet** and **loud** verbs, fifteen in each list.

	Quiet	Loud		Quiet	Loud
1.	_____	_____	9.	_____	_____
2.	_____	_____	10.	_____	_____
3.	_____	_____	11.	_____	_____
4.	_____	_____	12.	_____	_____
5.	_____	_____	13.	_____	_____
6.	_____	_____	14.	_____	_____
7.	_____	_____	15.	_____	_____
8.	_____	_____			

bang	patter	sob
blare	peal	squeak
boom	purr	swish
clatter	rattle	thud
crash	ring	thunder
gurgle	rumble	tick
hiss	rustle	tinkle
howl	shriek	twitter
hum	sigh	whimper
low	slam	yelp

WATCH YOUR LANGUAGE!

Did you notice how some 'sound' verbs can be either loud **or** quiet depending on the situation in which they are used? For example, a child could **sob** quietly or loudly, depending on whether it wished to be heard or not!

Exercise 2
Choose an appropriate sound verb from your lists to complete the following sentences:
1. The baby _____ contentedly in its pram.
2. The wind _____ round the corner of the house.
3. The puppy _____ in pain when the boy kicked him.
4. The champagne glasses _____ as the old ladies smiled and _____ the old melodies of their youth.
5. The rain _____ on the roof, and we _____ for sun and blue skies.
6. The head chef _____ out of the kitchen while the youngest trainee _____ quietly in a corner.
7. He remembered how her gown had _____ and _____ as she danced.

Exercise 3
Choose five 'quiet' verbs and five 'loud' ones and write a continuous piece of prose, **or** a short poem (8–10 lines), in which each verb is used only once or twice. Be imaginative. Consider the context in which the sound might be made, the kind of person, animal or object **associated** with that sound. Try to create an **atmosphere**.

Stage 3

'IT'S ALL TALK!': TALKING VERBS

Believe it or not, there are more ways of speaking than simply 'say' or 'tell'. Here are 30 really vibrant talking verbs:

babble	jeer	roar
bark	lisp	scream
bawl	moan	shout
chat	murmur	snap
cry	mutter	snarl
drone	natter	stammer
exclaim	pray	stutter
gossip	preach	utter
grunt	rant	whisper
harp	rave	yell

Exercise 1
Fill in the blanks in the following sentences with a suitable 'talking' verb from the above list. (Some verbs must be written in the past simple tense.)

VOCABULARY: ACTION WORDS

1. 'Heavens above!' he _____. 'I can't possibly eat all that!'
2. He _____ something about losing his wallet, but it wasn't very clear.
3. 'Help!' she _____. 'I can't get out!'
4. He never stopped _____ all through the play. It was really irritating.
5. I wish Harry practised what he _____.
6. The Principal _____ on about discipline for 20 minutes.
7. Maurice doesn't actually speak. He merely _____ whenever he wants something.
8. Barbara is forever _____ on about her boyfriend. It's a real bore.
9. They _____ him all the time about his clothes. It was deliberately cruel.
10. I love to _____ with my mates at the weekend.

Exercise 2

Read carefully the following extract from George Orwell's *1984*, and answer the questions which follow.

> 'Thirty to Forty group!' yapped a piercing female voice. 'Thirty to Forty group! Take your places please!'
>
> Winston sprang to attention in front of the telescreen, upon which the image of a youngish woman, scrawny but muscular, had already appeared, dressed in a tunic and gym-shoes.
>
> 'Arms bending and stretching!' she rapped out. 'Take your time from me. One, two, three, four! One, two, three, four! One, two, three, four!'
>
> As Winston mechanically shot his arms backwards and forwards, he wore the look of grim enjoyment on his face, which was considered proper during the Physical Jerks.
>
> 'Stand easy!' barked the instructress, a little more genially.
>
> Winston sank his arms to his sides and slowly refilled his lungs with air, but the instructress had already called them to attention. 'And now let's see which of us can touch our toes!' she said enthusiastically. 'Right over from the hips please. One, two! One, two!'
>
> He loathed this exercise, which sent shooting pains all the way from his heels to his buttocks and often ended by bringing on another coughing fit.
>
> 'Smith!' screamed the shrewish voice from the telescreen. '6079, Smith W.! Yes, you! Bend lower please! You can do better than that! You're not trying. Lower, please! That's better, much better. Now stand at ease, the whole squad, and watch me!'

1. Can you identify the 'talking' verbs in the above extract? Underline each one.
2. What impression do they give us of the instructress? Why does she speak the way she does?
3. Write a short piece of **dialogue** or **narrative** (150–200 words), in which you use as many of the talking verbs from this section as possible. Try not to repeat a verb. Here is a 'starter' sentence (but you are free to create your own, of course):

    'You're not afraid of me, are you?' she murmured, as she passed his chair . . .

WATCH YOUR LANGUAGE!

Stage 4

'ACTION PLEASE!': DRAMATIC VERBS

In the following exercises, we will look at how verbs can be **dramatic**, creating a sense of tension, mystery or violence. These are truly **action** words, giving life to the text, creating an immediate excitement for the reader.

Exercise 1

Read the following passage from *Cider with Rosie* by Laurie Lee. It describes Miss B., the Head Teacher. (I think you'll agree that she was absolutely terrifying!) Answer the questions which follow.

> Miss B., the Head Teacher, to whom I was now delivered, was about as physically soothing as a rake. She was a bunched up and punitive little body and the school christened her Crabby; she had a sour yellow look, lank hair twisted round her ears, and the skin and voice of a turkey. We used to be afraid of the gobbling Miss B.; she spied, she pried, she crouched, she crept, she pounced — she was a terror.
>
> Each morning was war without declaration; no one knew who would catch her attention next. We used to stand to attention, half-crippled in our desks, till Miss B. walked in. She had a habit of whacking the walls with her ruler, and then fixed us with her squinting eye. We would sometimes say a prayer; but scarcely had we bellowed the last Amen than Crabby coiled, uncoiled and sprang, and knocked some poor boy sideways.

1. Underline those verbs the writer uses to describe Miss B.
2. What did she do with her ruler?
3. How did the class say the last Amen of the prayers?
4. '. . . than Crabby **coiled**, **uncoiled** and **sprang**, and knocked some poor boy sideways'. What do you think 'coiled' and 'uncoiled' refer to, in terms of Miss B.? Is 'sprang' **dramatic**, and why? (30–50 words)

Exercise 2

Here is another short passage, describing the **violence** of an attack upon a house, during a burglary.

> In a burglary in Meadow Drive last night, considerable damage was done to interior fittings and decorations. Doors were ripped off their hinges, soft furnishings were slashed, mirrors and pictures were broken, and paint daubed over walls and carpets. The intruders made off with a small collection of valuable paintings. Items of jewellery were also stolen. A Garda investigation is under way and it is believed that two men are being held for questioning.

(a) Which verbs convey the **violence** of the attack?
(b) Write a similar report (the same number of words), using the **same** verbs but placing the attack in a different **situation**, and changing the details accordingly.

VOCABULARY: ACTION WORDS

Exercise 3

The exam. Poetry.
Read the poem, and then answer the questions which follow.

The House at Night

1. Some stealthy spider is weaving round my bed
   and mice are nibbling the curtains overhead.
   Weird footsteps make the floorboards crack,
   the staircase creaks,
   chill draughts thrill down my back
   from some forgotten window out of sight
   this is the house at night.

2. There's a whispering on the landing
   where a creepy tropic plant is standing,
   and the coatrack in the hall
   lets fall a scarf — a long, soft fall:
   a snake's loose coils that rapidly grow tight
   this is the house at night.

3. From the distant kitchen come the notes of dripping taps
   plink-plonking secret codes
   I cannot get the meaning of: a sudden
   icy shudder — the refrigerator groans — a hidden
   oven, cooling, ticks in rustling ember-light
   this is the house at night.

4. But even stranger is my own tense breathing
   as I lie here speechless looking at the ceiling
   that seems to swim all round like falling snow.
   I can hear my eyelids batting gently, slow
   then quick as heartbeats as I freeze with fright
   at something in the mirror shining bright
   has someone left the telly on all night?
   No, thank heaven, it's all right,
   it's only the moon's pale, spooky light
   touching my tangled sheets with chalky white
   yes, this is the house at night.

JAMES KIRKUP

WATCH YOUR LANGUAGE!

1. Concentrate on the **verbs** in this poem. Underline each one. You should find 24 (excluding 'is').
2. 'Chill draughts **thrill** down my back'. What do you think the verb 'thrill' means here? Look up a thesaurus to find other words for thrill, and a dictionary for other meanings.
3. Comment on the verb in the image 'the refrigerator **groans**'. Is it a good way to describe the fridge? What exactly is it describing?
4. Choose **ten to fifteen verbs** from this poem and write (a) a poem, (b) a continuous piece of prose, or (c) a piece of dialogue in which each verb is used just once. Include also some movement, sound and talking verbs from the rest of this unit.

UNIT 7

Grappling with Grammar

THE PAST TENSE 2

The final two past tenses to be considered are the **past perfect simple** (**had** done) and the **past perfect continuous** (**had been** doing).

Stage 1
THE PAST PERFECT SIMPLE

Example   John **had worked** in Cork, before he came to Dublin.

In this example, two actions occurred in the past, one **before** the other. The first action is in the past perfect simple ('had worked'), the second in the past simple ('came'). The past perfect tense is especially important when you want to stress that one event **finished** before another began. This tense is very useful when you are writing a story. It makes it clear to the reader when **exactly** things happened in relation to each other in the past.

Example   He **had visited** his aunt in Portlaoise, where he **had lived** as a child, **before** he arrived in Dublin.

Exceptions

There are **two** situations when it is best to use the **past simple** instead of the **past perfect simple**.
1. When the second action happens as a result of the first.
   Example   When Sorcha **arrived**, we **opened** a bottle of wine.
2. When there is a **sequence of events** in a story, in the past.
   Example   When the alarm went off, the burglar **panicked**. He **raced** out the door and **fell** over a motorbike outside, and a policeman promptly **arrested** him.

WATCH YOUR LANGUAGE!

Exercise 1

Complete these sentences with the **past perfect simple** of the verbs in brackets.

> **Example** Sheila returned to Ireland after twenty years in the States, to find that many things _____ (change). **had changed**

1. Her best friend, Mary, was no longer there. She _____ (go) away.
2. Most of her family were no longer there, either. They _____ (leave) many years before.
3. The local hotel was no longer open. It _____ (close) down in 1985.
4. Dr. Harris was no longer alive. He _____ (die) six months before.
5. She didn't recognise the town. It _____ (change) completely.

Exercise 2

Enlarge on the skeleton notes in the brackets, as in the following example, using the **past perfect simple** tense.

> **Example** Susan didn't want to come to the cinema with us. (She/already/see/film/twice)
> She **had** already **seen** the film twice.

1. Mam wasn't at home when I arrived. (She/just/go/out)
2. We arrived at the pitch late. (The match/already/begin)
3. Donna wasn't hungry when I rang. (She/just/finish/her fifth doughnut!)
4. Mick invited Tina to dinner last Saturday, but she couldn't go. (She/already/arrange/go out with/someone else)
5. I was really delighted to see Maura again. (I/not/see/her/for years)

Stage 2

THE PAST PERFECT CONTINUOUS

Now look at this sentence:

> **Example** They **had been** play**ing** for half an hour when there was a terrible thunderstorm and the match was stopped.

We use the **past perfect continuous** to say **how long** something **had been going on before** something else happened. This may also refer to **habitual** actions in the past.

> **Example** Joan **had been** smo**king** for twenty years before she finally saw sense.

With this tense, the action is always continuous, that is, going on for some time in the past.

Exercise 1

Read the following situations and then follow each one with a **sentence** in the **past perfect continuous** tense.

> **Example** Teresa was very tired, so she went to bed much earlier than usual. (She/study/hard/all day)
> She **had been studying** hard all day.

Your turn!

GRAMMAR: THE PAST TENSE 2

1. The two boys came home, one with a black eye and the other a cut lip. (They/fight/in the schoolyard)
2. When Mr. Butler walked into the room, it was empty, but there was a distinct smell of cigarette smoke. (Some students/smoke/there during lunchbreak)
3. When Paula came back from a session on the sunbed, she looked very red. (She/lie/under it/for too long)
4. I arranged to meet Peter in a pub, but after a while, I realised that I had come to the wrong one! (I/wait there/for 20 minutes) before I realised my mistake.
5. Donna woke up terrified in the middle of the night because she didn't know where she was. (She/dream/about a giant-sized doughnut) which had taken over the world!

Exercise 2
Answer the following questions with a sentence in the **past perfect continuous** form.

Example What had you been doing before you had the crash?
I had been talking to my girlfriend on my mobile phone.

You may use your imagination in your answers to these questions, as there are many possibilities.

1. Where had she been working before she came to Galway?
2. Who had he been speaking to before the accident?
3. How long had they been playing before the rain started?
4. Why had you been thinking about it for so long?
5. What had you been doing before you started this unit?

Stage 3

Exercise 1
Do you remember Donna? She's the one who has popped up in a number of the exercises in this unit! She is addicted to doughnuts! Read this mini-saga about her, and **identify** each past tense as you read. You will find examples of all **six** past tenses (from this unit and Unit 6).

1. Donna **ate** ten doughnuts yesterday. (Tense:_____)
2. Donna **has eaten** doughnuts every day since she was a kid. (Tense:_____)
3. She **was eating** her fifth doughnut at about six o'clock when her boyfriend, Paul, rang. (Tense:_____)
4. 'Donna? It's me, Paul. Have you **been eating** doughnuts again all day?!' he asked. (Tense:_____)
5. 'Who? Me?!' said Donna, guiltily, stuffing a sixth doughnut behind a cushion on the sofa. 'No, way, Paul! I'm giving them up, honest. I **had eaten** just one little one before you rang. No more, I swear!' (Tense:_____)
6. Paul sighed. He **had heard** it all before. (Tense:_____)
7. 'I don't believe you, Donna! You sound like you're stuffing your face this very minute! Come on. Own up! Just how many doughnuts **had you been eating** before I rang?!' (Tense:_____)

WATCH YOUR LANGUAGE!

Exercise 2

Did you spot all of the six tenses in Exercise 1? Good! Now, answer the following questions about Donna in the **tense** of the question. Be very careful with the wording.

> **Example** What do you think Donna **did** the moment she put the phone down?
> I think she **ate** the sixth doughnut hidden behind the cushion on the sofa. (past simple)

Now you do it.
1. What **did** she do **after** she ate the sixth doughnut?
2. What **has she done** so many times already?
3. What **was she doing** when her Mum and Dad came home from work?
4. What **has she been doing** since she was a little girl?
5. What **had she done** just before Paul rang?
6. What **had she been doing** all day?

Exercise 3

The exam. Reading comprehension.

Here are some short extracts of the type used in the Reading and Fiction sections of the Junior Cert. exam papers. **Identify the tenses** of the verbs in bold, and then answer the questions which follow. Write a complete sentence in the **same tense** as the question.

1. He **had been** a tall man. From feet to neck **covered** a long space. His head **lay** beside him. When she **pushed back** the leaves and layers of earth and debris Moya **saw** that **he'd had** large white teeth, all of them cracked or broken, long fingers, and very big bones. All his clothes **had rotted away** except some threads of blue denim from his overalls. The buckles of the overalls **had turned green**.

    (a) Had he been a small man?
    (b) Where did his head lie?
    (c) What had his teeth been like?
    (d) What had happened to his clothes?

2. The bull **seemed** to take no notice of me as I **edged** my way into the stable. He just **turned** with awesome slowness and **made his way** into the stall. There Harry **dropped** the rope over Monty's horns and **tied** it tightly to a huge iron bar in the wall outside. I **opened** the door of his stall and as I **passed along** his massive body I **sensed** the terrible power of this animal. I **ran** my fingers along its massive neck to find the vein from which I would take the blood. The skin was hard and leathery and it would take a good jab to pierce it. The bull **stiffened** but **did not move** as I **plunged** the needle in and with relief I **saw** the blood flowing into the syringe. I **was withdrawing** the needle and thinking how simple the job was after all when everything **started to happen**. The bull **gave** a tremendous roar and **whipped** his head around at me with incredible speed.

GRAMMAR: THE PAST TENSE 2

(a) How did the bull react as the vet edged his way into the stable?
(b) What did Harry do?
(c) What did the vet do with the needle?
(d) What happened as he was withdrawing the needle? (Begin with 'As he was . . .')

3. The trend towards co-education **has gathered pace** this century as women **have fought** for equal rights and opportunities. The vast majority of schools in England are now mixed and **it has long been thought** correct to say that co-education is right for everyone. However, this argument is unjust to good single-sex schools. **Changes have been made**, especially in the last couple of decades, to face up to weaknesses in the system. Girls' schools, for example, **have made** great strides in ensuring that a broad choice of subjects is available, including a wider range of sciences, design and technology, information technology and sports.

(a) What has gathered pace this century?
(b) What have women fought for?
(c) Has it always been thought that co-education is correct for everyone?
(d) What changes have been made in girls' schools, for example?

VERBS IN THE PAST TENSE — SUMMARY

Examples	Tense
1. I **wrote** to Paul **last week**.	Past simple
2. I **was waiting** for Nora for two hours.	Past continuous
3. I **have** just **moved** house.	Present perfect simple
4. I **have been** dreaming of this house for years.	Present perfect continuous
5. I **had read** the book before I saw the film.	Past perfect simple
6. I **had been** looking forward to that moment for a long time.	Past perfect continuous

When understood and practised, these tenses will make your expression clearer, more precise and more varied. Students often use only the past simple or the present tense in their writing, and these mixed together wrongly most of the time! Try to avoid 'would' when describing things in the past, even **habitual** actions. It becomes repetitive and boring. Use it **once** to introduce a memory, for example, and then continue in the **past simple**, the **past continuous**, or the **past perfect** forms. This will result in much better writing. Watch those tenses!

WATCH YOUR LANGUAGE!

Punctuation Please!

DASHES AND HYPHENS

Question What's the difference between a dash and a hyphen?
Answer Good question! Both are written as short lines, and they look alike, but the dash is longer than the hyphen.
> **Example** Dash: You know what will happen — you'll lose your way.
> Hyphen: This is very up-to-date information.

They each have different uses, too. Let's deal with the **dash** first.

Stage 1

DASH

Uses

1. A single dash marks a **sharp break** in a sentence.
   > **Example** Books, copies, notes — he threw them all in the bin.
2. Two dashes can be used in order to provide **extra information**.
   > **Example** Come to me after class — don't forget your French copy — and I'll try to explain the bit you've missed.
3. Dashes can be used **instead of brackets** ( ) to enclose words giving extra information. They give **more emphasis** to the words between them than brackets do.
   > **Example** Shoes — which must be brown — will be worn at all times.
4. Dashes are used to introduce a **comment** or an **explanation**.
   > **Example** (a) (comment) Soccer star Alan Shearer has been transferred for a record fee — £2 million.
   > (b) (explanation) I like vegetables — carrots, peas, broccoli, anything.

   In Example (b) the dash **explains** what you mean by vegetables. You would not use a dash if you simply wrote: I like carrots, peas, broccoli, anything.
5. A dash shows a **break in speech**.
   > **Example** (a) Sheila picked up the knife and screamed: 'Get out of here or I'll kill you, you —'
   > (b) 'Really, now you ask me,' said Alice, very much confused, 'I don't think —' 'Then you shouldn't talk,' said the Hatter. (*Alice in Wonderland*, by Lewis Carroll)
6. A dash may be used to add an **element of surprise**, an **unexpected turn of thought**, or a **witticism**.

PUNCTUATION: DASHES AND HYPHENS

Example 'There is always an easy solution to every human problem — neat, plausible and wrong.' (H. L. Mencken)

7. A **longer** dash (called a 3-em dash) may be used to indicate a word or **part** of a word that's been left out.

    Example 'You're a d——— fool!'

Finally . . . be careful how you use dashes. They are often used as excuses for bad punctuation. Students sometimes put them between two words when they don't know whether to use a comma, colon or semi-colon. Dashes should be used **sparingly**, and when they **end** a sentence, for example, all other punctuation marks are omitted.

Let's exercise them.

Exercise 1

Rewrite the following sentences inserting one or two dashes in the correct place in each one.
1. He thought Paris was the most beautiful city in the world until he saw Florence.
2. The Mayor launched the new lifeboat which slid gracefully into the water and crashed into another boat.
3. I have made some plans not very detailed ones for the trip to Rome.
4. I appreciate your offer will you really manage without it?
5. You must handwrite your essay typing will not do and hand it up tomorrow.
6. Put the baby to bed don't forget her bottle and I'll ring later to check how she is.
7. As Tom charged out the door, Mr. Brown roared after him: 'Don't forget your'   But his words were drowned out by Tom's motorbike.
8. We were happy to eat *pâté de foie gras* we changed our minds when Ian told us how the geese were force-fed.
9. There are 30 students in my class ten of them are girls.
10. Mary burst into the loo to tell her mate the news only to realise she was in the gents toilet.

Exercise 2

Add one or two dashes and any necessary commas to these sentences.
1. The 1798 commemoration ceremony it was the biggest event ever held in the town was attended by over two thousand people.
2. Joe Mullery was fined for having six adults and two children in his mini three in the front three in the back one child on the floor in the front one child lying across the window.
3. My grandmother the one who died before I was born travelled all over Europe and America.
4. Many countries Ireland was one of them did not qualify for the World Cup in 1998.
5. Complete this application don't forget to sign it and post it off quickly.
6. Peggy was quite happy to share a room with Denise until she heard about her pet snake sharing it too.

7. We had to wait two hours for the train cows had wandered on to the track at Arklow.
8. The class is divided on this issue half agree with the uniform half don't.
9. Sunscreen sunglasses sunhat she left them all behind on the bed.
10. Tennis star Pete Sampras has had his hands insured for a colossal sum $3 million.

Stage 2

HYPHEN

'Our hyphens are in a mess.' (E. Whitaker-Wilson, *How to Punctuate*)

Uses

1. A hyphen is used to join two words together. It changes the meaning of both words. The two words together are then known as a **compound** word.

   Example side + show = side-show
   seat + belt = seat-belt
   jelly + babies = jelly-babies

2. A hyphen is used to mark the division of words at the end of a line **in print**. The break should be a **syllabic** one.

   Example 'sing-' (at the **end** of one line) followed by 'ing' (at the **beginning** of the next line)

   However, in **handwriting**, this use should be avoided altogether.

3. Combinations of **three words** divided by **two** hyphens are quite common in English.

   Example brother-in-law, commander-in-chief, up-to-date, Stratford-upon-Avon

4. A hyphen is used to break up:
   (a) telephone numbers (046-28351)
   (b) account numbers (Acc. No. 3030-6145-2332)
   (c) continuous numbers in street addresses and pages (10-15 St. Stephen's Green, pages 138-155)

5. Hyphens are used in **compound adjectives** before nouns.

   Example a light-blue shirt, a well-known politician

6. Hyphens help to avoid confusion in the **spelling** of some words.

   Example mis-spell, hair-raising, hitch-hike, stock-still, stage-struck

7. Hyphens help to avoid **mispronunciation**:

   Example co-operate, pre-eminent, co-ordinate

8. Hyphens always feature with certain **Latin** prefixes:

   Example ex-champion, non-smoker, sub-committee, vice-captain

Finally . . . as with dashes, the hyphen should be used with **care**. 'The hyphen is not an ornament but an aid to being understood, and should be employed only when it is needed for that purpose.' (H. W. Fowler, *A Dictionary of Modern English Usage*)

Let's exercise it.

PUNCTUATION: DASHES AND HYPHENS

Exercise 1

Match a word from List A and one from List B to form a **compound word**, requiring a hyphen. Write out the newly formed words — with hyphens, of course!

List A	List B
spirit	off
cross	hearted
audio	fiction
sky	west
half	blank
law	level
non	examine
south	visual
play	abiding
point	high

Exercise 2

In pairs.

Look back to Use 3 on hyphens. How many more **three-word** combinations requiring **two hyphens** can you come up with? You may consult your dictionary. Time limit: fifteen minutes. The pair who have written out the most examples within the time limit win.

Here's a starter: cul-de-sac.

Exercise 3

Write at least **three** compound words for each of the following 'starter' words. Don't forget the **hyphen**.

Example   cross-reference

1. cross- _____   4. non-   _____
2. self-   _____   5. short- _____
3. well-   _____

Stage 3

DASHES AND HYPHENS

Exercise 1

Fit the following hyphenated words into the correct sentence below.

back-breaking   mouth-watering
hair-raising   heart-breaking
heart-warming

1. He found that picking grapes for seven hours was _____ work.
2. It was _____ to get the letter from home, saying they missed her.

WATCH YOUR LANGUAGE!

3. Taking the roller coaster ride on 'Space Mountain' was a _____ experience.
4. Although we were on a diet, we couldn't resist the chocolate cake — it looked so _____.
5. It was _____ to watch the little girl crying over her broken dolly.

Exercise 2

Now write sentences of your own, using the five compound words from Exercise 1, plus the following compounds and the stimulus words provided in brackets:

1. all-round (athlete)
2. Anglo-Irish (Agreement)
3. cross-examination (witness)
4. free-range (hens)
5. hitch-hike (Cork)
6. fifty-fifty (the Lotto)
7. law-abiding (citizen)
8. North-South (relations)
9. play-off (match)
10. post-war (Europe)

Exercise 3

The exam. Personal writing.

(a) In his books, the Irish writer, Roddy Doyle, uses **dashes** instead of quotation marks when writing dialogue. Read the following extract from his Booker Prize award-winning novel *Paddy Clarke Ha Ha Ha* and comment briefly on his use of dashes. For example, do you think the dialogue is easier to read with dashes rather than quotation marks? If so, **why** is this?

> We loved marching. We could feel the boards hopping under us. We put so much effort into slamming our feet down that we couldn't keep in time. She made us do this a couple of times a day, when she said we were looking lazy.
> While we marched this time Miss Watkins read the proclamation.
> — Irishmen and Irishwomen: In the name of God and of the dead generations from which she receives her old tradition of nationhood, Ireland, through us, summons her children to her flag and strikes for her freedom.
> She had to stop. It wasn't proper marching any more. She hit the blackboard.
> — Suígí síos.*
> She looked annoyed and disappointed.
> Kevin put his hand up.
> — Miss?
> — Sea?**
> — Paddy Clarke said his granda's Thomas Clarke on the tea-towel, Miss.
> — Did he now?
> — Yes, Miss.
> — Patrick Clarke.
>
> * Sit down.
> ** Yes.

— Yes, Miss.
— Stand up till we see you.
It took ages for me to get out of my desk.
— Your grandfather is Thomas Clarke?
I smiled.
— Is he?
— Yes, Miss.
— This man here?
She pointed at Thomas Clarke in one of the corners of the tea-towel. He looked like a granda.
— Yes, Miss.
— Where does he live, tell us?
— Clontarf, Miss.
— Where?
— Clontarf, Miss.
— Come up here to me, Patrick Clarke.
The only noise was me on the floorboards.
She pointed to a bit of writing under Thomas Clarke's head.
— Read that for us, Patrick Clarke.
— Ex — eh — executed by the British on 3 May, 1916.
— What does Executed mean, Dermot Grimes who's picking his nose and doesn't think I can see him?
— Kilt, Miss.
— That's right. And this is your grandfather who lives in Clontarf, is it, Patrick Clarke?
— Yes, Miss.
I pretended to look at the picture again.
— I'll ask you again, Patrick Clarke. Is this man your grandfather?
— No, Miss.
She gave me three on each hand.

(b) Try writing a short piece of dialogue of your own. It should be about the same length as the extract above and based on one of the following situations:
- ◆ A row with one or both of your parents
- ◆ A discussion on the World Cup 1998
- ◆ An argument over who should pay for something
- ◆ Any situation involving conflict of some kind

Remember to use **dashes** throughout, instead of quotation marks.

WATCH YOUR LANGUAGE!

How Do You Spell . . . ?

DOUBLE LETTER WORDS 2

In this unit, you will be exercising double letter words from 'm' to 't'.

1. Double 'm' and 'n' words

Double 'm'	Double 'n'
accommodate	annual
common	beginning
grammar	channel
immediately	innocence
recommend	tyranny

It would be useful to **underline** the double 'm' or 'n' section of each word in the above list as a way of reminding yourself that there are two 'm's or 'n's. These words are often misspelt.

Exercise 1

(a) Study the ten words above for ten minutes in class. Remember it will be easier to learn these spellings because each word contains a **double** 'm' or 'n' and they are written in **alphabetical** order.

(b) When the ten minutes are up, your teacher will call out each word in the order in which you have learned them. Write them out, one underneath the other, in a list, being very careful with those **double** 'm's and 'n's!

(c) Exchange your copy with the person next to you. You will now correct his/hers, and he/she will do likewise with yours. Please refer to the **original spelling list** when correcting each word.

(d) Give **one** mark for each word spelled correctly, and a total mark out of ten.

(e) If a word has been spelled **incorrectly**, cross it out and write the **correct** spelling of the word beside it, again checking from the original list.

(f) Take back your own copy and write out any words **you** have spelled incorrectly, **five times** each.

Exercise 2

Can you unjumble these words from your double 'm' and 'n' list?
1. LNHCANE
2. DMROMECNE
3. RAMGAMR
4. YEMILDEMIAT
5. NIBGNIENG

SPELLING: DOUBLE LETTER WORDS 2

Exercise 3
Write **two** sentences each for the remaining **five** words, using the word in a different situation/context in each sentence.

Example   annual
   Sentence 1.   'I see Mrs. Flanagan is off on her **annual** holiday again. That'll be her tenth, you know.'
   Sentence 2.   The Dublin 15 Arts Festival in an **annual** event now.

2. Double 'p' words

   appeal   approach
   appear   opportunity
   appearance   opposite
   appetite   support
   applied   supporter

This list should be quite easy to learn as the first six words begin with 'app', the next two with 'opp', and the final two with 'supp'.

Exercise 1
As for double 'm' and 'n' words.

Exercise 2
Do you remember the **cloze style** exercise for double 'd' words in Unit 4? Read the notes and instructions again, and do exactly the same with these words from the double 'p' list.

(a) 1. ___earance   (c) 1. ___etite   (e) 1. ___osite
    2. app_____   2. app____   2. opp____
    3. appear____   3. appet__   3. oppos__
    4. _____ance   4. _____ite   4. _____ite
    5. _____   5. _____   5. _____
(b) 1. ___orter   (d) 1. _____ity
    2. supp__er   2. opp__unity
    3. ___ort__   3. ___ort_____
    4. _____er   4. opport_____
    5. _____   5. _____

Remember! This exercise is designed to help you to **spell** better. It is not a test in comprehension. It is simply a way of learning to spell a word **in stages**.

Exercise 3
Write **five** sentences, using **two** of the list words in each sentence. Try to make them as imaginative and as interesting as possible. Be careful with the spelling of these double 'p' words.

WATCH YOUR LANGUAGE!

3. Double 'r' words

arrange	horrible
arrive	irritable
barrier	marriage
correspondence	quarrel
embarrass	terrible

The words 'embarrass' and 'marriage' are often misspelt. Underline that part of the word where the spelling error usually occurs:
- the 'ia' in marriage (often misspelt as 'ai'), and
- the double 'r' and 's' in embarrass.

Exercise 1
As for double 'm' and 'n' words.

Exercise 2
Fill in the gaps in the following piece of dialogue with suitable words from the list of double 'r' words.

Mr. Dawson: Did we receive any _____ from that Sheridan man, Pamela?

Pamela: No, Sir. I did try to _____ a meeting with him, for next Wednesday, but he declined.

Mr. Dawson: Really! The cheek of the man! Is he deliberately trying to _____ me, in front of my colleagues?! Why is he creating this _____ between us, do you know?

Pamela: I've no idea, Sir.

Mr. Dawson: Well, let me know the moment any letters _____ in for me, will you?

Pamela: Of course, Sir.

(Exit Mr. Dawson. Phone rings.)

Pamela: Hello, Mr. Dawson's secretary speaking. Who's calling, please?

Mr. Sheridan: Hello, gorgeous! How's my favourite girl, then? Is that _____ old sod, Dawson, working you too hard again? Come away with me, my lovely. Ours could be a _____ made in heaven!

Pamela: Oh, Mr. Sheridan! You're a _____ man!

Mr. Sheridan: Yes, well, you've a _____ life with that bully. If you worked for me, I bet, we'd never have as much as one _____. Come on, Pamela. What do you say? Will you marry me?

Exercise 3
Continue the above dialogue, using **all ten** double 'r' words once again. Keep the same characters: Pamela, Mr. Dawson and Mr. Sheridan. You may write the dialogue between just **two** of these characters, if you wish.

SPELLING: DOUBLE LETTER WORDS 2

4. Double 's' words

discuss	message
essay	necessity
express	passenger
impossible	pressure
issue	scissors

Did you notice how all the above words have a vowel letter immediately in front of the double 's'? Underline these letters. It will help you to remember how to spell them.

Exercise 1
As for double 'm' and 'n' words.

Exercise 2
(a) Having learned the spellings, can you **unjumble** these double 's' words?
   1. ENCSYISET
   2. ILSPMOSEIB
   3. ESGSPNREA
   4. RSIOSCSS
   5. SEPUSRER

(b) Here are synonyms (words of similar meaning) of the remaining five double 's' words. Can you match them up?
   1. converse   _____
   2. convey   _____
   3. composition   _____
   4. concern   _____
   5. communication _____

   Use a thesaurus or a dictionary, if you can't figure them out. All of them beginning with 'c' should help!

Exercise 3
Now that you have your dictionary out (!), write an alphabetical list of double 's' words, beginning with 'a'.

> **Example**   'a' for address
> 'b' for boss
> and so on

You can forget 'x', 'y' and 'z', but there is a 'w' word with 'ss' in it.

5. Double 't' words

attack	cottage
attempt	lettuce
attitude	matter
attractive	motto
battle	settlement

Notice that the first four words in this list begin with 'att'. This is quite common for double 't' words. You will find a lot of 'att' words in your dictionary. Note too how the double 't' in battle and matter is preceded by 'a' also.

WATCH YOUR LANGUAGE!

Exercise 1

As for double 'm' and 'n' words.

Exercise 2

Here are some **definitions**, from the *Concise Oxford Dictionary*, of the words in the double 't' list. Place the correct word after each one.
1. a small simple house, especially in the country. _____
2. the act or an instance of settling. _____
3. seek to achieve or complete (a task or action). _____
4. a prolonged fight between large organised armed forces. _____
5. a composite plant, *Lactuca sativa*, with crisp edible leaves used in salads. _____
6. attracting or capable of attracting; interesting. _____
7. a sentence inscribed on some object and expressing an appropriate sentiment. _____
8. to act against with force, to seek to hurt or defeat. _____
9. a physical substance in general, as distinct from mind and spirit. _____
10. a settled opinion or way of thinking. _____

Exercise 3

Now write one sentence for each word in the double 't' list, in which the meaning/definition **as given in Exercise 2** is clear. Words may have several meanings. I have given only one definition for each word. Do look up all the other possibilities in your own dictionary.

Summary: double-letter words (Units 4 and 7)
1. Remember the point I made at the beginning of Unit 4: 'One of the most common errors made in spelling double-letter words is to leave out one of the two letters.' Having exercised lots of this type of word, you should now be able to avoid making this error.
2. Make your own **personal** list of double-letter words — ones **you** frequently misspell — and practise writing them in simple, clear sentences.
3. Take any short story or section from a novel that you have read and **underline** any double-letter words you find. This will make you more **aware** of them, and reinforce the spelling at the same time.
4. Finally . . . watch that **spelling**!

VOCABULARY: WORDS WITH ATTITUDE

Words at Work

WORDS WITH ATTITUDE

1. Expressing your opinion: talks, debates
2. Sexism in words
3. More formal words: job applications, CVs

Stage 1

EXPRESSING YOUR OPINION: TALKS, DEBATES

In conversations with your friends, you constantly state your opinion of, or your attitude to, all manner of things. It's easy in speech, isn't it? You don't have to worry about your grammar, punctuation, spelling or vocabulary. In the exam, however, you are required to express yourself in writing. You have to stop and really think about what you want to say. If you are asked to state your opinion or attitude, you can't simply reply (as you might in conversation) — 'That's stupid!' — and leave it at that. Explaining exactly **why** something is 'stupid' — if that is truly your opinion — requires a good deal more thought. You don't have a lot of time, so the words you use must be well considered and clearly expressed.

Here are some 'words with attitude' to get you started:

1. **Agreeing**:
    - I couldn't agree more with . . .
    - I take your point.
    - Yes, to a certain extent, that's true . . .
    - I absolutely endorse that opinion.
    - The point about (topic) is extremely relevant . . .
    - That's certainly an excellent point/idea . . .
    - Exactly!
    - It is a very good idea to . . .
    - I cannot but agree with . . .
    - I am fully in agreement with . . .

2. **Disagreeing**:
    - I couldn't disagree more with . . .
    - I don't accept the point that . . .
    - I can't accept that . . .
    - On the contrary, I . . .
    - I'm afraid I think that's absolute rubbish/nonsense.
    - I must seriously question/dispute that point.
    - Absolutely not!
    - I disagree entirely with . . .
    - I refuse to accept that . . .

3. **Giving your point of view**:
    - As far as I'm concerned . . .
    - It's quite clear to me that . . .
    - Let me explain why I feel this way.
    - First of all I'd like to explain . . .
    - I can see your point of view, but . . .
    - I'm certain/convinced that . . .

- It's obvious that . . .
- I cannot emphasise enough how . . .
- I do not dispute the fact that . . .
- It's my sincere belief that . . .
- There can be no doubt/question that . . .
- I feel very strongly that . . .
- I think it is essential/necessary/important that I/we . . .

Make sure your opinion/attitude is argued sensibly, and not mere prejudice. If, for example, you were asked what could be done to reduce smoking among teenagers, it might not be too intelligent to reply: 'Shoot the tobacco manufacturers!' More reasoned arguments, supported by statistics for example, would make a better impression on the examiner.

Exercise 1 Oral.
(a) In a class of 30 students, your teacher will divide you up into six teams — five students per team.
(b) Your teacher will ask each team to choose a number, from 1 to 3. Each team must then prepare to **debate** the topic that accompanies that number — no matter what it is. No choice! Your teacher will decide whether your team is for (agrees with) or against (disagrees with) the motion.
(c) Once given your topic, you have **five minutes** only to prepare **three** arguments and select students from your team to debate them.
(d) The students chosen **must** use the expressions from the 'Agreeing', 'Disagreeing' and 'Giving your point of view' lists, while making their points.
(e) After five minutes, your teacher will call upon two teams, of his/her choice, to debate their particular motion.

The process:
- Student 1 from Team A must make an opening argument in under one minute, to be opposed by Student 1 from Team B, within the same time limit.
- Then on to Student 2 from Team A, and then Student 2 from Team B.
- The final speaker (Student 3) on each team must sum up all his/her team's arguments — in under two minutes.
- The whole process should not take longer than ten minutes.

On a show of hands, the rest of the class — the audience — will decide which team has won the debate, on the basis of how **often** and how **well** the individual team members used the expressions from the lists! The process continues, with your teacher now choosing the next two teams to debate, and then finally the last two. The third debate could be held over to the next class, and all three topics then thrown open to the 'floor' for discussion. Remember to use the expressions. They are the hooks on which you will hang your own excellent points of argument.

Exercise 2
Complete the following conversation with the most appropriate expression from the box below. (The numbers in brackets indicate the number of **words** in the expression.)

VOCABULARY: WORDS WITH ATTITUDE

Donna: You sound a bit tired. Are you OK?
Tracy: No. I'm _____(1) exhausted!
Donna: Another work-out in the gym, I suppose. _____(1), Tracy, _____(3) I think you're overdoing it, I really do.
Tracy: Yes, but _____(1) I'll have a great figure at the end of it. Just _____(1) how everyone will envy me!
Donna: Everyone? Greg, you mean. I _____(1) it's for him you're doing all this body-building. _____(2) I think you're mad. _____(5) he's not worth it.
Tracy: Well, _____(1) there's no point in talking to you. You just don't understand.
Donna: Oh, I understand very _____(1), Tracy! _____(4), that Greg is taking you for a right mug, and _____(1) you can't see it!
Tracy: You're wrong. You'll see. _____(5) I'm meeting him Wednesday after school. _____(2) I should be studying for my Maths test, but _____(3) I'm _____(1) going to fail it anyway.
Donna: Oh well, that's _____(1) your problem, Tracy. _____(1) my dear, I don't give a damn! See ya!

honestly, hopefully, presume, obviously, between you and me, as a matter of fact, to be honest, definitely, frankly, probably, strictly speaking, apparently, clearly, personally speaking, imagine, in my opinion, absolutely, as far as I'm concerned

Exercise 3

The exam. Functional writing. (1998 Junior Cert. Higher Level paper)
> 'You have been asked to give a 5 minute talk on why we should do Media Studies in school. Write out the talk you would give.'

Read this article on the media from *The Irish Times*. It will provide some information and points for discussion. Complete the set task in 20 minutes, using as many of the words and expressions from this unit as possible. Refer to the article, if you wish, in order to support your points.

MEDIA

THE FLICK of a button and we banish the starving, fly ridden child . . . Enter the happy game show, the 'real life' soap. The flick of a wrist and we have turned the page, skipping over the analysis of the beef tribunal in favour of the latest sports news.

We all select what we read, what we view, what we listen to. The type of newspaper we read or don't read, the television programmes we watch or choose not to watch, the radio station we tune into or ignore, all shape our view of the world. Or do they? Do we believe what we read, see or hear at second hand? Should we believe what we read, see or hear at second hand? Are we getting all the facts or a selective number which change the picture subtly? How important is the camera angle, the photo caption, the reporter's own prejudices?

Do we want to know the 'truth'? Is it not more exciting to read a sensationalised murder story or sex scandal rather than an account of the latest controversy over the siting of a heritage centre? What do we actually want from the media?

WATCH YOUR LANGUAGE!

Stage 2

SEXISM IN WORDS

Exercise 1 Oral and/or written.

Discuss this statement:

> 'Almost from the moment you are born you are taught how to be a male or how to be a female . . . you were taught that being a boy is one thing, being a girl another. This is what is meant by sex-role stereotyping.'
>
> *(The Gender Trap, Book 1, by C. Adams and R. Laurikietis)*

You might like to consider some of the following questions:
1. How do parents **dress** their children from babyhood on?
2. Do we use different **language** for boys and girls?
3. We give boys and girls different **toys**. Why?
4. Does our **education system** foster equality of the sexes?
5. Is it possible to avoid **sexism**?

Exercise 2

Sexist	Neutral
chairman	chairperson
salesman	salesperson
air hostess	flight attendant
housewife	homemaker
actor/actress	actor
Mrs./Miss	Ms.
he . . .	he or she/they . . .

Make a table with the following headings: **Male**　**Female**　**Neutral**

Put the words below under the individual headings, depending on whether you think they apply to one heading more than another. Then write a brief **comment** on the choices you made for each heading.

beautiful	competitive	chatty	powerful
ambitious	kind	efficient	caring
quiet	nagging	strong	handsome
aggressive	confident	gentle	charming
shy	sympathetic	cry	confrontational
complaining	polite	rude	brutal
brave	argue	talk	discussion
gossip	weak		

VOCABULARY: WORDS WITH ATTITUDE

Exercise 3

Would you like to change sex for a day?

(a) Take ten minutes to think about how you would spend the day as a member of the opposite sex. Make notes about what you would do and how you would behave. Would your personality change? How would it be affected? Prepare a three-minute talk on the imagined experience. Use the language of this unit when formulating your thoughts — not only the words from Exercise 2, but also the 'attitude' words and expressions from Stage 1.

(b) Comment on the caption which accompanied this cartoon from an American magazine (*Collier's Weekly*) of 1903. How relevant is it to relations between the sexes today, as we approach the millennium? Is this a good cartoon in your opinion? Give reasons to support your answer — using as many 'attitude' words as possible from this unit.

'What now, little man?'

Stage 3

MORE FORMAL WORDS: JOB APPLICATIONS, CVS

In conversation with our friends, we use informal, casual language and phrasing. However, when applying for a job, this is not appropriate. We must adopt a more formal style when we wish to present ourselves as serious and responsible candidates for a particular position. Look at this letter, written by 'Sloppy Sam' to a friend of his Dad's who runs a restaurant. Sam is looking for a holiday job.

Would you give Sam a job? I don't think so!

> Friday
>
> Howya Tony!
>
> Dad says there's a job going in your place. Can I have it? (Gis a job, yeh!!) I'm dead cool with most people and I'd say the bistro's a bit of a laugh. I'll give you a shout Tuesday to see what the story is. OK?
>
> Yours — whatever!
> Sam

WATCH YOUR LANGUAGE!

A job application, written to someone in this casual manner, and whom you should be trying to impress, requires a different **register**. (The 'register' is the style of language you use for a particular setting or circumstance.) Using the correct register is vital. It is not a matter of being pretentious or dishonest about who you are. It simply means that you are showing consideration and respect for the person you **hope** may employ you!

Exercise 1

Here is a simple letter of the type that might give 'Sloppy Sam' a better chance of getting that job. I have left some blank spaces. Write out the letter into your copybook, **neatly** and very **carefully**, and fill in the blanks with words from the box below. Be especially careful with your **handwriting** and **spelling**!

Sample letter of application

> 2, Meadow Grove
> Brookhaven
> Blanchardstown
> Dublin 15
> 28 June 1999
>
> The Manager
> Mac's Bistro
> Bell Lane
> Dublin 8
>
> Dear Sir or Madam,
>   I wish to _____ for the _____ of temporary waiter, as _____ in the *Dublin Herald* on 26 June.
>   I am 15 years old, and have just _____ 3rd year in Brookhaven Community College, Blanchardstown. I have just taken the Junior Certificate examination. I am _____ the results.
>   For the past year, I have had a part-time job in a local café, where I have _____ some _____ of working with the public. My _____ are: cookery, athletics and football. I am a member of my local youth club and I have helped to _____ for the members at club functions.
>   I can supply _____ from the _____ of my school, Ms. A. Brennan, and from the _____ of Clooney's Café, Mr. J. Kelly.
>   I am _____ for _____ at any time.
>
>   I look forward to meeting you.
>   Yours _____,
>   Samuel Hyland

awaiting, experience, apply, manager, advertised, cater, references, interests, interview, gained, position, faithfully, completed, available, principal

VOCABULARY: WORDS WITH ATTITUDE

Here is a sample **Curriculum Vitae**. The words come from the Latin, meaning the 'course of one's life'. Make sure that you learn to spell these two words correctly.

A Curriculum Vitae (or CV) is a list of your personal details, qualifications and experience. Layout and presentation are very important. Remember that a good CV is your passport to a job interview.

Sample Curriculum Vitae

Personal details
Name	Anne Redmond
Address	Main Street, Charleville, Co. Cork
Telephone number	024-12345
Date of birth	14 August 1983
Place of birth	Cork

Educational record
Primary	1987–1995	Charleville National School
Secondary	1995–1998	Charleville Secondary School

Examination results

Junior Cert. June 1998

Subject	Higher level	Ordinary level
English		C
Irish		C
Maths		B
French		B
Home Economics	A	
Science		A
Geography		C
History		C

Work experience

Summer 1997 — General Services Ltd., Main St., Charleville. Duties: reception, secretarial, filing, switchboard

Achievements
Captain, Charleville Basketball Team
Class Prefect, 1994/1995
Assistant Manager, Charleville School Bank
Chairperson, Charleville Youth Club

Interests
Basketball, Swimming, Reading, Music

Referees
Mrs. Patricia Leahy, Office Manager,
General Services Ltd., Main St., Charleville, Co. Cork
Telephone: 024-21493
Miss Aisling Sullivan, Principal,
Charleville Secondary School, Charleville, Co. Cork
Telephone: 024-56508

Exercise 2

Write out your own CV, first in neat handwriting into your copy, checking every word for correct spelling. This is really important if you want to make the right impression on a prospective employer. Then type it up on one of your school's computers. The computer will probably have a spell-check facility, but this is not enough on its own! So, check those spellings again!

WATCH YOUR LANGUAGE!

Sample covering letter

When you are applying for a job, you will need to write a short **covering letter** to accompany your CV. It should look like this.

> (your address)
>
> (date)
>
> The Manager (or name if you have it)
> (address)
>
> Dear Sir or Madam,
>   I wish to apply for the position of (job) as advertised in (paper) on (date).
>   I enclose a copy of my Curriculum Vitae, giving my personal details, educational record and work experience. I am available for interview at any time, and can be contacted at (phone number or address).
>   Thank you for your consideration, and I look forward to meeting you.
>
> Yours faithfully,
> (name)

Exercise 3

Write a covering letter, enclosing a CV, in reply to the following advertisement:

Graham O'Sullivan

Due to expansion in Dublin City Centre, Graham O'Sullivan Ltd are recruiting

GENERAL ASSISTANTS
Full-Time & Part-Time
Positions Available
for our cafes

Competitive rates of pay.
Full training will be given.

Please ring **6767297** for further details or send a copy of your CV to 14 Lr. Baggot Street, Dublin 2.

Exercise 4

The exam. Functional writing. (1998 Junior Cert. Higher Level paper)
You are applying for the position of Bank Manager of your school bank. Make out the brief CV you would submit, and write an accompanying letter of application for the job.

UNIT 8

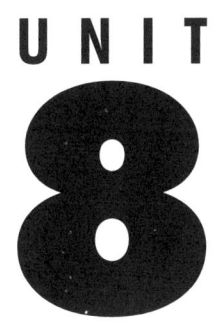

Grappling with Grammar

PREPOSITIONS AND CONJUNCTIONS

Question What is a preposition?
Answer It is a word which:
1. links nouns and pronouns to the other words in a sentence.
   Example Mary met her friend **at** the bus stop.
2. can be attached to an adjective.
   Example 'good at': Donna is very good **at** sport.
3. can be attached to a verb.
   Example 'climb up': I climbed **up** the hill in record time.

   As you can see, prepositions are usually very small words.

Question What is a conjunction?
Answer It is a word which links or connects two parts of a sentence.
   Example We ate fish **and** chips for weeks.

'And' is the most commonly used conjunction. Here are some more:
   as, although, but, because, either, or, neither, nor,
   however, unless, until, that

Stage 1
PREPOSITIONS

Exercise 1

In pairs. Oral.
(a) Decide who's A and B.

WATCH YOUR LANGUAGE!

(b) Your teacher will select pairs of students at random and call out a preposition, for example 'at'. Student A must compose the first half of a sentence, and Student B must then complete it, using the preposition 'at'.

(c) A time limit of 20 seconds will apply each time. If a pair of students fail to complete the task in the set time, their turn passes to the next pair of students, and so on.

(d) The pair of students who compose the most sentences **with** prepositions — win!

Exercise 2

Individual.

This crossword is composed entirely of prepositions or words to which prepositions are attached. You have ten minutes to complete it. The student who finishes first wins!

Clues Across

1. Jim smokes too much! It's time he __ ____. (3,4)
5. % or __ cent. (3)
7. It's __ use crying over spilt milk! (2)
8. I feel ____ a break. (4)
9. You can't ____ __ the weather in Ireland. (4,2)
12. Unfortunately he isn't getting __ with his boss. (2)
13. __ sooner said than done. (2)
14. Would you __ me a favour? (2)
15. I'm thinking __ going to the USA next year. (2)
16. Take it or leave __. (2)
18. The police couldn't ____ __ where the man lived. (4,3)
21. It took him a long time to ____ out the answer. (4)
23. I __ it to my Dad (money). (3)
25. He talked so quickly that she couldn't ____ up. (4)
26 & 22. Down. He couldn't face __ __ the fact that his girlfriend had left him. (2,2)
27. Don't forget to __ out the cat. (3)

Clues Down

1. Some people do Yoga when they want to ____ ____. (4,4)
2. What are you going to ____ up as a career. (4)
3. It all depends __ what he says. (2)
4. Now that the anaesthetic has ____ off, my tooth hurts. (4)
5. Can you lend me £5? I'll __ you back tomorrow. (3)
6. The car stopped because it had __ __ of petrol. (3,3)
10. She trusted her boyfriend but he __ her ____ badly. (3,4)
11. The footballers kept __ playing, despite the blizzard. (2)
12. The wedding was put __ because the bride was ill. (3)
16. It is the ambition of many to take part __ the Olympic Games. (2)
17. After the accident the car was a ____ off. (5)
19. He had difficulty __ learning Chinese. (2)
20. The couple soon made __ after their quarrel. (2)
22. see 26 Across.
24. What a surprise! I can't __ over it! (3)

162

GRAMMAR: PREPOSITIONS AND CONJUNCTIONS

Exercise 3

(a) **Identify** and **underline** the prepositions in the following passage.

Sean O'Brien was very lonely and bored. He lived by himself in an old house on the edge of town and rarely spoke to anyone. Everyone thought he should have a pet for company, but the only animal he ever let into the house was a mangy mongrel with only one ear, which he christened 'Radar'. The first time he saw it, it snarled at him and Sean shouted back, 'Go on, then, you miserable one-eared mutt, get out of my yard!' To his surprise the dog immediately stopped snarling and slunk over to the corner of the house, where it sat eyeing him up from a safe distance. Mr. O'Brien stared at the dog for a while and finally said, 'Ah well, go on, then. You might as well stay, I suppose. But don't expect me to . . .'

(b) Now write your own **ending** to this short tale (100–120 words). Use the following prepositions:

in, at, to, under, over, after, until, with, before, off

Exercise 4

(a) Choose the **preposition** from Column B which goes with the **adjective** in Column A.
(b) Then compose **a complete sentence** for each one, which **concludes** with the words from Column C.

Example 9. That chair is similar **to** the one we have at home.

Column A	Column B	Column C
1. ashamed		everything you have done for us
2. different	of	harm
3. bound		the bad weather
4. capable	from	himself
5. grateful		washing powders

6. safe	for	everyone's safety
7. due		Limerick
8. responsible	to	what I had expected
9. similar		doing much better
10. allergic		the one we have at home

Different prepositions may be used after certain frequently used adjectives and verbs, depending on the context. Be careful with these, as they are often misused.

> **Example** bad at: He's **bad at** communication.
> bad for: Smoking is **bad for** you.

Exercise 5

Write a **short** sentence for each of the following adjectives and verbs plus prepositions, which clearly shows the difference in meaning between them:

1. good at: _____
   good with: _____
   good for: _____
2. familiar with: _____
   familiar to: _____
3. annoyed at: _____
   annoyed with: _____
   annoyed about: _____
4. decide to: _____
   decide on: _____
5. sensitive to: _____
   sensitive about: _____
6. disgusted at: _____
   disgusted with: _____

Stage 2

CONJUNCTIONS

The words 'and' and 'but' are the most frequently used conjunctions, but there are others! Try to avoid overusing 'and' in particular, as the result is often a long, rambling sentence that merely confuses the reader.

Exercise 1

Link the situations in Column A to those in Column C, with a conjunction from Column B. Write one complete sentence each time, underlining the conjunctions.

GRAMMAR: PREPOSITIONS AND CONJUNCTIONS

Column A	Column B	Column C
1. We got wet through	even though	I ate a huge lunch.
2. Our team seldom wins	so	ugly.
3. He never changes his mind	because	you're ready or not.
4. She's not leaving	or	it didn't matter.
5. We often go to a disco	but	I can afford it.
6. Arnie is tall, dark	and	he's decided something.
7. I'm still hungry	unless	Tuesday.
8. Dad's leaving now	until	a club at the weekend.
9. I haven't got it	once	the others give up.
10. I run an expensive car	whether	sue me!

Exercise 2
Insert conjunctions in the following story:

Cormac and Elaine lived in the States _____ five years. _____ they were living there, Elaine had twins. She was attending university at the time, _____ it was difficult coping with the twins _____ study. _____ she had her degree, they decided to come home _____ both Cormac and Elaine felt they wanted to bring the kids up in Ireland. _____ they had _____ save a lot of money, they were happy. Elaine worked _____ a computer firm _____ Cormac _____ a building society.

Exercise 3
Use these ten conjunctions in the sentences below.

as far as, wherever, during, providing, as long as, as if, therefore, however, although, whereas

1. _____ I go, I seem to bump into my ex-boyfriend.
2. He looked _____ he'd seen a ghost.
3. You can borrow books from the library _____ you bring them back.
4. Where's Hannah? In class, _____ I know.
5. They really shouldn't talk _____ the concert.
6. Tom works really hard _____ Anne just couldn't be bothered.
7. _____ you're here, you may as well give me a hand.
8. There has been no rain for ages. _____ we have to be careful how much water we use. (Two sentences)
9. _____ I hated study, I decided to stay on at school.
10. There's no talking to him _____ hard I try.

Exercise 4
Write a short piece of dialogue (one A4 page or two copybook pages) between two characters, which takes place **before**, **during** or **after** one of the following situations:

WATCH YOUR LANGUAGE!

1. a family wedding
2. a confrontation of some kind
3. a visit to an elderly relation
4. a first date
5. a job interview

Use as many **conjunctions** as you can, but **avoid** repeating 'and' and 'but'! Try to use these two only once, if possible.

Stage 3

PREPOSITIONS AGAIN

Look at these two sentences:
1. I'm interested in collect**ing** posters. (gerund)
2. I'm interested in **posters**. (noun)

Certain prepositions can be followed by a verb with 'ing' (the gerund) **or** by a noun.
Here are the most common ones:

good at	tired of	bad at
responsible for	keen on	anxious about
fond of	capable of	afraid of
sick of		

Exercise 1

Can you complete the following sentences with the gerund ('ing') **and** a noun, in each case?

Example   good at: George is very good at play**ing** the concertina.
                      George is very good at Maths.

	Gerund	Noun
1. Rita is keen on	(a) _____	(b) _____
2. Gráinne is fond of	(a) _____	(b) _____
3. Tom is afraid of	(a) _____	(b) _____
4. The principal is responsible for	(a) _____	(b) _____
5. Sometimes, teenagers are bad at	(a) _____	(b) _____
6. Mum is anxious about	(a) _____	(b) _____
7. Horror films are capable of	(a) _____	(b) _____
8. Irish people are sick of	(a) _____	(b) _____
9. I'm really tired of	(a) _____	(b) _____

Verbs plus prepositions

Look at these two sentences:
1. He drank **in** the beauty of the scene.
2. He drank **to** his daughter's success.

Again, we see that a change in preposition results in a change in meaning.

GRAMMAR: PREPOSITIONS AND CONJUNCTIONS

Exercise 2
Complete the following sentences with a suitable preposition after the verb. Be very careful which one you choose (in, at, to, etc.). Don't just guess! Check your dictionary if you're not sure.
1. Burglars broke _____ their house.
2. Kevin broke _____ the champagne after the match.
3. He congratulated me _____ passing my exam.
4. They died _____ their beliefs.
5. Children in the Sudan are dying _____ starvation.
6. She's always comparing me _____ him.
7. Shakespeare compared her _____ 'a summer's day'.
8. David was leaning _____ the car.
9. Simon was leaning _____ David for support.
10. Uncle Shane provided _____ her in his will.
11. Tim provided his sister _____ a car.
12. Colm swore _____ the man for his bad driving.
13. She swore _____ the Bible she was telling the truth.
14. Susan was treated _____ her acne in Dublin.
15. Betty treated her friend _____ a meal.

Exercise 3
Replace the words in bold in the following sentences with a prepositional phrase from the box below. Be careful! As you can see from the example, some of the prepositions will be followed by 'ing' on the verb, and the word order may also change.

Example   All those **who think we should go** to France this year, raise your hands.
              All those **in favour of** going to France this year, raise your hands.

1. **If you believe what it says in** the papers, we are in for an economic boom.
2. **Taking into consideration** the number of absences, our principal has decided to write to all parents.
3. **Even though there was** deep snow everywhere, Fred decided he'd go to work.
4. Everyone in the class **with the exception of** Mrs. Ó Maolmhuire liked the idea of no homework for a week.
5. **Having decided not to** wait for the others, Mark went on ahead.
6. **She was not only kind enough to** visit me in hospital, she also looked after my house.
7. Saturday's show has been cancelled; **this is because there has been** a lack of interest.
8. **If a fire breaks out**, sound the alarm at once.
9. **Speaking as a representative of** the committee, I would like to thank you for coming tonight.
10. We have exercised many of the prepositions and conjunctions used in speech and writing **but we have excluded** those which are obscure or rarely encountered.

according to, in spite of, on behalf of, apart from, other than, in addition to, instead of, due to, in case of, in view of

WATCH YOUR LANGUAGE!

Exercise 4

The exam. Functional writing.

Read this letter to Shirley and highlight or underline the prepositions and conjunctions. Then write a reply in 120–180 words, giving your advice to the correspondent. Use prepositions and conjunctions carefully and appropriately throughout your letter. Make good use of all those you've exercised in this unit.

> **Where does my duty lie?**
>
> Dear Shirley
>
> I am 13 and madly in love with the boy who lives in the villa next door.
>
> Unfortunately, our parents don't get on, and mine have forbidden me to have any contact with him. The local vicar has agreed to marry us secretly, and I am on the point of agreeing to this, as my parents are insisting that I marry a friend of the family, whom I hate.
>
> I would rather die than leave the man I love. What should I do? Should I give up family and home for him, or should I bend to my parents' wishes?
>
> Lovesick J. Verona.

And finally . . . a joke!

    Teacher: What will you get if you use too many conjunctions, Peter?
    Peter: Conjunctionitis, Sir!

(I know! I know! Sad! — author.)

Punctuation Please!

BRACKETS, BLOBS AND DOTS

Stage 1

BRACKETS

Question When do we use brackets (also called parentheses)?

Answer
1. When adding **extra information**.
   > **Example** The Second World War (1939–1945) cost millions of lives.
2. When inserting **an explanation**.
   > **Example** Fiona (Peter's boss) is in London.
3. When giving **references**.
   > **Example** A discussion of field tactics is given below (see p. 46).
4. When enclosing **optional** words.
   > **Example** There are many (obvious) problems.

   In this example, the 'optional' word means that the problems **may** or **may not** be obvious.
5. When explaining foreign words, especially Latin phrases:
   > **Example** My attitude to life is *carpe diem* (seize the day).

PUNCTUATION: BRACKETS, BLOBS AND DOTS

Warning! Be wary of brackets. Many students use them to support badly written sentences. Instead of crossing out the entire sentence and starting over, they stick in a bracket or two, in order to sort out their thoughts. However, this often results in confused, misshapen expression, which looks dreadful and is difficult to read.

Example Sandra (who didn't know it at the time) was being two-timed by Simon (who already had a girlfriend in Waterford) but nobody (not even her best friend) would tell her (poor Sandra!).

Here is how the above should read:

Example Sandra didn't know it at the time, but Simon was two-timing her. He already had a girlfriend in Waterford but nobody (not even her best friend) would tell her.

The second version is clearer, and makes one long sentence into two more balanced ones. Using brackets once is quite acceptable. So the rule is: use brackets only where absolutely necessary or correct in terms of usage, as in Uses 1–5 above.

Exercise 1
Insert appropriate **extra information** into the brackets in the following sentences:
1. During the Second World War (_____) Ireland remained neutral.
2. Mary McAleese (_____) is visiting the States at the moment.
3. The subjects I like most are History (_____) and French.
4. Cork (_____) is the capital of the South.
5. Mick McCarthy (_____) is scouting for new players.

Exercise 2
Insert an **explanation** into the brackets in the following sentences:
1. Mr. Mulvihill (_____) was busy putting up Fire Safety notices.
2. My Grandad used to always say *tempus fugit* (_____).
3. She (_____) re-vamped her image yet again for the film *Evita*.
4. So the students (_____) came up with a great idea.
5. Mark (_____) is leaving school.

Exercise 3
(a) Insert brackets where **appropriate** in the following sentences:
1. Susie told me but I can't believe it that Mr. Mason is in love with Miss Breen.
2. The guard at least I think he was a guard told me I couldn't go in.
3. Ireland's main striker Niall Quinn despite a painful knee injury turned out for the match against Scotland.
4. For a discussion of the effect on the environment of pesticides see below Ch. 4, p. 73.
5. The Tour de France last year 1998 boosted tourism in Ireland and excited much interest in the international media.

(b) Now write five sentences of your own, in which you insert brackets only once per sentence, in order to provide **extra information** or an **optional word**.

WATCH YOUR LANGUAGE!

Stage 2

BLOBS

Question When do we use blobs (also called bullet points)?

Answer Actually, there are no set rules here! One writer referred to this punctuation mark as 'the invasion of the blobs'. They are a fairly recent phenomenon, having 'invaded' newspapers some years ago. You'll now find them in magazines, advertisements and word-processing packages. Most books on punctuation don't mention them at all. But since they seem to be here to stay, you might as well learn how to use them!

We use blobs when we are giving information which is suited to being presented in list form.

Example The town has many tourist attractions:
- stunning scenery
- a beautiful sandy beach
- a heritage centre
- a reputation for good *craic*.

Remember! Use blobs to **clarify** your work. Don't use them for decoration.

Exercise 1

(a) Rewrite the following instruction and list of items with **one** colon (:) and **four** blobs.

If you intend eating corn-on-the-cob without getting butter all over your face, you'll need a large plate strong grips for the cob a very absorbent napkin equally messy friends.

(b) Rewrite the following, deciding for yourself how many blobs are required (one colon is also necessary).

Let me make some final comments about painting wash the brushes immediately after painting replace the lids tightly on the cans wash your hands thoroughly with spirit and soap don't lick the paint brushes wash the dog.

Exercise 2

Here is an advertisement for the Ferrycarrig Hotel in Wexford. Can you **rewrite** the information contained in the ad into **seven** blob points? The first one is done for you.

- Every luxurious bedroom and suite enjoys a spectacular view over the wonderful Slaney estuary.

Check out our views before you book your next break.

At the Ferrycarrig Hotel Wexford, every luxurious bedroom and suite enjoys a spectacular view over the wonderful Slaney estuary. In addition we've a fabulous health and fitness club and golf on our clifftop course at St Helen's Bay. Our cuisine is as stunning as the views from both our beautifully appointed restaurants. Located just two hours from Dublin, it's our view that no other hotel can compare for your next break. To find out more about our great Spring and Summer offers call us on 1890 51 61 71 now.

FERRYCARRIG HOTEL

The peace of Ireland you've been dreaming of

PUNCTUATION: BRACKETS, BLOBS AND DOTS

Exercise 3

Here is another advertisement for two hotels, using blobs to highlight points of information. This time, rewrite **one** of these lists of blob points in the form of a longer, more explanatory piece of prose (as in the Ferrycarrig Hotel ad) on the attractions of the hotel, in **full sentences**.

Sinnott
HOTELS

Connemara Coast
HOTEL ★★★★
Furbo, Galway
Tel. (091) 592108
- Breathtaking Views
- Grounds sweeping down to the shores of Galway Bay
- Leisure Centre
- Black & White Hotel Bar of the Year
- 10 mins. from Galway City

Connemara Gateway
HOTEL ★★★
Oughterard, Co. Galway
Tel. (091) 552328
- Indoor heated pool & sauna
- Various walking and driving routes
- Cottage Style Bar
- Fishing & Golf nearby
- 20 mins. from Galway City

Stage 3

DOTS

Question When do we use dots (also called points of ellipsis)?
1. When we want to show that:
   (a) words have been left out, as in a **quotation**, for example.
   Example '. . . man, proud man,
   Dress'd in a little brief authority, . . .'
   (William Shakespeare)
   (b) a **statement** is deliberately left **unfinished**.
   Example Even before the match was half over, I thought, 'Well . . .'
2. In **advertising**, between short groups of words for emphasis (but this is not acceptable in more formal writing).
   Example Don't hesitate . . . send for your free brochure today.
3. In textbooks, examination papers and business correspondence to indicate **words** to be filled in.
   Example Textbook: Here are some sentence starters for letters:
   ◆ I am delighted to inform you that . . .
   ◆ I regret to inform you that . . .
   Exams: The four kinds of citrus fruits are . . .
   Business: Enclosed please find £ . . . for . . . videos at £ . . . each.

Rules
1. Writers always use **three** dots. There is absolutely no reason for this number, but it has become standard practice.
2. A **full line** of dots indicates that a **whole paragraph** or more has been left out from a quoted passage. It may also show the omission of one or more **lines of poetry**.
   Example I wandered lonely as a cloud . . . .
   . . . . a host of golden daffodils.

WATCH YOUR LANGUAGE!

3. Dots are always placed **inside** quotation marks, whether they fall at the beginning or end of the sentence.
   Example   Tom said, '... and let me assure you, I wouldn't have done that even if ...'

Exercise 1
Which words (indicated by dots) have been left out of these well-known quotations?
1. 'Beside the lake, ... in the breeze.'
   (poem 'The Daffodils' by William Wordsworth)
2. 'Romeo, Romeo ... Romeo?'
   (play *Romeo and Juliet* by William Shakespeare)
3. 'To be ... question.'
   (play *Hamlet* by William Shakespeare)
4. 'I am ... world!'
   (Leonardo DiCaprio in *Titanic*)
5. A bird in the hand ... bush.
   (Proverb)
6. 'Ask not ... for you, but what you ... country.'
   (John Fitzgerald Kennedy, President of the USA)
7. All work ... a dull boy.
   (Proverb)
8. 'All the world's a stage, ... merely players.'
   (play *As You Like It* by William Shakespeare)
9. 'Nothing ... you.'
   (song, sung by Sinead O'Connor)
10. Greater love hath no man ... for his friends.
    (John 15:13)

Exercise 2
Write the last sentence of five different stories ending in three dots, suggesting that more will follow.
Example   It was at that precise moment that I realised I could die ...
Then exchange copies with your neighbour and write possible **endings** to each other's sentences.

Exercise 3
The exam. Reading comprehension/fiction.
In exams, you are often asked to refer to, or quote from, a text. Students often make the error of quoting whole chunks of text, and wasting valuable time in the process. Employing dots to indicate the area of text you are discussing is a useful tactic and a practical, time-saving device.

Read the following newspaper article on Leonardo DiCaprio. Answer the questions below, **employing dots**, where appropriate, to make your points.

PUNCTUATION: BRACKETS, BLOBS AND DOTS

HOW HOT is Leonardo DiCaprio? Combustible enough to warrant a stratospheric salary for future projects, industry observers say.

'Depending on the success of *The Man in the Iron Mask* (which has grossed $49 million so far), Leo could command $25 million for his next film. 'Hollywood is just quaking in its boots about it,' says Jae Kim, an entertainment analyst.

That's because big bucks for *Titanic's* DiCaprio could lead to salary inflation for heavyweights like Jim Carrey, Tom Cruise, Tom Hanks, John Travolta, Bruce Willis and Arnold Schwarzenegger — all of whom are said to be members of the $20 million club.

Just what is DiCaprio's current asking price, and has he been flooded with scripts?

'We don't give out that information,' says a mildly exasperated Cindy Guagenti, the actor's rep. 'We feel that he is overexposed right now. . . . We want to pull him way, way back.'

Teen magazine editors don't. Seems their readers can't get enough. 'We've never gotten a response like this to any young celebrity,' says Beth Mayall, editor of *All About You!*, a publication for girls ages 11 to 15.

She says DiCaprio has been featured in every issue since November, from pullout posters and gossip about Leo sightings to quizzes with questions as 'Is your boyfriend as cute as Leonardo DiCaprio?'

'He's definitely the barometer by which teens measure the object of their affection,' Mayall says with a laugh. (DiCaprio peers out from April's *All About You!*, the first time a male has been on the cover.)

'WE FEEL THAT HE IS OVEREXPOSED RIGHT NOW. . . . WE WANT TO PULL HIM WAY, WAY BACK.'

And *Seventeen's* May issue features two separate DiCaprio covers. 'We honestly liked them both and figured we'd let the readers choose,' spokeswoman Julie Stonberg says. Newsstands will sell both; subscribers will randomly get either cover.

Four books about the *Titanic* star are on Best-Selling Book lists in America and Europe, and another one is on the way. *Lovin' Leo: Your Leonardo DiCaprio Keepsake Scrapbook* is due in May from Scholastic Trade Books. 'We expect this one to be a really big hit,' Scholastic's Alan Cohen says. 'Girls can't get enough of him.'

And in the unlikeliest of places. A rumour had DiCaprio attending 9 am Sunday Mass at Padre Serra Parish in Camarillo, California. Church attendance, usually 1,000, increased by about 300 one recent Sunday. 'We had people who never had set foot in our church before, most of them teen-age girls,' says the jovial Rev. Liam Kidney. 'At least these kids are looking for this guy in a church. They could be looking for him in a bar.'

Was DiCaprio there? 'I'm not at liberty to say,' the pastor says. 'Only Jesus knows for sure.'

1. What could happen in the movie industry if Leonardo DiCaprio earns a lot of money from *Titanic*?
2. What was Cindy Guagenti's (the actor's rep) reaction to the question: 'Just what is DiCaprio's current asking price, and has he been flooded with scripts?'
3. What has Beth Mayall (editor of *All About You!*) to say about DiCaprio?
4. What does Alan Cohen of Scholastic Trade Books have to say about a book due out in May?
5. Briefly describe the scene at Sunday Mass in the Padre Serra Parish in Camarillo, California.

WATCH YOUR LANGUAGE!

How Do You Spell . . . ?

SILENT LETTER WORDS 2

1. **Silent 'k' words**

knack	knob
knapsack	knock
knee	knot
knife	know
knit	knowledge

Notice how all the above words begin with 'kn', and except for 'knapsack' and 'knowledge', they are all words of **one syllable**.

The word 'know' is often misspelt as 'now', so watch that one! Again, **underline** the 'k' in each word. It will really help you to remember it.

Exercise 1
(a) Study the ten words above for ten minutes in class. Remember it will be easier to learn these spellings because each word contains a **silent 'k'** and they are written in **alphabetical** order.
(b) When the ten minutes are up, your teacher will call out each word in the order in which you have learned them. Write them out, one underneath the other, in a list, being very careful with those **silent 'k's**!
(c) Exchange your copy with the person next to you. You will now correct his/hers, and he/she will do likewise with yours. Please refer to the **original spelling list** when correcting each word.
(d) Give **one** mark for each word spelled correctly, and a total mark out of ten.
(e) If a word has been spelled **incorrectly**, cross it out and write the **correct** spelling of the word beside it, again checking from the original list.
(f) Take back your own copy and write out any words **you** have spelled incorrectly, **five times** each.

Exercise 2
(a) Complete the pattern as shown in the example.

Example	knit	knits	knitted	knitting
1. know	_____	_____ *	_____
2. knock	_____	_____	_____
3. knot	_____	_____	_____
4. kneel	_____	_____ *	_____
5. knead	_____	_____	_____

* Be careful with these two, they're **irregular**!

SPELLING: SILENT LETTER WORDS 2

(b) Write just **one** question and **one** answer to that question, using the following silent 'k' words only once each:

knife, knew, knack, knickers, knot

Compare your question and answer with your neighbour's. Give a mark out of ten for humour and originality!

Exercise 3

Supply the missing silent 'k' word for each of the following sentences — without referring to the above list. (Nos. 1, 3 and 4 have **slight** variations in spelling.)

1. In Home Economics class last week, Darren _____ over a whole pan of pancake batter.
2. He'd _____ you as soon as look at you!
3. 'Get _____!' he said, rudely.
4. Sheila hates _____. She prefers to buy jumpers in a shop.
5. It's common _____ that Ireland is a very popular holiday destination.
6. Colm did his _____ in, playing rugby.
7. Dad is always promising to fix the _____ on that door, but he never does.
8. There's a real _____ to making a good Irish coffee.
9. Tom doesn't _____ that Julie fancies him.
10. 'Oh no! I think I've left my _____ on the bus!'

Now, **check** your list to see if you've spelled the words correctly.

2. Silent 'l' words

balm	calf	chalk	could
calm	half	walk	should
			would

Notice that the above words are not written in alphabetical order, but in three rhyming pairs and one trio of rhyming words. This should make it easier to learn the spellings.

Exercise 1

As for silent 'k' words.

Exercise 2

(a) Complete the rhyme:
chalk,   walk,   t_____
balm,   calm,   p_____

(b) Write one sentence in which 'could', 'would' and 'should' are used.
    Example   'If I could afford to go I would, as you should realise by now.'

(c) Write a sentence in which 'calf' and 'half' are each written just once.

(d) Unjumble the following words from the silent 'l' list, and write them into the space provided:
   1. D U O W L   _____   4. A H K L C   _____
   2. L F A C   _____   5. H L D S O U _____
   3. M L B A   _____

WATCH YOUR LANGUAGE!

Exercise 3

Write a short piece of **dialogue** in which each of the silent 'l' words is used just once and is underlined. Here is an opening sentence to get you started, but you may of course compose your own.

Pat: You're being very **calm** about this, aren't you?

3. Silent 'n' and 'p' words

Silent 'n'	Silent 'p'
autumn	cupboard
condemn	pneumonia
damn	psalm
hymn	psychic
solemn	receipt

1. Notice that all the silent 'n' words have an 'm' in front of them — so the ending is 'mn'. Link the 'm' and 'n' together in your mind, and you should get the spelling right.
2. Silent 'p' words are difficult to spell correctly, so learn these well. Underline the 'p' in each word. 'Receipt' and 'cupboard' need special care, as they are often misspelt.

Exercise 1

As for silent 'k' words.

Exercise 2

I have taken out the silent 'n' or 'p' in the following words. Rewrite each one, putting its correct silent letter back in. Then write one question style sentence for each completed word.

Example   Did she give you a receipt?

colum	receit
sychology	neumatic
rasberry	salm
dam	solem
hym	condemed

Exercise 3

Quiz. What is it, then?
Here are definitions of some silent 'n' and 'p' words, taken from the *Concise Oxford Dictionary*. Can you find them? (Your teacher may allow you to work on these in pairs, or give it to you for homework as an individual challenge.)

Clue: **Some** of them are from your list, but don't cheat by looking back at it! Learn the **spellings first**, before you do this exercise.

SPELLING: SILENT LETTER WORDS 2

1. a journalist contributing regularly to a newspaper. _____
2. a fictitious name, especially one assumed by an author. _____
3. a skin disease marked by red scaly patches. _____
4. condemnation to eternal punishment, especially in hell. _____
5. an upright cylindrical pillar often slightly tapering and usually supporting an arch, or standing alone as a monument. _____
6. considered to have occult powers, such as telepathy, clairvoyance, etc. _____
7. a large extinct flying birdlike reptile with a long slender head and neck. (Last seen in Jurassic Park!) _____
8. serious and dignified; accompanied by ceremony. _____
9. a song of praise, especially to God in Christian worship. _____
10. a recess or piece of furniture with a door and shelves, in which things are stored. _____

4. Silent 's' and 't' words

Silent 's'	Silent 't'	
aisle	bustle	listen
Carlisle*	castle	mistletoe
demesne**	christen	mortgage
island	fasten	thistle
isle	hustle	whistle

* A town in Cumbria, England.
** Pronounced: dem-aine.

1. There are very few silent 's' words, but they are often misspelt. The silent 't' words are more numerous. Did you notice that in six of the list words, the 't' is followed by 'le'; in three of the words by 'en', and the odd man out is 'mortgage'?
2. How do you say the word 'often' — pronouncing the 't' or not? Both ways are correct, but you must always remember to **spell** it with 't'!

Exercise 1
As for silent 'k' words.

Exercise 2
Answer the following questions with words from the silent 's' and 't' lists.
1. Which list word rhymes with 'bustle'? _____.
2. Which list word rhymes with 'thistle'? _____
3. What do we kiss under at Christmas? _____
4. What should we do with seat-belts? _____
5. What does the bride walk up, to reach the altar? _____?
6. What is land attached to a mansion or estate called? _____

177

WATCH YOUR LANGUAGE!

7. What can we build from sand? _____
8. What must we pay for 20 or 25 years, when we buy a house? _____
9. What is the symbol of Scotland? _____
10. Can you complete the phrase, 'clean as a _____'?

Exercise 3

Can you place two or more of the list words together with some words of your own, so that they make sense as the **title** or heading of a **newspaper or magazine article**?

> **Example**   Carlisle Castle: the legend unfolds
> Christmas hustle and bustle

Try to write ten titles/headings, or more if you can! Use your imagination, but remember to **spell** the list words correctly.

5. Silent 'u' words

biscuit	guest
building	guide
buoy	guitar
colour*	honour*
guarantee	labour*

* These words are often misspelt, because **American** English does not have a 'u' in them.

Lots of silent 'u' words begin with 'gu', as do four of the above. Also, you will always find a 'u' after the letter 'q', for example queue, quest.

Exercise 1

As for silent 'k' words.

Exercise 2

(a) Complete the pattern as shown in the example.

> **Example**   colour   colours   coloured   colouring

1. guarantee _____ _____ _____
2. guide _____ _____ _____
3. honour _____ _____ _____
4. labour _____ _____ _____
5. build _____ _____* _____

* Be careful! An irregular one.

(b) Write **one** question and **one** answer for each of the remaining five words on the list.

> **Example**   'Which **biscuits** do you prefer, Monica?'
> 'Oh, I like chocolate **biscuits**, Tom.'

Exercise 3

Use your **dictionary** to find the words defined below. They all begin with 'gu'. Write them into the spaces provided, being very careful with the **spelling**.

SPELLING: SILENT LETTER WORDS 2

1. a dish of mashed avocado pears mixed with chopped onion, tomatoes, chilli peppers and seasoning. _____
2. to watch over and defend or protect from harm. _____
3. a defender, protector, or keeper. _____
4. a small tropical American tree, bearing an edible pale yellow fruit with pink juicy flesh. _____
5. a breed of dairy cattle from an island of this name. _____
6. a member of a small independently acting (usually political) group taking part in irregular fighting against larger forces. _____
7. to estimate without calculation or measurement, or on the basis of inadequate data. _____
8. the chief monetary unit of the Netherlands. _____
9. a machine with a heavy knife-blade sliding vertically in grooves, used for beheading. _____
10. culpable of, or responsible for, a wrong. _____

6. Silent 'w' words

wrap	wrinkle
wreck	wrist
wren	write
wrestle	writing
wriggle	wrong

Notice that each word begins with 'wr', and the sound is 'r'. Just remember to put the 'w' in front! Underline the 'w' in each word. Keep it **visible**, so you don't forget it, when learning the spellings.

Exercise 1
As for silent 'k' words.

Exercise 2
(a) Which five words from the above list are hidden in the boxes? Each word is in two parts. Spell out the completed word, and write it into the space beside the boxes.

K L E	I N G	1. _____
G G L E	W R	2. _____
W R I T	W R	3. _____
A P	W R I N	4. _____
O N G	W R I	5. _____

(b) Now make your own boxes for the remaining five words in the list. Swop copies with your neighbour. Give yourselves a time limit of one minute to figure out the words, and to **write them out**. The one who finishes first, and whose words are **spelled correctly**, wins!

WATCH YOUR LANGUAGE!

Exercise 3

Write one complete sentence for each of the ten silent 'w' words on your list. Vary the type of sentence by writing:
- Three **question** style sentences
- Three **statement** style sentences
- Three **negative statement** style sentences
- One of your **own choice**

Words at Work

WORDS AT PLAY: PUNS, PROVERBS AND QUOTABLE QUOTES

Stage 1

PUN FUN

What's made from custard and jelly, stands in the middle of Paris and wobbles?
The Trifle Tower.

What do French kids eat for breakfast?
Huit heures bix.

What do cats eat for breakfast?
Mice Crispies.

Which cake wanted to rule the world?
Attila the Bun.

Teacher: What does illegal mean?
Dick: A sick bird of prey.

Jokes are a good place to start, because many of them depend on **puns** — the use of words that **sound** the same, but have different meanings. We often say that 'puns' are words that **play** on two or more meanings. The word 'pun' itself dates from the seventeenth century, and may have come from the now obsolete word, 'pundrigion', meaning 'a fanciful formation'. The jokes above are certainly that!

Exercise 1

In pairs. Oral and written.
(a) Your teacher will call out the **first** part of a joke which depends on a pun. You must supply a funny/smart **answer** to it in under **one minute**. If you can't, your turn passes to the next two students. Your teacher will select pairs at random — so you must be quick-thinking!

VOCABULARY: PUNS, PROVERBS AND QUOTABLE QUOTES

(b) Each pair of students will write down **all** the answers they hear and award a mark out of ten each time.

(c) At the end, the marks will be added up and the pair with the highest marks and/or the funniest pun, win!

Exercise 2

(a) The titles of these books all relate to the names of their authors. Match each title to its most suitable author, from the box below.

   Example *The Burglar* by Robin Banks

   1. *Asking Questions* by _____
   2. *Punctuality Please* by _____
   3. *Songs for Assembly* by _____
   4. *Cliff Walks* by _____
   5. *Feet First* by _____
   6. *Greeting your Class* by _____

   O. Wye, T.O. Proudfoot, A.L. Wayslate,
   L.O. Kidz, Hal E. Looyah, Lee Anne Dover

(b) Now invent some funny titles of your own for the following authors.

   Example Mary Higginbottom, *Mystery at Rear End*

   1. Eva Brick   _____
   2. Luke Warm   _____
   3. L.R. Driver   _____
   4. Mona Lott   _____
   5. I. Basham   _____

Exercise 3

(a) Complete these sentences by adding a person's name from the box below. Remember your answers must reflect the use of a pun. Say the names **aloud** before you make your choice.

   Abigail, Jack, Ernest, Isobel, Bridget, Robin, Herman

   1. 'Can you help me change this wheel?' asked _____.
   2. 'Zat is my voman!' yelled _____.
   3. 'I burgle banks,' said _____.
   4. 'Ring me at six,' said _____.
   5. 'Are you really serious about this?' asked _____.
   6. 'It'll be windy tonight,' remarked _____.
   7. 'I cross that river every day,' said _____.

(b) Now, compose your own sentences, using the following names:

   Kerry, Ray, Colm, Grant, Cathy, Diane, Spike, Aileen

   Remember! A pun depends on the connection you make in terms of sound and/or meaning between the name and the message of the sentence.

WATCH YOUR LANGUAGE!

Stage 2

PUNS IN NEWSPAPERS AND ADVERTISING

Newspaper headlines frequently use puns to catch the reader's attention.

> **Example**
> The Budget: A Matter of Life and Debt
> Smoking Bill comes under fire
> Hod-zilla!
> Zidane the Man!
> France for the Coup!
> Strikers set to bring trains to a standstill

In the last example, we see how **alliteration** is used for the same purpose. In this case, we notice the same sound or letter at the beginning of two or more words, as in 'strikers', 'set' and 'standstill'. This is quite common in poetry also.

Exercise 1

Here are some more examples of alliterative puns from newspapers. They are numbered 1–5.

1. **SONIA SHINES BY THE LEE**
2. **CHILE CON-CARNAGE**
3. **BUZZING BELFAST**
4. **Hingis in a hurry**
5. **THE BEAUTY OF BALI**

(a) Two of them (1 and 4) refer to people. Who and what do you think each headline is referring to?
(b) What does the word 'carnage' mean in No. 2? How might it relate to the word 'Chile'? What type of situation or event might it refer to?
(c) Could No. 3 be from a Northern Ireland tourism promotion? If so, what might 'buzzing' mean in this context?

Exercise 2

(a) Find five newspaper headlines which use alliterative puns in this way.
(b) Cut them out and stick them into your copy or notebook.
(c) Write a brief comment on the meaning/significance of the pun in each one, in the context of its original article. (20–40 words each)

VOCABULARY: PUNS, PROVERBS AND QUOTABLE QUOTES

Exercise 3
Look at these captions from a 1992 SDS (Special Distribution Services of An Post) advertising campaign and explain each of the puns.

1. Blades for Swords
2. Scent to Coventry
3. Duplicates for New York, New York
4. Anything for Adare
5. Tin Openers for Cannes
6. Kettles to Boyle

The campaign actually comprised over 30 separate ads, with the universal theme that a company could deliver anything, anywhere via SDS.

Exercise 4
(a) What product or service do you think is being referred to in the captions below? The word being punned (or played on) is in bold.
(b) Explain the pun in each case.

1. The **mane** event
2. **Specs** appeal!
3. **Focus** on value
4. Throw in the **trowel**!
5. **Gnome** Man's Land
6. **Pout and pucker** up
7. Cool **Clobber** by Carol
8. **Inn** fact. £43 per room.

Stage 3

PROVERBS AND QUOTABLE QUOTES

Proverbs

This cartoon is an example of a well-known **proverb**. No doubt you have quoted it many times yourself in order to persuade your parents that you're working too hard!

Proverbs are sayings in common use that contain a widely accepted truth, or 'pearl' of wisdom. There is an adjective — 'proverbial' — which is often used to describe someone or something as well known as a proverb, for example 'his proverbial honesty', or something that is typical, for example 'our proverbial summer weather!'

All work and no play makes Jack a dull boy.

WATCH YOUR LANGUAGE!

Exercise 1

Let's see how many you know! Complete these fifteen proverbs, in under two minutes. Your teacher will time you.

1. Too many cooks . . .
2. You can't have your cake . . .
3. Don't put all your eggs . . .
4. Hunger is . . .
5. The family that prays together . . .
6. It's a long lane that . . .
7. Birds of a feather . . .
8. One man's meat is another man's . . .
9. The proof of the pudding is . . .
10. Half a loaf is . . .
11. It's no use crying . . .
12. All's well that . . .
13. People in glasshouses . . .
14. Empty vessels . . .
15. A bad workman always . . .

Swop copies with your neighbour and correct each other's work. Your teacher will call out the endings. Award one mark for each correctly completed proverb. The student with the most marks is . . . a proverbial proverb person!

Exercise 2

(a) Explain what each of the proverbs below means in one or two sentences.
(b) Then write a short piece of dialogue in which each proverb is used just once.

1. Blood is thicker than water.
2. Don't look a gift horse in the mouth.
3. Little children should be seen and not heard.
4. Never say die.
5. It never rains but it pours.

Sometimes proverbs are misquoted and completed in a humorous way.

> **Example** 'Where there's a will, there's a way.' could become:
> 'Where there's a will, there's a relative.'
> or
> 'He who hesitates is lost.' could become:
> 'He who hesitates is . . . er . . . er!'

Exercise 3

Individual or in pairs.

Try completing these proverbs in a humorous way. (Your teacher might allow you to work in pairs on this, either in class or as an assignment to be completed in a few days, for example.) Your classmates and teacher will judge which student or students have produced the funniest proverb.

You can be as silly as you like as long as the two halves of your proverb **relate** to each other in some way — as with **puns**.

> **Example** A rolling stone . . . is an ageing rocker!

VOCABULARY: PUNS, PROVERBS AND QUOTABLE QUOTES

1. Many hands make . . .
2. A bird in the hand . . .
3. Better late . . .
4. Too many cooks . . .
5. There's no smoke . . .
6. When in Rome . . .
7. An apple a day . . .
8. Absence makes . . .
9. Great minds . . .
10. A rolling stone . . .

Quotable quotes

Quotations are extremely useful, especially when writing essays, preparing debates/talks, and supporting points being made in exercises or exams. When stuck for an opening (or a conclusion) to an essay, for example, a quotation can encapsulate or summarise the key issue or mood of the piece. It will focus the attention of the reader on the point being made.

Quotations need not always be taken from literature. Songs, cartoons, jokes, magazines, advertisements, TV, billboards, witty remarks by famous people — all are valid.

Here are some that may appeal to you, followed by some suggestions on how you might use them.

DOROTHY PARKER (American wit in the 1930s)
'People ought to be one of two things, young or old. No — what's the use of fooling? People ought to be one of two things, young or dead.'

Suggestions:
- Debate: 'Youth is wasted on the young' or 'Ageism is rampant among the young' or 'Young people despise the old'
- Personal writing (Junior Cert. Higher Level paper, 1998): 'The Generation Gap'

'Four be the things I'd been better without. Love, curiosity, freckles, and doubt.'

Suggestions:
- Debate: 'Teenagers are obsessed with themselves'
- Personal writing (Junior Cert. Higher Level paper, 1998): 'You have been asked to write a humorous article or essay for the school magazine and have been given the freedom to choose your own title. Write out the article/essay you would submit.'

MAGAZINE
'The name's Bond — James Bond. Licensed to, er, thrill.'

Suggestions:
- Debate: 'It's still a man's world'
- Article: 'Boring males **or** females I have known'
- Essay: 'Bores'

DAVID BOWIE (singer)
'I'm an instant star, just add water and stir.'

Suggestions:
- Essay: 'Famous lives'
- Article: 'Stars in their eyes'
- Debate: 'Pop idols are not real. They're custom-made machines.'

WATCH YOUR LANGUAGE!

ZSA ZSA GABOR (actress)
'Macho does not prove mucho.'
> **Suggestions**:
> - Debate: 'Macho males do not impress' or 'Man is more than his muscles'

BOB DYLAN (singer)
'No one's free — even the birds are chained to the sky.'
> **Suggestions**:
> - Essay: 'What freedom means to me'
> - Article: 'Prisoners of conscience, Amnesty International'
> - Poem inspired by this quote.

VERNON NAISMITH (American wit)
''Twas in a restaurant they met,   He had no cash to pay the debt,
Romeo and Juliet,   So Romeo'd while Juliet.'
> **Suggestions**:
> - Discussion: 'The relevance of Shakespeare today'
> - A four-line funny poem about **another** two characters from a Shakespearean play, or any play.

AMY LOWELL (poet, 1874–1925)
'All books are either dreams or swords: you can cut, or you can drug, with words.'
> **Suggestions**:
> - Essay: 'The power of the leabhar'
> - Debate: 'Literature is a load of dead people in books'
> - Poem: Write eight or ten lines entitled 'WORDWARP', or anything to do with words.

BRENDAN BEHAN (*The Hostage*, Act 2)
'I wish I'd been a mixed infant.'
> **Suggestions**:
> - Debate: 'Co-education is best'
> - Essay: 'Memories of primary school' or 'My funniest childhood memory'
> - Discussion: 'Mixed-up kids and mixed-up adults'

BRIAN ALDISS (writer; from *Barefoot in the Head*, 1969 — last two lines of concluding poem 'Charteris')
'Keep violence in the mind
Where it belongs.'
> **Suggestions**:
> - Debate: 'Violence in society is out of control'
> - Poem: 'Violence in my head' (8–10 lines)
> - Essay: 'The many faces of violence today'
> - Article: 'Violence in our schools'

UNIT 9

Grappling with Grammar

REPORTED SPEECH

Question What is reported speech?

Answer It is direct speech, that is, someone's actual words, being commented on or reported by someone else.

Example 'It's only a joke!' (direct speech)

Anne said that it was only a joke. (reported speech)

Study these examples. Note the changes in tense from direct speech to reported speech.

Direct speech	Reported speech
1. 'I **love** chips!'	Dave said (that) he **loved** chips.
2. 'I **am eating** curry chips at the moment.'	Dave said (that) he **was eating** curry chips at the/that moment.
3. 'I **have** already **eaten** three bags.'	Dave said he **had** already **eaten** three bags.
4. 'I **ate** three bags **yesterday**, too!'	Dave said he **had eaten** three bags **the day before** too.
5. 'I **will** eat more for my dinner.'	Dave said he **would** eat more for his dinner.
6. 'I **can** eat more chips than anybody!'	Dave said he **could** eat more chips than anybody.
7. 'I **may** just eat chips until I burst!'	Dave said he **might** just eat chips until he burst.

Did you notice that:
- 'I' in direct speech becomes he/she in reported speech?
- the 'time adverbials' — as they are called — also change? For example, 'yesterday' changes to 'the day before'.

Time adverbials

Direct speech	Reported speech
today	that day
this afternoon	that afternoon
this evening	that evening
tonight	that night
tomorrow	the following/next day
yesterday	the day before
now	then, at that time
last night	the night before
last week, year, etc.	the week, year, etc. before
next week, year, etc.	the following week, year, etc.
two weeks ago	two weeks before/previously

Although you may use these correctly in speech, it's very easy to become careless with them in your writing. This results in sloppy unclear reporting. The Functional Writing and Media sections of the Junior Cert. paper often ask you to write letters or reports, so it is important to exercise this skill.

Stage 1

Exercise 1
Oral, in pairs.
(a) Choose a partner. Decide who's A and B.
(b) Your teacher will select pairs of students at random and call out a direct speech statement, followed by a name.
> **Example** 'Sheila lives in Cork.' Thomas.
(c) A and B then confer, and A replies: 'Thomas said that Sheila **lived** in Cork.' You will be given fifteen seconds to compose your **reported speech** sentence.
(d) Student B in each pair **writes down** all the reported statements.

Expect to hear direct speech statements in a range of tenses from **present simple** ('lives') to **present continuous** ('is living') to **future** ('will live'), as well as a variety of verbs **and** time adverbials!

Exercise 2
(a) Compose five **direct speech** statements in three minutes.
(b) Exchange your copy with another student. Write out each other's examples, in **reported speech**.
(c) Swop copies again, and **correct** each other's work. Check with your teacher if you're unsure about any of them. Keep your statements simple — no hidden traps!

GRAMMAR: REPORTED SPEECH

Exercise 3

Put the following statements into reported speech.

Example 'I'm really tired at the moment,' Karen said.
Karen said that she was really tired at the/that moment.

1. 'I'm really fed up at the moment,' Karen said.

2. 'I'm going to have my eyebrows shaved,' Bobby said.

3. 'I've seen that film four times,' Roy said.

4. 'I can't go. Auntie Marge is coming to tea tomorrow,' Rita explained.

5. 'We're coming home tomorrow,' the girls said.

6. 'I will start working really seriously tomorrow,' Mary promised.

7. 'We may never return,' the aliens said.

8. 'I can always finish it next week,' Joe said.

9. 'I've done everything I can,' explained the doctor.

10. 'We've finished our work, Miss,' the students said.

Stage 2

REPORTED QUESTIONS

In reported questions, the word order changes, as well as the tense.

Example Direct: 'When **does** the bus **leave**?'
Reported: **She asked me** when the bus **left**.
Direct: 'When **did** the bus **leave**?'
Reported: **She asked me** when the bus **had left**.

Exercise 1

Put the following questions into reported speech, introducing each statement with:
'He asked me if . . .' or 'She asked me if . . .', depending on the context.

1. 'Do you like Oasis?' Mark asked.

WATCH YOUR LANGUAGE!

2. 'Are you meeting Paul at the weekend?' Katy asked.
   _____

3. 'Have you heard about Dick and Shauna?' Tina asked.
   _____

4. 'Will you go over this Geography with me?' Tom asked.
   _____

5. 'Can you mind the baby tomorrow night?' Mum asked.
   _____

6. 'Have you thought about my idea?' Sarah asked.
   _____

7. 'Did he really hate me?' Sorcha asked.
   _____

8. 'What will you buy with the money?' Gerard asked.
   _____

9. 'Have you finished the exercise?' the teacher asked.
   _____

Exercise 2

Here are some questions you might be asked in a job interview. **Report** the questions back to a friend.

> **Example** 'How old **are** you?'
> She asked me how old I **was**.

1. Where do you live?
2. How much experience do you have?
3. What have you done before?
4. How much do you earn at your present job?
5. Why are you interested in this work?
6. What are your grades like in English?
7. Can you work at weekends?
8. Do you use our products?
9. What do you know about our firm?
10. When will your exams be finished?

Exercise 3

A rather nosy woman at the bus stop asked Rhona these questions:

1. Has the 39 bus already gone?
2. Where do you live?
3. How long have you been at your school?
4. Do you like it there?
5. Are the teachers nice?
6. Do you get much homework?
7. Have you seen that film *Godzilla*?
8. Is there a young man in your life?
9. Did you colour your hair yourself?
10. Will you be here again tomorrow?

GRAMMAR: REPORTED SPEECH

Rhona is telling her Mum about the woman. Write out Rhona's **reporting** of the woman's questions. Begin like this:

First, she asked me if the 39 bus . . .

Stage 3

REPORTED COMMANDS, WARNINGS AND ADVICE

Commands, warnings and advice can be reported in the following way:
1. Command: 'Lock the door, please.'
   Reported: She **told me to lock** the door.
2. Warning: 'Cigarettes can kill you.'
   Reported: The doctor **warned me that** cigarettes **could** kill me.
3. Advice: 'See your doctor, if the symptoms persist, Mr. Murphy.'
   Reported: The chemist **advised him to** see his doctor if the symptoms **persisted**.

Other reporting verbs for commands, warnings and advice are:

order, command, forbid, remind

Exercise 1

Here are some more examples of commands, warnings and advice. Write them in reported speech. Use the reporting verbs from the list above and the examples.

1. 'Do your homework now!' (Mum)

2. 'Stay out of trouble this time, son.' (the police)

3. 'Take some pain killers every four hours.' (doctor)

4. 'Be more careful with your money.' (horoscope)

5. 'Wash those hands immediately!' (Dad)

6. 'Stay away from that place.' (friend)

7. 'Don't take any risks on Saturday.' (horoscope)

8. 'Use a dictionary to check your spellings.' (author of this book!)

9. 'Don't snack between meals.' (dietician)

10. 'Stop writing now!' (teacher)

WATCH YOUR LANGUAGE!

Exercise 2
Read this notice:

> **COUNTRY CODE**
> 1. In estates and farmland, do not climb over walls and fences.
> 2. Close gates that you open.
> 3. Do not leave litter.
> 4. Keep dogs under control.
> 5. In forests, do not smoke and do not light fires.
> 6. In mountainous terrain, plan your climb carefully. Be properly equipped and carry enough food with you. Keep together. Tell people where you are going and when you will be back.

1. What does the code tell you to do?
2. What does it warn you not to do?

Write your answers in the present tense, in reported speech.

Exercise 3
The exam. Functional writing.

Question 1 on the 1998 Higher Level paper reads:

'A letter has appeared in a daily newspaper claiming that "teenagers nowadays have no moral standards". Write a letter of reply in which you respond to the charge.'

Here are some of the comments one imagines may have been made in the letter of complaint:
1. Teenagers nowadays don't care about authority.
2. They are extremely selfish and immature.
3. They drink and smoke with no thought of the consequences.
4. They are irresponsible and bad-mannered.

Write your reply, using **reported speech**.

Example   The writer of the letter said that . . ., stated . . ., complained . . ., criticised . . .

Try not to use emotive language. Be objective and answer the imagined criticisms one by one, in clearly expressed points.

Exercise 4
The exam. Poetry.

Read the following poem, and then answer the questions which follow, in reported speech as far as possible.

GRAMMAR: REPORTED SPEECH

What the Doctor said

He said it doesn't look good
he said it looks bad in fact real bad
he said I counted thirty-two of them on one lung before
I quit counting them
I said I'm glad I wouldn't want to know
about any more being there than that
he said are you a religious man do you kneel down
in forest groves and let yourself ask for help
when you come to a waterfall
mist blowing against your face and arms
do you stop and ask for understanding at these moments
I said not yet but I intend to start today
he said I'm real sorry he said
I wish I had some other kind of news to give you
I said Amen and he said something else
I didn't catch and not knowing what else to do
and not wanting him to have to repeat it
and me to have to fully digest it
I just looked at him
for a minute and he looked back it was then
I jumped up and shook hands with this man who'd just given me
something no one else on earth had ever given me
I may even have thanked him habit being so strong

RAYMOND CARVER

1. What did the doctor say about one lung?
2. What was the patient's response to this?
3. What questions did the doctor ask him then? (Use reported speech.)
4. How did the patient reply to those questions?
5. Was the doctor sorry for him? What did he say exactly?
6. What didn't the patient want to do?
7. What did he say the doctor had just given him?
8. What do you think the poet meant in the last line of the poem? Begin with: 'I think he was saying that . . .'

WATCH YOUR LANGUAGE!

Punctuation Please!

ALL OF IT: CHALLENGE TIME!

In Units 1–8, you exercised the following punctuation marks:

Unit 1. capital letters and full stops
Unit 2. commas
Unit 3. semi-colons and colons
Unit 4. question marks and exclamation marks
Unit 5. apostrophes
Unit 6. quotation marks
Unit 7. dashes and hyphens
Unit 8. brackets, blobs and dots

Do you understand how important punctuation is, Gary?

Oh yes, sir, I'm always on time.

Expect quite challenging exercises in this 'Test Yourself' unit. A variety of punctuation marks will be required each time. If you are unsure about how to use any of the above, it would be wise to revisit the individual unit before attempting these exercises. This is 'proof of the pudding' time, so good luck!

Exercise 1

The following is an extract from the Fiction section of the 1997 Junior Cert. Higher Level paper. (It is taken from the novel *The Flither Pickers* by Theresa Tomlinson.) I have removed all **capital letters**, **full stops** and **commas**. Can you write it out again, replacing each one? Then check with the actual paper to see how you've done! Reminder: The first word within a piece of dialogue takes a capital letter, as does each word at the beginning of a sentence.

> grandpa shook his head again 'women? it takes strong men to launch that boat aye and plenty of 'em'
> 'hannah knows what to do she's helped before'
> 'nay we've never had women in those racks ye'd not stand a chance'
> irene covered her face with her hands near despairing
> mam spoke firm again 'now listen you here isaac welford if you can be coxswain and those lads can man her then we can launch her'
> at last grandpa seemed to gather himself together a spark of his old self gleamed in his face and he laughed out loud
> 'all right my lass all right if you lot can launch her then we will man her now get me out of this bed'

PUNCTUATION: CHALLENGE TIME!

Exercise 2

(a) Punctuate the following extract from *Angela's Ashes* by Frank McCourt. I have removed all the **capital letters**, **commas** and **full stops**.

cyril benson dances he has medals hanging from his shoulders to his kneecaps he wins contests all over ireland and he looks lovely in his saffron kilt he's a credit to his mother and he gets his name in the paper all the time and you can be sure he brings home the odd few pounds you don't see him roaming the streets kicking everything in sight till the toes hang out of his boots oh no he's a good boy dancing for his poor mother

mam wets an old towel and scrubs my face till it stings she wraps the towel around her finger and sticks it in my ears and claims there's enough wax there to grow potatoes she wets my hair to make it lie down she tells me shut up and stop whinging that these dancing lessons will cost her sixpence every saturday which i could have earned bringing bill galvin his dinner and god knows she can barely afford it i try to tell her ah mam sure you don't have to send me to dancing school when you could be smoking a nice woodbine and having a cup of tea but she says oh aren't you clever you're going to dance if i have to give up the fags forever

if my pals see my mother dragging me through the street to an irish dancing class i'll be disgraced entirely they think it's all right to dance and pretend you're fred astaire because you can jump all over the screen with ginger rogers there is no ginger rogers in irish dancing and you can't jump all over you stand straight up and down and keep your arms against yourself and kick your legs up and around and never smile my uncle pa keating said irish dancers look like they have steel rods up their arses but i can't say that to mam she'd kill me

there's a gramophone in mrs o'connor's playing an irish jig or a reel and boys and girls are dancing around kicking their legs out and keeping their hands to their sides mrs o'connor is a great fat woman and when she stops the record to show the steps all the fat from her chin to her ankles jiggles and i wonder how she can teach the dancing she comes over to my mother and says so this is little frankie? i think we have the makings of a dancer here boys and girls do we have the makings of a dancer here? we do mrs o'connor

mam says i have the sixpence mrs o'connor

ah yes mrs mccourt hold on a minute

she waddles to a table and brings back the head of a black boy with kinky hair big eyes huge red lips and an open mouth she tells me put the sixpence in the mouth and take my hand out before the black boy bites me all the boys and girls watch and they have little smiles i drop in the sixpence and pull my hand back before the mouth snaps shut everyone laughs and i know they wanted to see my hand caught in the mouth mrs o'connor gasps and laughs and says to my mother isn't that a howl now? mam says it's a howl she tells me behave myself and come home dancing

(b) Although the writer has chosen not to use **quotation marks**, are there moments in this extract where they could have been used? Insert **quotation marks** where appropriate, in your opinion.

Exercise 3
(a) Select a piece of writing of about 300–350 words from **one** of the following sources:
 1. a newspaper article
 2. a favourite magazine
 3. a book
 4. your class textbook.
(b) Read it carefully and highlight every **capital letter, full stop** and **comma**.
(c) Attempt to write a **summary** of the piece, in approximately **one-third** of the number of sentences. For example, if your piece contains 30 sentences, then you will be writing ten. Watch those capital letters, full stops and commas. Remember: good punctuation is all about **care**.

Exercise 4
Punctuate the following edited extract from *Three Men in a Boat*, by Jerome K. Jerome. You will need to insert: **capital letters, full stops, commas, semi-colons, colons, quotation marks** and **question marks**.

we pulled out the maps and discussed plans we arranged to start on the following saturday from kingston harris and i would go down in the morning and take the boat up to chertsey and george who would not be able to get away from the city till the afternoon (george goes to sleep at a bank from ten to four each day except saturdays when they wake him up and put him outside at two) would meet us there

should we camp out or sleep at inns

george and i were for camping out we said it would be so wild and free so patriarchal like

harris said how about when it rains

you can never rouse harris there is no poetry about harris — no wild yearning for the unattainable harris never weeps he knows not why if harris's eyes fill with tears you can bet it is because harris has been eating raw onions or has put too much worcester over his chop

if you were to stand at night by the seashore with harris and say hark do you not hear is it but the mermaids singing deep below the waving waters or sad spirits chanting dirges for white corpses held by seaweed harris would take you by the arm and say i know what it is old man you've got a chill now you come along with me i know a place round the corner here where you can get a drop of the finest scotch whisky you ever tasted — put you right in less than no time

PUNCTUATION: CHALLENGE TIME!

harris always does know a place round the corner where you can get something brilliant in the drinking line i believe that if you met harris up in paradise (supposing such a thing likely) he would immediately greet you with so glad you've come old fellow i've found a nice place round the corner here where you can get some really first-class nectar

in the present instance however as regarded the camping out his practical view of the matter came as a very timely hint camping out in rainy weather is not pleasant

rainwater is the chief article of diet at supper the bread is two-thirds rainwater the beefsteak-pie is exceedingly rich in it and the jam and the butter and the salt and the coffee have all combined with it to make soup

after supper you find your tobacco is damp and you cannot smoke luckily you have a bottle of the stuff that cheers and inebriates if taken in proper quantity and this restores to you sufficient interest in life to induce you to go to bed

Exercise 5

This is a passage from the Fiction section of the 1995 Junior Cert. Higher Level paper. (The passage, in edited form, is from the novel *Huckleberry Finn* by Mark Twain.) Punctuate it. You will need to insert: **capital letters, full stops, commas, exclamation marks, quotation marks, dots** and **colons**. When you have finished the exercise, correct it from your own set of exam papers.

on his epic journey down the mississippi the young boy huckleberry finn (huck) witnesses many happenings for instance the following

boggs comes a tearing along on his horse whooping and yelling like an injun he was drunk and weaving about in his saddle he was over fifty years old and had a very red face everybody yelled at him and laughed at him and sassed him and he sassed back and said he'd attend to them later but he couldn't wait now because he'd come to town to kill old colonel sherburn

i was scared but a man says

he don't mean nothing he's always carrying on like that when he's drunk he's the best-natured old fool in arkansaw — never hurt nobody drunk or sober

boggs rode up before the biggest store in town and yells

come out here sherburn come out and meet the man you've swindled you're the hound i'm after and i'm a-goin to have you too

by and by a proud-looking man about fifty-five — and he was a heap the best-dressed man in that town too — steps out of the store and the crowd drops back on each side to let him come he says to boggs mighty calm and slow — he says

i'm tired of this but i'll endure it till one o'clock mind — no longer if you open your mouth against me only once after that time you can't travel so far but i will find you *but boggs does not heed the warning and later* here comes boggs again — but not on his horse there was a friend on both sides of him hurrying him along he was quiet but was doing some of the hurrying himself somebody sings out

  boggs

  i look over there to see who said it and it was that colonel sherburn he was standing perfectly still in the street and had a pistol raised in his right hand — not aiming it but holding it out with the barrel tilted up towards the sky when they see the pistol the two men jumped to one side and the pistol barrel come down slow and steady to a level — both barrels cocked boggs throws up both of his hands and says o lord don't shoot bang goes the first shot and he staggers back clawing at the air — bang goes the second one and he tumbles backwards onto the ground heavy and solid with his arms spread out

  colonel sherburn he tossed his pistol onto the ground and turned around on his heels and walked off

Exercise 6

Punctuate the following extract from the Drama section of the 1998 Junior Cert. Ordinary Level paper. (It is taken from the play *The Whiteheaded Boy* by Lennox Robinson.) Insert the following punctuation marks: **capital letters**, **full stops**, **commas**, **question marks**, **exclamation marks** (3) and **apostrophes**.

Mrs Murphy and her daughter Kate are preparing a table in the parlour. Denis, her youngest child and only son, is due home from university in Dublin. Mary, the eldest daughter, helps out. She is engaged to Pat. It is five o'clock on a cold winter's evening.

Mrs Murphy:	hand me down the silver teapot kate (**smells teapot**) theres a sort of musty smell from it
Kate:	sure we havent used it since denis was here in the summer
Mrs Murphy:	(**points**) put it there (**thinks**) well have to get some fresh eggs for denis
Kate:	there was a duck egg left over from the dinner
Mrs Murphy:	a duck egg dont you know denis hates duck eggs
	(**enter mary the eldest daughter carrying a small bunch of nearly withered flowers**)
Mary:	these were all I could find in the garden
Mrs Murphy:	theyre not much put them in the middle of the table theres a mans voice — denis — tis denis (**hurries to open door**) ah its only pat
Pat:	(**entering room**) good night all
Mary:	good night pat
Pat:	good night mary (**trying to talk to mary**) have you had your tea
Mary:	I havent
Pat:	I wanted you to come across to the community centre to the concert swallow your tea and come on
Mary:	oh pat id like to but you see denis is coming on the six oclock bus
Pat:	yerra denis will keep get your coat and come on

PUNCTUATION: CHALLENGE TIME!

Mrs Murphy: (**overhearing**) whats that pat mary where are you going
Mary: nowhere mother pat wanted me to go to the concert with him
Mrs Murphy: she couldnt go out tonight pat she must be here to look after denis
Mary: id better stay pat
Mrs Mruphy: tomorrow night now shed be delighted maybe denis would go with the two of you that would be nice now
Pat: oh faith that would be grand — grand entirely only you see theres no concert tomorrow night
Mrs Murphy: isnt that a pity and denis so fond of music i left a jug of cream on the kitchen table get it for me kate
Mary: stay and have a cup of tea pat
Mrs Murphy: sure pat had his tea an hour ago mary
Pat: i had indeed mrs murphy ill say good night to you take care of denis
Mary: ill see you as far as the door pat (**mary and pat leave the room**)
Mrs Murphy: what was mary thinking of — asking a stranger to stay for tea tonight
Kate: what stranger is it pat sure hes like one of the family and he will be the day he marries mary
Mrs Murphy: im wondering sometimes what sort of a husband he will make her

Exercise 7

Punctuate the following article from the *Sunday Independent*. Write it out, in paragraphs, as in the printed piece. You will find occasion to use all of the punctuation marks you've practised so far, plus **dashes** and **hyphens**.

SO YOU THINK YOU'RE FUNNY

ciara dwyer falls for channel 4s latest irish comic recruit graham norton

i saw him on stage in edinburgh it was love at first sight he is graham norton camp comedian

he was wearing a persil-white suit his brown eyes twinkled and he had the most divine beauty spot he swished onto the stage divilment written all over him do you like the suit he started it was skin-tight and spotless then he gave us that look a sidewards glance a bulging of the eyes and a raised eyebrow all at once we howled

in nortons world its the little frivolous things that count he took off his jacket folded the arms together and hung it on the microphone stand a tidy stage is a happy stage we loved him

he singles out nora from the audience a middleaged greyhaired woman wearing glasses nora looked a bit like a civil servant or someones mother at least

graham norton is the sort who can sanitise a curse word the sort who can be as camp as michael barrymore julian clary and kenneth williams in one and still be good clean fun

WATCH YOUR LANGUAGE!

nora was not offended

with his gaudy kittycat phone norton collected messages from the advertisement he had placed in a singles column he ordered a pizza and when the delivery man appeared graham leered at his leathers whats your name norton asked neil the leathered one replied what a lovely name norton squealed that look was back

norton didnt do anything extraordinary on stage but his ordinary world was very funny

graham nortons new comedy show so graham norton started on channel 4 last friday night its supposed to be chat showish norton revealed weve come up with other things and now theres less room for guests

born in dublin and brought up in bandon graham studied speech and drama in london most of us know him as noel the youth worker priest in father ted but the boy has brains when ned sherrin was on holidays norton hosted radio four's loose ends no mean feat

now we venture into grahams world every friday the show wont be about issues of world importance unless its in a very superficial way it sounds like a line out of noel cowards private lives lets be superficial and pity the poor philosophers lets blow trumpets and squeakers and enjoy the party as much as we can coward would be mad about the norton boy

How Do You Spell . . . ?

CONFUSING WORDS: HOMONYMS AND HOMOPHONES

Question What's the difference between a **homonym** and a **homophone**?

Answer Good question! It is very easy to confuse these two, but there is a real difference. Read the following definitions:

- A **homonym** (from two Greek words: **homo**, meaning 'same', and **nym**, meaning 'name') is a word with the **same spelling** as another word, but **with a different meaning**.

  Example   coach: (a) Tom is a football **coach**.
  (b) We hired a **coach** for the school tour.

- A **homophone** (from two Greek words: **homo**, meaning 'same', and **phone**, meaning 'sound') is a word which has the **same sound** as another word, but a **different spelling** and a **different meaning**. Warning! These are the ones that cause the most confusion with spelling.

  Example   meet: I'll **meet** you at six.
  meat: She doesn't eat **meat**.

SPELLING: HOMONYMS AND HOMOPHONES

Stage 1

HOMONYMS

Pupil: What's the orchestra reading, Miss?
Teacher: The score.
Pupil: Really?! Who won?

Exercise 1

Write two short sentences for each of the following words, which clearly show the difference in meaning between them:
1. bank (of a river)   bank (for borrowing money)
2. arms (body)   arms (weapons)
3. bark (sound)   bark (of a tree)
4. fine (OK)   fine (money paid)
5. jam (for eating)   jam (traffic)

Exercise 2

Homonyms can be nouns, adjectives or verbs.

Example Dad cut the wood with his electric **saw**. (noun)
I **saw** him doing it. (verb)

(a) Write twelve **sentences** using each of these words as a noun and as a verb.

   race, tie, lie, catch, coach, ground

   Example watch: 'That's a lovely **watch**, Anne.' (noun)
   '**Watch** your spelling!' (verb)

(b) Write five **questions** using each of these words as an adjective.

   plain, light, fine, utter, sound

   Example grave: 'Is she really in grave danger?'

You will find many examples of homonyms in your dictionary. They are usually indicated by a small number (1, 2, 3) to show the different meanings of the word.

Example lock (1): tuft of hair; lock (2): fastening of door or drawer; lock (3): part of a canal shut off for boats; lock (4): wrestling, a hold that keeps an opponent's limb fixed; etc.

Exercise 3

(a) Look in your dictionary and find **two** more meanings for each of these homonyms:
   1. club: 1. organisation
              2. _____
              3. _____

WATCH YOUR LANGUAGE!

2. fair: 1. just
          2. _____
          3. _____

3. break: 1. separate into pieces, under a blow or strain
          2. _____
          3. _____

4. nerve: 1. fibres in the body, carrying messages
          2. _____
          3. _____

5. see: 1. perceive with the eyes
          2. _____
          3. _____

(b) Write **one** sentence per word in which the word is used **twice** — but with a different meaning each time.

> **Example** see: I can **see** you've put a lot of work into this sculpture, but I don't quite **see** what it's all about.

Stage 2

HOMOPHONES

'Grate Sail! Bye Now! Everything Going Cheep!'

Although homophones can cause problems in spelling, they can also lead to some funny jokes, so let's start with a bit of fun! Here are some homophone jokes:

What do gnomes do after school?   Where did Sir Lancelot study?
Gnomework!   At knight school!

Where are the Great Plains?
At the great airport!

Exercise 1

In pairs, now make up your own funny answers to the following questions. Remember, the joke depends on a deliberate but witty **misspelling** of the word.

1. Who wrote Alice in Cucumber Land?
2. How is Paddington bearing up?
3. What language do they speak in Cuba?
4. What's the capital of Canada?
5. Where would you find a square root?
6. Which animals cheat in exams?
7. What kind of vessel does Dracula travel in?
8. What do you call the study of shopping?

SPELLING: HOMONYMS AND HOMOPHONES

9. What do you get if you cross a sheepdog with a vegetable?
10. What do you call a camel with three humps?

Your teacher will have some of his/her own answers to the above.

Exercise 2 (The serious bit!)
(a) Sort these words into pairs of homophones:

                                                                     pairs

coarse	knot	
meet	cellar	
not	herd	
write	principle	
seller	thought	
heard	loose	
principal	aloud	
taught	course	
lose	meat	
allowed	right	

(b) Write one sentence for each pair, in which both words are shown to have separate **meanings** and **spellings**.
    Example   by/buy: Carol went **by** herself to **buy** the car.

Exercise 3

Complete these sentences, choosing the correct spelling from the words in brackets, according to its meaning in the sentence.

1. The _____ (principle, principal) actor was killed off in the last _____ (scene, seen) of the play.
2. He _____ (knows, nose) I only want some _____ (piece, peace).
3. If you don't _____ (practice, practise) you won't win _____ (there, their) scholarship.
4. It's a _____ (waste, waist) of time trying to make myself _____ (herd, heard) over you lot!
5. The Tour de France afforded some amazing _____ (sites, sights) as the _____ (hole, whole) of Ireland turned out to greet the cyclists.
6. The kids _____ (through, threw) stones at passing cars, and at people on bicycles _____ (two, too).
7. We can _____ (here, hear) them from _____ (here, hear).
8. Denise _____ (past, passed) me _____ (by, bye) on the street.
9. I can't _____ (bare, bear) the _____ (thought, taught) of him leaving.
10. Dr. Ross has _____ (grate, great) _____ (patients, patience) with his _____ (patients, patience)!

WATCH YOUR LANGUAGE!

Stage 3

NEAR HOMOPHONES

In a pair of near homophones the sound is not exactly the same in both words but is so close that it is still easy to misspell them.

Example   accept/except, affect/effect

Exercise 1

Here are some more. Write sentences to show the distinct difference in meaning between each pair of near homophones. Use your **dictionary**. Be very careful with the **spelling** of the words in each case.

1. immigrant: _____
   emigrant: _____
2. formally: _____
   formerly: _____
3. border: _____
   boarder: _____
4. personal: _____
   personnel: _____
5. weather: _____
   whether: _____
6. breath: _____
   breathe: _____
7. bought: _____
   brought: _____
8. desert: _____
   dessert: _____
9. envelop: _____
   envelope: _____
10. angle: _____
    angel: _____

Exercise 2

Draw a line down the centre of your copy or A4 notepad. Write the word **Homonyms** on the left and the word **Homophones** on the right. Underneath these headings, write out all the homonyms and homophones you have read and exercised in this unit. Think of it as a **spelling** exercise and be really careful.

♦ With the **homonym** list, write the **meaning** in brackets beside each word — as they are all **spelled the same**, remember!

   Example   bear (1) (Paddington); bear (2) (carry); bear (3) (put up with)

SPELLING: HOMONYMS AND HOMOPHONES

◆ With the **homophone** list, be extra careful with the **spelling** as it is not the same! Write the meaning also, in a bracket beside each word.

   Example   taught (past of 'to teach'); thought (past of 'to think')

   This exercise will concentrate your mind on these confusing and often confused words!

Exercise 3

Here are some extracts from an American article entitled 'The World According to Student Bloopers' (an American colloquialism for errors). The author — a history teacher — pasted together a 'history' of the world from student spelling bloopers, collected by teachers throughout the US.

(a) Read it carefully, and underline or highlight all the bloopers.
(b) When you have finished laughing, go back and reread the passage, inserting the **correct spelling** for each blooper.

> The inhabitants of Ancient Egypt were called mummys. They lived in the Sarah Dessert and travelled by camelot. They built the Pramids; they are a range of mountains between France and Spain.
>
> The Bible is full of interesting caricatures. In the Book of Guinnesses, Adam and Eve were created from an apple tree. One of Jacob's sons, Joseph, gave refuse to the Israelites.
>
> Without the Greeks we wouldn't have history. They had myths. A myth is a female moth. Homer wrote the Iliad and the Oddity. Socrates was a famous Greek teacher who went a round giving people advise. They killed him. Socrates died from an overdose of wedlock. In the Olympic Games, Greeks ran races, jumped, hurled biscuits and threw the java.
>
> Then came the Middle Ages. King Arthur lived in the age of shivery. In midevil times most of the people were alliterate.
>
> During the Renaissance, Martin Luther dyed a horrible death, being excommunicated by a bull. It was the age of grate inventions. Sir Walter Rally invented cigarettes. Sir Francis Drake circumcised the world with a 100-foot clipper.
>
> The government of England was a limited mockery. Queen Elizabeth's navvy went out and defeated the Spanish Armadillo.
>
> The greatest writer of the Renaissance was William Shakespear. He lived at Winsor with his Mary wives, riting tragedees, comedees, and errors. Romeo and Juliet are an example of a heroic couplet. Miguel Cervantes was writing at the same time as Shakespear. He wrote Donkey Hote. The next great otter was John Milton. He wrote Paradise Lost. Then his wife died and he wrote Paradise Regained . . . (to be continued).

(c) Now, write a short article of your own with **deliberate** bloopers, the intention being to provide your long-suffering teacher, parent or friend with a good laugh!

Words at Work

WORD MIX

1. Using your dictionary
2. Foreign words and phrases
3. Malapropisms and misprints

Stage 1

USING YOUR DICTIONARY

'Neither is a dictionary a bad book to read. There is no cant in it, no excess of explanation, and it is full of suggestion — the raw material of possible poems and histories.'
RALPH WALDO EMERSON

If you want to improve your word power, you must develop a serious relationship with your dictionary! Invest in a good one, like the *Concise Oxford Dictionary*, or the *Concise Oxford School Dictionary* (the Irish edition).

You must then learn how to use it, so that you can find a word quickly. Dictionaries can be intimidating, but once you understand alphabetical order and the various symbols which accompany each word, you will have few difficulties. Let's begin.

Alphabetical order

'If I could write the alphabet, I'd put 'U' and 'I' together.'

You will be familiar with the term 'alphabetical order' because you can see its use in textbooks, telephone directories, address books, record stores, etc. It is a very useful way of locating items quickly. Words in your dictionary are also in alphabetical order, of course. It's easy enough to find the word 'abacus', for example, as it's on page 1 of most dictionaries! However, finding the word 'amusement' means you have to work your way through from 'ab' to 'am', and then through all the 'ama's, 'amb's, etc. until you get to 'amu'. This is not as tedious as it sounds. At the top of each page in a dictionary there are two words in bold black letters. These are **index words**. They are the **first** and **last** words on that page, and will help you locate your word more quickly.

Exercise 1

With the help of your dictionary, arrange these words in strict alphabetical order:

abbey	bargain	crash	deer
abacus	baby	comb	dear
acrobat	breathe	cloud	dual
acting	blaze	clothes	dryer
altogether	buyer	cynical	disk

VOCABULARY: WORD MIX

Exercise 2

In pairs.

Create your own exercise for **another** pair of students, by composing four lists of five words each, as in Exercise 1. Select your words from any letters, from 'e' to 'w'.

(a) Time limit of ten minutes to select and write up the lists — with the order of the words in each list mixed up, of course.
(b) Swop copies with another pair of students.
(c) Rearrange their words in strict alphabetical order, in ten minutes.
(d) Take back your own copy and **correct** the exercise done by the other pair, by checking the word order in your dictionary. Time limit of five minutes.
(e) The pair of students who finish first are the winners.

Understanding your dictionary's symbols and letters

Study these dictionary entries. The numbers 1–8 represent the various parts of the entry, as follows:

1. headword
2. phonetic script
3. definition
4. countable
5. noun
6. cross-reference
7. the same as
8. example

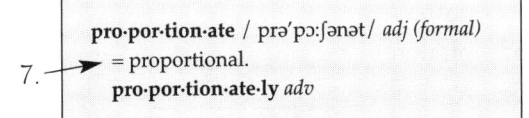

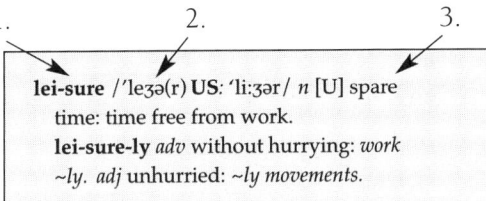

1.
lei-sure /'leʒə(r) US: 'li:ʒər/ n [U] spare time: time free from work.
lei-sure-ly adv without hurrying: work ~ly. adj unhurried: ~ly movements.

2.
3.

5.   4.   8.
wage¹ /weɪdʒ/ n [C] payment made or received for work or services: His ~ s are £50 a week. The postal workers have asked for a ' ~ increase/rise of £25 a week. (Note: usually pl except when wage is used as an adjective: a ~ freeze.) → fee(1). pay¹ salary.

6.

7.
pro·por·tion·ate / prə'pɔ:ʃənət/ adj (formal)
= proportional.
pro·por·tion·ate·ly adv

Exercise 3

Now say which part of a dictionary entry you can use to help you with these areas of English:

1. spelling   _____   5. parts of speech   _____
2. pronunciation   _____   6. synonyms   _____
3. usage   _____   7. meaning   _____
4. grammar   _____   8. associated words   _____

207

WATCH YOUR LANGUAGE!

Exercise 4

Select any five words from your own dictionary, and identify the various parts of the entry in each case, using some or all of the reference words 1–8 from Exercise 3.

Example	student (from *Concise Oxford Dictionary*, page 1210)
	1. **student** = headword
	2. stju:d(ə)nt = phonetic script
	3. n. = noun
	4. a person who is studying esp. at university or another place of higher education = definition

Exercise 5

As you saw with 'n.' for noun, dictionaries use abbreviations in order to save space; these are generally listed at the front of your dictionary. Find out what each of these abbreviations means, and write out the full word in the space provided.

1. adj. _____
2. adv. _____
3. aux. _____
4. Bibl. _____
5. (C) _____
6. colloq. _____
7. compar. _____
8. conj. _____
9. demons.adj. _____
10. demons.pron. _____
11. esp. _____
12. ex. _____
13. exc. _____
14. F. _____
15. f. _____
16. fem. _____
17. gen. _____
18. incl. _____
19. infin. _____
20. irreg. _____
21. masc. _____
22. metaph. _____
23. mod. _____
24. n. _____
25. neg. _____
26. obj. _____
27. opp. _____
28. perh. _____
29. pl. _____
30. prep. _____
31. pron. _____
32. pronunc. _____
33. ref. _____
34. rel. _____
35. rel.pron. _____
36. sing. _____
37. sl. _____
38. superl. _____
39. syn. _____
40. v. _____

VOCABULARY: WORD MIX

Stage 2

FOREIGN WORDS AND PHRASES

At least 80 per cent of English words are borrowed from other languages, the main ones being Latin and French. Other contributors are Italian, German, Greek and Spanish. Even some Russian words are widely used today! Here is a list of words and phrases in common use in English, numbered 1–130, under their particular language heading. How many of them do you understand?

Latin
1. ad infinitum
2. ad nauseam
3. agenda
4. alias
5. alma mater
6. alter ego
7. bona fide
8. circa
9. contra
10. crux
11. curriculum
12. dictum
13. et cetera (etc.)
14. gratis
15. in camera
16. in memoriam
17. memorabilia
18. modicum
19. mores
20. non compos mentis
21. nota bene (NB)
22. opus
23. per annum
24. per capita
25. per se
26. post mortem
27. re
28. requiem
29. status quo
30. sub judice
31. subpoena
32. terra firma
33. thesaurus
34. ultra
35. verbatim
36. versus
37. vice versa

French
38. apropos
39. avant-garde
40. bistro
41. blancmange
42. blasé
43. carte blanche
44. cartel
45. chef
46. chez
47. chic
48. clique
49. connoisseur
50. cortège
51. coup d'état
52. crèche
53. critique
54. cul-de-sac
55. déjà vu
56. denouement
57. dossier
58. en bloc
59. en masse
60. exposé
61. fait accompli
62. faux pas
63. gaffe
64. genre
65. grand prix
66. haute couture
67. impasse
68. macabre
69. né(e)
70. par excellence
71. résumé
72. sabotage
73. sachet
74. séance
75. tête-à-tête
76. toupet
77. vis-à-vis

Italian
78. alfresco
79. bravo
80. confetti
81. diva
82. fiasco
83. gala
84. gusto
85. incognito
86. influenza
87. madonna
88. maestro
89. mafia
90. manifesto
91. marina
92. nuncio
93. novella
94. stanza
95. studio
96. tempo
97. virtuoso

Greek
98. diaspora
99. dogma
100. ethos
101. eureka!
102. logos
103. phobia
104. trauma

Spanish
105. aficionado
106. bonanza
107. don
108. fandango
109. fiesta
110. hacienda
111. hombre
112. incommunicado
113. junta
114. machismo
115. macho
116. mañana
117. paella
118. patio
119. sombrero

German
120. angst
121. kaput
122. kitsch
123. poltergeist
124. rucksack/knapsack
125. schmaltz
126. wanderlust

Russian
127. glasnost
128. intelligentsia
129. pogrom
130. sputnik

WATCH YOUR LANGUAGE!

Exercise 1
Group work. Class of 30.
The class will divide into five groups of six students. The sixth student in each group will report back to the teacher and class on the group's work. This is what you must do.

(a) Group One will work with the words numbered 1–26
   Group Two with words numbered 27–52
   Group Three with words numbered 53–78
   Group Four with words numbered 79–104 and
   Group Five with words numbered 105–130. (Each group has 26 words.)
(b) Everyone in each group studies all the words you have been assigned. Make a list of those you understand and their meanings. (10 minutes)
(c) Consult your dictionary for those you **don't** understand, and write out the meanings. (10 minutes)
(d) As a group, select three words or phrases from your list, and compose a sentence for each one which clearly shows its meaning and usage. (5 minutes)
(e) Student 6 from each group reads out the group's three sentences to the whole class. (10 minutes)

Exercise 2
Fill in the blanks in the following sentences with a foreign word or phrase from the list.
1. Richard made a terrible _____ when he asked Sandra how Greg was. Didn't he know they'd split up?
2. Preserving the _____ seems to be all he cares about.
3. The mad general came to power after a violent and bloody _____.
4. He never stops talking about football. He goes on and on about it _____.
5. I'd like to talk to you tomorrow, Carmel, _____ the proposed changes in the uniform.
6. It's a little difficult to eat _____ in this weather!
7. Maophil was delighted to hear that she had been given _____ to organise a venue for the Christmas party.
8. Ciarán had a very interesting _____ with his six-year-old son last week, on the subject of women.
9. Ex-President Mary Robinson was very fond of talking about the Irish _____.
10. We'll have to buy a new hoover. This one is definitely _____.
11. Paul and Laura really believed they had a _____ in their house.
12. I'll never go there again! The whole thing was a dreadful _____.
13. Don't bother trying to get any sense out of him. He's strictly _____.
14. This time next week Sharon will be sitting in her hacienda eating _____.
15. Students abandoned their classes _____ when they heard that Leonardo DiCaprio was in the Principal's office!

VOCABULARY: WORD MIX

Exercise 3

Write a short piece of dialogue, **or** a humorous poem, **or** a report, which uses each of the following foreign words or phrases just once.

| Chez Maurice | kitsch | crux | bravo | confetti |
| post mortem | tempo | machismo | incognito | trauma |

Stage 3

MALAPROPISMS AND MISPRINTS

Question What's a malapropism?

Answer There is a play by Richard Brinsley Sheridan called *The Rivals*, in which there is a character called **Mrs. Malaprop**. She constantly confuses and misuses words which look and sound alike.

Example 'Illiterate him, I say, quite from your memory.'

'Illiterate' should be 'Obliterate'!

The intention is humorous, of course, and this kind of amusing error is called a 'malapropism'.

Students often make mistakes like this too, but they're more commonly known as 'howlers' or 'bloopers' (American).

You can have great fun with malapropisms and increase your word store at the same time. There is a strong element of punning, as with Unit 8.

Exercise 1

In pairs, or from one student to the next around the class.

Used as a game, malapropisms can be spoken by one player to another, who has to guess the **correct** word or phrase.

Example Student A: Correct the malapropism in this sentence: 'You must keep your nose to the tombstone.'

Student B: It should be 'grindstone'. Correct this malapropism: 'She had an operation on her foot and it went sceptic.'

Student A: It should be 'septic'. Correct this malapropism . . .

Now you do it, using the following idioms and proverbs as inspiration:
1. Let the cat out of the bag.
2. Take the bull by the horns.
3. To kill two birds with one stone.
4. To be at a loose end.
5. To feel under the weather.
6. To stick your neck out.
7. To skate on thin ice.
8. To put your foot in it.
9. Like a red rag to a bull.
10. Like a bear with a sore head.
11. Look before you leap.
12. The early bird catches the worm.
13. A friend in need is a friend indeed.
14. Out of the frying pan into the fire.
15. Don't put all your eggs in one basket.

The student (or students) who produces the funniest malapropism gets a huge round of applause!

WATCH YOUR LANGUAGE!

Exercise 2

Do you remember 'The World According to Student Bloopers'? Here are some more extracts. Identify the 'bloopers' by underlining them as they occur, and write what you believe is the **correct** word over each one.

Christopher Columbine was a great narrigator who discovered America while cursing about the Atlantic. Later, the Pilgrims crossed the ocean, and this was known as the Pilgrim's Process.

They were met by Indian squabs carrying their porpoises on their backs. During the Revolutionary Wars the colonists won the mane war and no longer had to pay for taxis.

Benjamin Franklin and Thomas Jefferson were two singers of the Declaration of Independence. Franklin died in 1790 and is still dead.

Under the American Constitution, the people enjoyed the right to bare arms.

Abraham Lincoln became America's greatest Precedent. He was born in a log cabin which he built with his own hands. He said 'In onion there is strength.'

The Clue Clux Clan lynched negroes and other citizens. It claimed to represent law and odour. One night in 1865, Lincoln went to the theatre and got shot in his seat by one of the actors in a moving picture . . . (to be continued).

Exercise 3

(a) Finally, here are some newspaper misprints. They happen all the time! Underline the misprint in each sentence, and write the correct word in the space provided.
   1. The accused had blond hair with a curly fridge. _____
   2. For sale: Three bra electric fire. Mint condition. £20. _____
   3. To give flavour to this dish, add a teaspoonful of curry powder, a small pinch of cinnamon and a couple of gloves. _____
   4. Mr. and Mrs. O'Brien announce the forthcoming marriage of their daughter, Gretta, to Mr. Mark Greene. The couple will exchange cows on May 23rd. _____
   5. John Morris, playing the role of Dr. Ross, has a terrific bedpan manner which is often funny. _____
   6. Red settee puppies for sale. Good pedigree. _____
   7. The suspect walks with a distinct limp and has a speed impediment. _____
   8. The old couple on the fourth floor found the stars too much for them. _____
   9. The holiday includes all food, wind, drinks, and leisure activities. _____
   10. The Phoenix Park is a conversation area and cannot be zoned for housing. _____

(b) Now, try writing some of your own! Your teacher may allow you to work in pairs on this! Or individually as homework.

UNIT 10

Bringing It All Together

GRAMMAR, SPELLING, VOCABULARY

With the exception of punctuation (which was tested in Unit 9), this last unit aims to challenge your knowledge of the language skills you have been exercising throughout this book: grammar, spelling and vocabulary. How well have you understood and exercised them? Let's find out.

Exercise 1

Grammar — proper nouns

Media studies. Extract from the 1995 Junior Cert. Ordinary Level paper.
(a) Read the following magazine article on the diary of Zlata Filopovic, underlining all the proper nouns as you read.
(b) Comment on the title of the article, using some proper nouns from the text.
(c) Which day's diary entry did you find the most moving? Give reasons for your answer — again using as many proper nouns as are appropriate.

Child of War

THE DIARY OF ZLATA FILOPOVIC

In late 1991, Zlata Filopovic, 10, a Bosnian girl, started a diary of her life in Sarajevo. It soon became a chronicle of horrors. Over the next two years, as the city came under intensifying attack, Zlata grew from an innocent child into a wise teenager. She compared herself to Anne Frank, the Dutch Jewish girl who was killed by the Nazis and who left behind a moving account of her life in hiding.

FRIDAY, 27th September 1991
I'm home from school and I'm really tired. It's been a hard week. Tomorrow is Saturday and I can sleep as long as I like. LONG LIVE SATURDAYS! Tomorrow night, I'm 'busy'. Tomorrow is Ivana Varunek's birthday party. I received an invitation today.

THURSDAY, 5th MARCH 1992
Oh God! Things are heating up in Sarajevo. On Sunday a small group of armed civilians (as they say on television) killed a wedding guest and wounded a priest. On Monday the whole city was full of barricades. We didn't even have bread.

MONDAY, 30th MARCH 1992
Hey Diary! You know what I think? Since Anne Frank called her diary Kitty, maybe I could give you a name too. What about: ASFALTINA, SEFIKA, MIMMY or something else???

I'm thinking, thinking . . . I've decided. I'm going to call you MIMMY.

All right, then. Let's start.

Dear Mimmy,
It's almost mid-term. We're studying for our tests. Tomorrow we're supposed to go to a classical music concert at the Skenderija Hall.

SUNDAY, 5th April 1992
Dear Mimmy,
I'm trying to concentrate so I can do my homework, but I simply can't. Something is going on in town. You can hear gunfire from the hills.

SATURDAY, 2nd MAY 1992
Dear Mimmy,
Today was truly, absolutely the worst day ever in Sarajevo. The shooting started around noon. Mommy and I moved into the hall. Daddy was in his office, under our apartment, at the time. We told him on the intercom to run quickly to the downstairs lobby where we'd meet him. The gunfire was getting worse and we couldn't get over the wall to our neighbours, the Bobars, so we ran to our own cellar.

THURSDAY, 7th MAY 1992
Dear Mimmy,
I was almost positive the war would stop, but today . . . Today a shell fell on the park in front of my house, the park where I used to play and sit with my friends. A lot of people were hurt. AND NINA IS DEAD. A piece of shrapnel lodged in her brain. She was such a sweet, nice little girl.

MONDAY, 29th June 1992
Dear Mimmy,
BOREDOM!!! SHOOTING!!! SHELLING!!! PEOPLE BEING KILLED!!! DESPAIR!!! HUNGER!!! MISERY!!! FEAR!!!

That's my life! The life of an innocent 11-year-old schoolgirl. A schoolgirl without a school, without the fun and excitement of school. A child without games, without friends, without the sun, without birds, without nature, without fruit, without chocolate or sweets, with just a little powdered milk. In short, a child without a childhood.

BRINGING IT ALL TOGETHER: GRAMMAR, SPELLING, VOCABULARY

Exercise 2
Grammar — collective nouns

Functional writing.

Exercise your imagination and write a short newspaper article, entitled 'The Collector' (150–200 words max.). It should describe a man or woman, boy or girl, who has an absolute mania for collecting all sorts of things, and/or animals, and/or insects. Look back at the many examples of collective nouns in Stage 1 and 2 exercises in Unit 1 and use as many of them as you wish for inspiration. Keep it credible!

Exercise 3
Grammar — parts of speech

(a) Here is an extract from the Fiction section of the 1998 Junior Cert. Higher Level paper. Identify the parts of speech in bold and write them under their correct headings in the table below. The extract (in edited form) is taken from the novel *Reading in the Dark* by Seamus Deane.

> *The narrator, who grew up in a Nationalist family in Northern Ireland in the 1940s, as a child shared a room with his brothers, the eldest of whom is called Liam. In the extract the boy recalls the first novel he ever read.*

The **first novel** I **read** had a **green** hardboard **cover** and was two hundred and sixteen pages long. It was called *The Shan van Vocht*, a **phonetic rendering** of an **Irish phrase** meaning The Poor Old Woman, a **traditional** name for **Ireland**. It was about the great **rebellion** of 1798, the **source** of **almost** half the songs we **sang around** the August bonfires on the Feast of the Assumption. In the **opening** pages, people **were talking** in **whispers** about the **dangers** of the rebellion as they sat around a **great** open-hearth fire on a **wild** night of **winter** rain and **squall**. I read and re-read the opening many times. Outside was the bad weather; inside was the fire, **implied** danger, a love **relationship**. There was something **exquisite** in this **blend**, as I **lay** in bed reading while my brothers **slept** and **shifted** under the light that **shone** on their eyelids and made their **dreams different**. The **heroine** was called Ann, and the hero was Robert. She was too good for him. When they **whispered**, she did all the **interesting** talking. He just kept on about dying and **remembering** her **always**, even when she was **there** in front of him with her **dark** hair and her deep golden-brown eyes and her **olive** skin. So I **talked** to her instead and **told** her how **beautiful** she was and how I wouldn't go out on the rebellion at all but just sit there and whisper in her ear and let her know that **now** was **forever** and not some time in the future when the **shooting** and the **hacking** would be over, when what was left of life would be spent **listening** to the night wind **wailing** on graveyards and **empty** hillsides.

WATCH YOUR LANGUAGE!

'For Christ's sake, put off that light. You're not even **reading**, you blank gom.' And Liam would turn over, **driving** his knees up into my back and **muttering** curses under his breath. I'd switch off the light, get back in bed, and lie there, the book still open, re-imagining all I had read, the various ways the plot might **unravel**, the novel **opening** into **endless possibilities** in the **dark**.

Noun	Adjective	Verb	Adverb

(b) Spelling

Here are some misspelled words from the text. Can you write the correct spelling in the space provided? Then correct your own work from the text. Only **one** letter is wrong in each case!

1. grate _____
2. possabilities _____
3. squal _____
4. exkuisite _____
5. waleing _____
6. unravell _____
7. traditionel _____
8. rebelion _____
9. noval _____
10. sourse _____
11. allways _____
12. rendring _____

(c) Sentence building

Now choose ten nouns, ten adjectives and ten verbs from the table above which would work well together in a sentence and make sense. Write ten sentences.

> Example   Ireland (noun), wild (adjective), told (verb)
> The old people **told** stories rooted in the **wild** untamed landscape of Celtic **Ireland**.

BRINGING IT ALL TOGETHER: GRAMMAR, SPELLING, VOCABULARY

Exercise 4

Grammar — reported speech

(a) Here is the Drama (Option 2) section of the 1992 Junior Cert. Higher Level paper. Can you rewrite it as a **report** of their conversation by a third person, in reported speech? The extract is taken from Act 2 of the play *The Power of Darkness* by John McGahern.

> **Example** Text: Eileen: *Sometimes I feel so surrounded that I could do away with myself. I feel things beating around the place.*
>
> **Report:** Eileen said that sometimes she felt so surrounded that she could have done away with herself. She felt things beating around the place.

Note how 'I' becomes 'she', and the present tense ('I feel') becomes the past simple ('she felt'). If you are unsure at any point, refer back to the past tense work in Units 6 and 7. Reported questions will begin 'Baby asked what was natural . . .'

Briefly, the story leading up to this scene is as follows:

The scene is set in the kitchen of aged and ill Peter King, a rich farmer. His young wife Eileen and her neighbour Baby are plotting against his life. Their aim is, first of all, to rob him, and then poison him. Eileen and Baby's son, Paul, are in love and it is the prospect of wealth for her son and herself that fuels Baby's murderous plans. Peter, as if he suspects something, has ordered his daughter Maggie (by an earlier marriage) to fetch his sister Martha, but Eileen blocks it. For the two plotters, the moment of decision has come . . .

Eileen:	*Sometimes I feel so surrounded that I could do away with myself. I feel things beating around the place.*
Baby:	*Don't worry about it, Love. But we haven't much time. We have to find the money. Then we'll give him what's good for him. The poor thing will be off like a bird.*
Eileen:	*I'm afraid. Isn't it better that he be let go natural?*
*Baby (**viciously**):*	*What's natural? Is it natural that he's trying to put his sister in charge over his lawful wife?*
Eileen:	*I don't know what way to turn.*
Baby:	*If you don't shift soon you'll find yourself out on the road and his sister will be cracking the whip.*
Eileen:	*I'd still have my rights as his wife.*
Baby:	*If he gives her charge of the money you can whistle for your rights.*
*Eileen (**panicking**):*	*I better go for Martha before he starts shouting. She'd be here already if Maggie had gone.*
Baby:	*Are you out of your mind? Here. Do what I tell you. Put on the kettle again here. We'll give him a good stiff drink.*

WATCH YOUR LANGUAGE!

Eileen: Suppose anything would happen?

Baby: There's no time for supposing. Just do what I tell you. Put on that kettle.

Eileen (**in awe and fear**): I'll put on the kettle.

Baby: That's more like it.

(Eileen stops in terror as Peter starts descending the stairs. Holding on to the wall, he gropes his way down. Baby retreats into the shadows of the room so that she can observe. Peter is too ill to notice her.)

Peter: Did you not hear me calling? Is there no way to make you hear? I might as well be dead up there for all anybody cares.

Eileen: Don't you know you're not fit to come down? Now we'll have to get you back up.

Peter: Did Maggie get back from Martha's yet?

Eileen: She didn't go yet. I told her I'd go myself.

Peter: I warned her to go at once. Has nobody any heed any more?

Eileen: I'm going for aunt Martha myself. Maggie is too giddy to go all that way on her own.

Peter: She's not half as giddy as what's left around here nowadays. I want my daughter to go. I want her to go this minute.

Eileen: Of course I'm not trusted to go. I'm just the skivvy.

(During the argument Baby stands in the shadows, a silent and sinister figure, unnoticed by Peter.)

(b) Functional writing

Imagine that the murder has been committed. You are the reporter for the local newspaper, who arrived first at the scene of the crime. Describe what you saw and heard, in detail. Be **objective** in your reporting — no sensational language. Begin like this:

> Mr. Peter King, a farmer, was found dead in the kitchen of his home on Sunday morning. The police are treating the death as suspicious . . .

Exercise 5

Using your dictionary — expanding your vocabulary

(a) Use your dictionary to check the meaning of these words **as they are used here**.

> **Example** My phone isn't **working**. — act or operate correctly or successfully.

1. The young girls **careered** down the corridor at breakneck speed.
2. Mr. O'Brien **trained** the clematis against the wall.
3. Our Art teacher is on six months' **leave**, travelling in India.
4. The business is looking for a young person with **drive** and energy.
5. She's a **retiring** sort of person.
6. Not everybody agreed with the idea **adopted**.

BRINGING IT ALL TOGETHER: GRAMMAR, SPELLING, VOCABULARY

(b) Write six sentences of your own in which each of the words in bold above is used in a different situation with a **different meaning**.

Exercise 6

Spelling — prefixes

re-, under-, over-, un-, mis-, dis-

Add one of the above **prefixes** to the verb in brackets in the sentences below, making any necessary changes to the spelling.

1. We were _____ (charge) for the wine.
2. The steak was so burnt, it was clearly _____ (cook).
3. I hate _____ (pack) my suitcase after the holidays.
4. You can always _____ (heat) it in the microwave.
5. He's wrong. He was obviously _____ (inform).
6. Don't _____ (estimate) him. He's very clever.
7. They _____ (connect) the electricity because they hadn't paid their bill in over a year.
8. Your essay is not good enough. It will have to be _____ (write).
9. The stain has completely _____ (appear).
10. Brian can neither tie nor _____ (tie) his shoelaces.

Exercise 7

Spelling — suffixes

-y, -ly, -like, -ful, -less

Make **adjectives** from these nouns, using one of the above **suffixes**.

1. coward _____
2. youth _____
3. fun _____
4. child _____
5. hope _____
6. success _____
7. filth _____
8. life _____
9. leisure _____
10. mind _____

Exercise 8

Sentence building

Write ten sentences of your own, using each of the following **prefixes** and **suffixes** just once.

re-, un-, mis-, dis-, over-
-ly, -ful, -less, -like, -y

Vary the type of sentence, that is, question, exclamation, negative, etc.

Exercise 9

Grammar. Vocabulary — sentence building

Read this poem carefully, and then answer the questions which follow. The poem is taken from *The School That I'd Like*, edited by Edward Bishen.

WATCH YOUR LANGUAGE!

Step with me into a future school

I'll show you around.
Even at a glance you've found
Things very different and strange.
    — Where are the clouds of white dust
    From the scraping chalk?
    Nobody sits on wooden chairs, at wooden desks,
    Listening to teachers talk.
    The framed blackboard is nowhere to be seen.
    Everything is clean.
    The rooms are bright,
    And large, and wide, and very light.

No one minds what we wear.
Clothes aren't considered important,
So usually our feet are bare.
No one minds about anything much, really.
    There is no whisper
    Of engraved desks, arranged in ranks.
    Or uniforms.
    How could you bear
    The drabness? Didn't you care
    That each child was an echo
    Of his neighbour?

We study at school for three days each week.
For the last hour of the third day
We hold discussions, in groups.
We talk on many things,
From religion to politics,
To our own personal problems.
We discuss human relationships,
And we look back, and see
What happened when knowledge gave man power.
Then we realize the importance
Of wisdom, as well.
    — These discussions are led
    By a student who is studying
    For A.O.Es.
    (Those are the Advanced Oral Exams.
    When a pupil has taken one,
    He writes a thesis on their improvement.
    Not many people are bright enough
    To take them all. I won't be.
    You have to be really clever, you see.)

It is a good school.
Hard work, sometimes,
But people always lend
A hand.
I can depend on someone
To help me understand.
There is so much to learn
That I will only touch the edge of it —
And simply sift the sand.
    — If I had a good brain
    I would dig really deep, and learn.
    But I am not shaped for that.
    I have as much to give
    As the bright ones.
    I know how to live
    Even if I never reach second in command.
    I have my purpose, too.
    If we were all brilliant,
    Who would be the crew?

There is a lot for me to do
To prepare me for whatever is in store.
But although I am a student and I learn,
I am not preparing for life.
I am alive now.
Learning is the start of something stretching
    before me,
And my heart
Says it will be great.
But I can wait.
This present learning tense suits me all right,
Although I'm not too bright.

                                                      MELANIE, 14

BRINGING IT ALL TOGETHER: GRAMMAR, SPELLING, VOCABULARY

(a) Underline all the nouns, verbs and adjectives in the **first two verses** of this poem (as far as 'neighbour?'), and then write them out in three lists under the headings below. Remember that '**is**', '**are**' and '**aren't**' are verbs too! You should have 21 verbs (some are repeated), 23 nouns and 18 adjectives (one is repeated).

Noun	Adjective	Verb

(b) Sentence building
Select ten examples of each part of speech, from your list, which you feel would work well together and make ten sentences — one noun, verb and adjective per sentence.
   Example   She couldn't **bear** (verb) the **drabness** (noun) of her **large** (adjective) flat any longer.

(c) Comprehension
Read from the line 'There is so much to learn' to the end of the poem. Try to summarise in your own words what Melanie is saying about school, and her own present and future. Quote from the poem to support your thoughts, and refer to earlier verses if you wish. (100–120 words)

WATCH YOUR LANGUAGE!

Exercise 10

Spelling — most frequently misspelled words

Here is my own alphabetical list of frequently misspelled words. It is based on those my own students often misspell, and also includes some that colleagues in other subject areas have suggested. 'Science', apparently, is very often misspelled! Note that the words are spelled in syllables, for easy learning.

Follow this **procedure** for all the spellings on the list — a **letter** at a time perhaps:
1. Learn the spelling, of an 'A' word for example.
2. Cover it, and write the word (in pencil) in the 'Spell it' space.
3. Check to see if it's correct. If it isn't, rub it out and relearn it, before writing it again.
4. Write a short sentence with this word in it, in the space provided.

	Word	Spell it	Short sentence
A	ab-so-lute-ly	absolutely	You're absolutely right.
	ac-ci-den-tal-ly		
	a-cross		
	ad-ver-tise-ment		
	af-fect		
	al-read-y		
	al-ways		
	a-mong		
	a-mount		
	ap-pear-ance		
	ar-gu-ment		
	au-thor		
	au-tumn		
B	beau-ti-ful		
	be-gin-ning		
	be-lieve		
	bi-cy-cle		
	bor-ing		
	bril-liant		
	bro-chure		
	bud-get		
	bun-sen		
	bus-i-ness		

BRINGING IT ALL TOGETHER: GRAMMAR, SPELLING, VOCABULARY

	Word	Spell it	Short sentence
C	cal-en-dar	_____	_____
	cam-paign	_____	_____
	can-celled	_____	_____
	ca-reer	_____	_____
	ca-tas-tro-phe	_____	_____
	cel-lo	_____	_____
	change-a-ble	_____	_____
	char-ac-ter	_____	_____
	choc-o-late	_____	_____
	christ-mas	_____	_____
	col-lege	_____	_____
	com-plete-ly	_____	_____
	con-cer-to	_____	_____
	con-science	_____	_____
	crit-i-cism	_____	_____
	crotch-et	_____	_____
D	def-i-nite-ly	_____	_____
	de-scribe	_____	_____
	de-scrip-tion	_____	_____
	de-ter-mined	_____	_____
	dis-ap-pear	_____	_____
	dis-ap-point-ed	_____	_____
E	e-con-om-ics	_____	_____
	ef-fect	_____	_____
	el-i-gi-ble	_____	_____
	em-bar-rass	_____	_____
	en-vi-ron-ment	_____	_____
	es-pe-cial-ly	_____	_____
	ex-ag-ger-ate	_____	_____
	ex-cept	_____	_____
	ex-cite-ment	_____	_____
	ex-haust-ed	_____	_____
	ex-hi-bi-tion	_____	_____
	ex-is-tence	_____	_____
	ex-pla-na-tion	_____	_____
	ex-traor-di-nary	_____	_____

WATCH YOUR LANGUAGE!

	Word	Spell it	Short sentence
F	fa-mil-iar	_____	_____
	fam-i-ly	_____	_____
	fas-ci-nat-ing	_____	_____
	fa-vour-ite	_____	_____
	Feb-ru-ary	_____	_____
	flu-o-res-cent	_____	_____
	for-eign	_____	_____
	for-tu-nate-ly	_____	_____
	for-ty	_____	_____
	friend	_____	_____
	fright-ened	_____	_____
G	gen-u-ine	_____	_____
	gor-geous	_____	_____
	gov-ern-ment	_____	_____
	grad-u-al-ly	_____	_____
	gram-mar	_____	_____
	grate-ful	_____	_____
	guar-an-tee	_____	_____
	guess	_____	_____
	gym-na-si-um	_____	_____
H	hand-ker-chief	_____	_____
	hand-some	_____	_____
	heard	_____	_____
	heav-i-ly	_____	_____
	heav-y	_____	_____
	hon-est-ly	_____	_____
	hor-ri-ble	_____	_____
	hos-pit-al	_____	_____
	hu-mor-ous	_____	_____
	hy-giene	_____	_____
I	im-me-di-ate-ly	_____	_____
	in-for-ma-tion	_____	_____
	in-no-cent	_____	_____
	in-tel-li-gent	_____	_____
	in-ter-est-ing	_____	_____
	in-vis-i-ble	_____	_____
	ir-rel-e-vant	_____	_____

BRINGING IT ALL TOGETHER: GRAMMAR, SPELLING, VOCABULARY

	Word	Spell it	Short sentence
J	jeal-ous		
	jew-el-ry		
	jour-ney		
	judge-ment		
K	kid-napped		
	kin-der-gar-ten		
	know-ledge		
L	lab-o-ra-tory		
	lei-sure		
	li-a-bil-i-ty		
	li-brar-y		
	lis-ten		
	lit-er-a-ture		
	live-li-hood		
	loose		
	love-ly		
	lux-u-ry		
M	man-age-a-ble		
	may-be		
	men-tion		
	mile-age		
	mis-chie-vous		
	mort-gage		
	mov-able		
N	nec-es-sar-y		
	neigh-bour		
	nei-ther		
	niece		
	nine-ty		
	no-tice-able		
O	o-be-di-ent		
	oc-ca-sion-al-ly		
	oc-curred		
	op-in-ion		

WATCH YOUR LANGUAGE!

Word	Spell it	Short sentence
op-por-tu-ni-ty		
op-po-site		
op-ti-mism		

P
par-al-lel		
par-lia-ment		
pas-sen-ger		
per-suade		
pleas-ant		
po-et		
pos-sess		
pre-cious		
prej-u-dice		
priv-i-lege		
pro-fes-sion		
psy-chol-o-gy		

R
re-al-ise		
re-al-ly		
re-ceipt		
re-cent		
rec-og-nise		
rec-om-mend		
ref-er-ee		
rel-e-vant		
re-spon-si-ble		
res-tau-rant		
rhyme		
rhythm		
ri-dic-u-lous		

S
safe-ty		
sand-wich		
scene		
scis-sors		
sep-a-rate		
sim-i-lar		
sin-cere-ly		
sol-dier		

BRINGING IT ALL TOGETHER: GRAMMAR, SPELLING, VOCABULARY

	Word	Spell it	Short sentence
	sol-emn	_____	_____
	speech	_____	_____
	sta-tis-tics	_____	_____
	suf-fi-cient	_____	_____
	sug-gest	_____	_____
	sup-pose	_____	_____
	sure-ly	_____	_____
	sur-prise	_____	_____
	sus-pi-cious	_____	_____
	sym-me-try	_____	_____
T	tech-ni-cal	_____	_____
	tech-nique	_____	_____
	tem-per-a-ture	_____	_____
	tem-po-rar-y	_____	_____
	ter-ri-ble	_____	_____
	their	_____	_____
	the-o-ry	_____	_____
	tired	_____	_____
	to-mor-row	_____	_____
	trag-e-dy	_____	_____
	tri-umph	_____	_____
	twelfth	_____	_____
U	un-doubt-ed-ly	_____	_____
	u-nique	_____	_____
	use-ful	_____	_____
	u-su-al-ly	_____	_____
V	vac-u-um	_____	_____
	val-u-a-ble	_____	_____
	veg-et-able	_____	_____
	ve-hi-cle	_____	_____
	vi-cious	_____	_____
	vil-lain	_____	_____
	vol-ume	_____	_____
W	weath-er	_____	_____
	Wed-nes-day	_____	_____

WATCH YOUR LANGUAGE!

Word	Spell it	Short sentence
weird	_____	_____
wheth-er	_____	_____
wom-en	_____	_____
wool-len	_____	_____

Y
yacht	_____	_____
yearn-ing	_____	_____
yes-ter-day	_____	_____
yield-ing	_____	_____
yo-gurt	_____	_____
young-ster	_____	_____

Z
za-ny	_____	_____
zeal-ous	_____	_____
zo-di-ac	_____	_____
zon-ing	_____	_____
zo-o-log-i-cal	_____	_____
zo-ol-o-gist	_____	_____
zo-ol-o-gy	_____	_____

And finally . . . a joke!

    Teacher: How many letters are there in the Space Alphabet?
    Bright student: 24. Miss — E. T. went home!

Exercise 11

Grammar — verbs. Comprehension — poetry
Read this poem carefully and then answer the questions which follow.

I am Tired of the Wind

    I am tired of the wind leaning against me,
        Let it lean somewhere else!
    On a brick wall that is too insensible to care,
        Or the trees on the common.

    Why should it shove me and elbow me?
        It is too familiar!
    I will lure it to the cliff edge, then jump aside
        For it to plunge over.

There! Now it screams down, flailing the sea;
   Smashes on rocks.
Grass does not stir across fields, smoke blur above chimneys.
   Oh, but suddenly I am afraid!

If the wind is a God's breath and I've murdered the wind,
   Will not that dead giant
More terrible then than in his platinum waking day
   Snort gustily in my dreams?

JOHN SMITH

1. Underline all the verbs in this poem. Write them out in a list in your copy.
2. How does the poet feel about the wind in the first two verses? Why? Support your answer by reference or quotation.
3. 'Oh, but suddenly I am afraid!' Why is he afraid? Explore the images in the last verse for your answer.
4. What is your favourite image of the wind from this poem? Explain your choice in a few sentences (20–30 words).

Exercise 12

Grammar — verbs.

Personal writing

Here are 20 unrelated half-sentences, with the verb in bold in each. As you can see, the verbs have been used in an imaginative and unusual way. Work as many of them as possible into a short nonsense story or poem of your own creation.

1. **purchased** a first-class ticket to Timbuctoo
2. **screamed** Sheila's mum
3. **carting** a load of bananas
4. a knife **quivered** in the door
5. **stuffing** another doughnut into her mouth
6. **screeched** Jimmy
7. **whined** Tommy
8. **oozed** onto the floor
9. spaghetti **dribbled** down the sides of the pan
10. **waving** a huge sword over his head
11. **galumphing** home
12. **chortling** all the way to hell
13. **plink-plonking**
14. eyelids **batting** at Greg
15. **gobbled** granny
16. **uncoiled** her hair for miles
17. **yelled** the bus driver
18. Eighteen! Eighteen! and don't **mix** them up!
19. **rumbling** tums and **tinkling** toes
20. **whispered** the lovely Alana Crabtree

WATCH YOUR LANGUAGE!

Exercise 13

Vocabulary — alliteration

Media studies

Here is an advertisement that uses alliteration very imaginatively.

(a) Identify the use of alliteration in each instance.
(b) Comment on the effectiveness of alliteration in this ad, in terms of selling its message to the consumer.
(c) Make up your own alliterative phrases for the following items:
- pears
- a deodorant
- the Hurling Final
- a chocolate bar
- a washing powder
- a chicken dish
- the Lotto
- a sun holiday
- a rock concert
- a front-page newspaper headline

THE PLEASURE OF PEACHES.

THE TEMPTATION OF TRUFFLES.

THE JOY OF JELLYBEANS.

THE INDULGENCE OF ICE CREAM.

THE ECSTASY OF ECLAIRS.

THE BLISS OF A BANK HOLIDAY SPENT

IN THE FOOD HALLS AT HARRODS.

This Bank Holiday Monday,
Harrods is open from 10am until 6pm.
So visit the Food Halls, our nineteen restaurants
or any of our 300 other departments.

Harrods
KNIGHTSBRIDGE

Exercise 14

Vocabulary — similes. Personal writing

(a) Underline the similes in the following passage.

Susie walked into the principal's office, trembling like a leaf. She was as white as a ghost and terrified. Mr. Brown on the other hand was as cool as a cucumber. He indicated a chair, and told her to sit down. Susie's heart was as heavy as lead. She knew she was in trouble and Mr. Brown was as hard as nails — everyone knew that.

'So, Susie . . .', Mr. Brown said, his arms folded over his chest. 'What's this I hear about you riding your bike like a maniac around the P.E. hall last Wednesday? The yard's not big enough for you, eh?' He glared at her, his eyes like ice, and Susie shook like a jelly.

'I'm . . . I'm really sorry, Mr. Brown. It's my friend. She's as mad as a hatter and she dared me to do it. Honest, I'd never have done it otherwise. I'm as weak as a kitten where she's concerned. She's always making me do daft things. It'll never happen again, I swear!'

'It had better not, young lady, or you'll be out of here as quick as a flash, do you hear?'

(b) Now, continue the story. Include some similes from those you exercised in Unit 4. Be as inventive as you can.

Exercise 15

Vocabulary — word building: using a thesaurus

Here are five entries from the *Bloomsbury English Thesaurus*. Choose three synonyms from each headword, and write **one** sentence per synonym, which clearly illustrates its particular usage and meaning.

| Example | certain | Three synonyms: positive, confident, convinced |

1. I'm **positive** it arrived on time.
2. Susan is **confident** she will succeed.
3. Terry is **convinced** that he's right about Sean.

Now, you do it!

---

beautiful *adj* charming, comely, fair, fine, exquisite, handsome, lovely, pretty.

beginning *n* arising, commencement, dawn, emergence, inauguration, inception, initiation, opening, outset, start, rise; origin, source.

funny *adj* amusing, comic, comical, diverting, droll, facetious, farcical, humorous, jocose, jocular, laughable, ludicrous, sportive, witty; curious, odd, queer, strange. * *n* jest, joke; cartoon, comic.

certain *adj* absolute, incontestable, incontrovertible, indisputable, indubitable, positive, inevitable, undeniable, undisputed, unquestionable, unquestioned; assured, confident, convinced, sure, undoubting; infallible, neverfailing, unfailing; actual, existing, real; constant, determinate, fixed, settled, stated.

furious *adj* angry, fierce, frantic, frenzied, fuming, infuriated, mad, raging, violent, wild; boisterous, fierce, impetuous, stormy, tempestuous, tumultuous, turbulent, vehement.

Exercise 16

Vocabulary — idioms

Study the photograph and text below. Then answer the questions which follow.

Back to his roots

A **DUTCH** soccer fan has decided to blow the final whistle on his football following career.

In a bit of a stew after Holland's 2-2 draw with their Group E rivals Mexico, he has decided to pack it all in and follow the gentleman's sport of rugby.

Apparently envious of those rugged chaps and their cauliflower ears, he decided to go a little better and, in a move reminiscent of Royal Ascot, he festooned his lobes with a few carrots.

And that, he told our intrepid reporter, was the root of his problem.

WATCH YOUR LANGUAGE!

1. What does the idiom 'Back to his roots' mean in the context of the photograph and the text?
2. What does it **usually** mean? Write one sentence to illustrate its more general use.
3. There are five other idioms in the text. Can you identify them? Write a brief comment on the meaning and usage of each one, in the context of the article.
4. Do you find this photo funny? If so, explain **why** you think so, in 30–50 words.

Exercise 17

Spelling — silent letter words

Do you remember those silent letter words? Study these examples and then add one more word for each silent letter from the box below.

Example	Silent 'b' — after 'm', as in another word	lamb thumb
1.	Silent 'e' — at the end of a word, as in	late _____
2.	Silent 'g' — before 'n', as in	gnat _____
3.	Silent 'h' — at the beginning of a word, as in	honest _____
4.	Silent 'gh' — at the end of a word, as in	neigh _____
5.	Silent 'k' — before 'n', as in	knee _____
6.	Silent 'l', as in	calf _____
7.	Silent 'n', as in	solemn _____
8.	Silent 'p', as in	physics _____
9.	Silent 's', as in	aisle _____
10.	Silent 'w', as in	wriggle _____

sign, though, half, psychology, gate, autumn, wrong, hour, knot, island

Exercise 18

Spelling — spelling traps

'able/ible' words. Do you remember them? Here's the test!
Write the endings of these words, with either 'able' or 'ible'. Don't guess! Go back and learn them before doing the test if you need to.

BRINGING IT ALL TOGETHER: GRAMMAR, SPELLING, VOCABULARY

1. sens____
2. cap____
3. comfort____
4. leg____
5. respons____
6. fashion____
7. soci____
8. gull____
9. miser____
10. account____

Exercise 19

Spelling — using your dictionary
'accept' or 'except'? Do you remember? Here's the test!
Put the correct word in each space.

1. accept/except?
   (a) We were all there _____ Sean.
   (b) Please _____ my invitation.
2. affect/effect?
   (a) The news of his death will _____ her badly.
   (b) Your stupid insults will have no _____ on me!
3. quite/quiet?
   (a) It's beautifully _____ in here, isn't it?
   (b) You're _____ right, of course.
4. principal/principle?
   (a) Sister Carmel is _____ of Loreto College, Swords.
   (b) 'A _____'s a _____.' (Mary, in *Juno and the Paycock*, by Sean O'Casey)
5. lightning/lightening?
   (a) Thunder and _____ really scare me.
   (b) This room could do with _____ up.

Exercise 20

Spelling — using your dictionary
One word or two? For example, 'maybe' or 'may be'?
Put the correct one in the spaces in these sentences. Don't guess! Check with your dictionary if you are not sure.

1. maybe/may be?
   (a) I _____ late home this evening. Don't wait up.
   (b) _____ she won't like it.
2. anyone/any one?
   (a) Has _____ seen Colm?
   (b) Which one do you want? _____, I don't mind.
3. into/in to?
   (a) Have you been _____ see the dentist yet?
   (b) He went _____ the staffroom five minutes ago.
4. sometimes/some times?
   (a) _____ in my life have been difficult.
   (b) Kids get fed up _____.
5. everyone/every one?
   (a) Will _____ be there?
   (b) Spots! I hate _____ of the little horrors!

WATCH YOUR LANGUAGE!

Exercise 21

Vocabulary — puns

Media studies. Functional writing.

To pun or not to pun! Do you remember 'Words at Play', Unit 8?

Study these two examples. Then answer the questions.

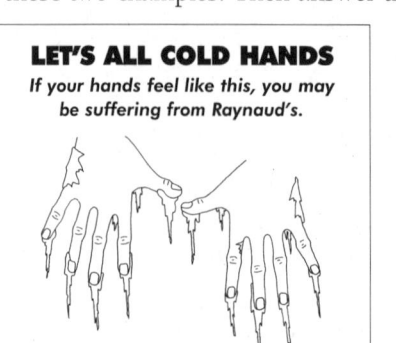

1. **LET'S ALL COLD HANDS**
   If your hands feel like this, you may be suffering from Raynaud's.

   1. Where is the pun in the caption?
   2. What is the original saying?
   3. How effective is the picture in conveying the message? Comment.
   4. What do you learn about Raynaud's disease from the picture and the text?

2. **Oh baby, it's well Dunne!**

   'VALUE Club for Baby' has just been launched by Dunnes Stores.

   It seems as though babies are the hippest thing as far as supermarket loyalty schemes are concerned. It's not long since Tesco launched a new loyalty card called 'Babyclub'.

   Extra

   Value Club for Baby will provide extra benefits to Dunnes Stores VALUE club members (of whom there are over 700,000) who have children under three years old.

   It will apparently provide a range of offers on a number of essential items.

   1. Where is the pun in the headline?
   2. How does it relate to the news story in the text?
   3. How will customers who have children under three benefit from 'Value Club for Baby'?

Exercise 22

Vocabulary — puns again

Functional writing.

Can you compose a witty 'pun' for this picture, which connects the image of the man and the book to the words: 'World Book Day 23 April 1998'?

World Book Day
23 April 1998

BRINGING IT ALL TOGETHER: GRAMMAR, SPELLING, VOCABULARY

Exercise 23

Grammar — past tenses

Write a story based on the following notes. Each section (1–5) represents a **paragraph** in your story, but you may write up to eight sentences per paragraph. Use the past tenses (simple, continuous, present perfect simple and continuous, past perfect simple and continuous) throughout. If in doubt about these, revisit Units 6 and 7 before you begin.

1. Last summer/Brenda and Paul/first holiday abroad, with their three children Sarah, Alan and Stewart.
2. First problem/plane delayed eight hours/sleep at airport. Middle of August/very hot/thousands of people. Paul suffers/claustrophobia. Alan ill. Not/good beginning to the holiday.
3. Plane overbooked/Paul and Brenda/different parts of plane. Brenda in smoking part with kids even though allergic to smoke. Kids/terrified/flying.
4. Get to holiday destination/local representative for travel agent very bad English/hotel dirty/miles from beach. Brenda terrified of rats/one night sees rat in bathroom. Paul gets food poisoning/very ill. Stewart/sunburn and food poisoning.
5. Really angry/extra charges/not mentioned in brochure. Decide never/go to that resort again. Sue travel company/return home.

Exercise 24

Personal writing. Functional writing. Media studies.

Here is a compelling advertisement from the National Drugs Helpline. Make use of it in **one** of the following ways:

(a) Personal writing. Dialogue.
   Write the conversation that takes place between two teenagers who have just read this advertisement. **One** of them has already experimented with ecstasy. The other has not.

(b) Personal writing. Debate/talk.
   Write out the arguments you would make for and against experimenting with drugs.

(c) Media studies. Advertising.
   1. How do you interpret the central message of the ad (Take ecstasy and you're experimenting on yourself)?
   2. Does the picture shock or startle you in any way? Why? How effective is it, in conveying the message?
   3. Examine the text. What is the **main** point being made?

WATCH YOUR LANGUAGE!

Exercise 25

Personal writing. Functional writing. Book review.

> The ancient force of Bealtaine blows on May Day, and fuses life into the scarecrow near Niamh and Daire Durkan's home. But Glasán isn't the only scarecrow to visit them. The Black One has also been awakened by the power of the Bealtaine winds . . . Niamh and Daire find themselves drawn into a dangerous attempt to destroy the evil powers of Greyfang and Deathtooth. And the wolves of Morrigan are in waiting . . .
>
> 'One of the year's most exciting books . . . fast, tense and one I didn't want to finish.'
> **SUNDAY INDEPENDENT**
>
> 'One of the best of its kind for many a long day.'
> **CONSUMER CHOICE**
>
> 'Riveting fantasy . . . a fast-moving tale where no words are wasted. From the awakening of the scarecrow, Glasán, the story moves at an ever-increasing pace with strange incidents, frightening gatherings and terrifying sequences in rapid succession. . . . Absolutely brilliant . . . exciting, funny and adventurous.
> **BOOKS IRELAND**
>
> A magical tale of power and revenge — a blend of high adventure and ancient Irish myth — the first in the Giltspur series.

(a) Read the summary of the plot of this book *The Battle Below Giltspur*, by Cormac Mac Raois, and the **reviews** beneath it.

(b) Write a summary and three mini-reviews (same length as those above) of **any** book you have read which impressed you. Remember to use dots and quotation marks where necessary, as in the above example.

Exercise 26

Vocabulary — word building
Rhyming couples. Just for fun!
The answers to the pairs of clues below rhyme. Can you work them out? (You might be allowed to do this in pairs, with a time limit of ten minutes.) Be warned! They're not all as easy as the example.

Example	large	porker	big	pig
1.	heaven	opposite of low	_____	_____
2.	for thinking	ditch for water	_____	_____
3.	working hard	short for Elizabeth	_____	_____
4.	antique	expensive metal	_____	_____
5.	contented	male parent	_____	_____
6.	to make for eating	this is one!	_____	_____
7.	opposite of warm	stupid/comic person	_____	_____
8.	Irish for book	strength	_____	_____
9.	has gills	plate	_____	_____
10.	agreeable	rodents	_____	_____
11.	greatest	nuisance	_____	_____

12.	boring	bird	_____ _____
13.	in the distance	famous person	_____ _____
14.	lots of boats	famous road	_____ _____
15.	you're here	swimming place	_____ _____

Exercise 27

Functional writing

Write a 'star profile' type article on one member of the group Boyzone for your school magazine **or** local newspaper. Do your research. Find out as much as you can about the person before you write it. If you are not a fan of this group, pick an individual performer or group of your own choice. (200 words approx.)

Exercise 28

Grammar — adjectives, adverbs, verbs

Functional writing

Read this film review, and then answer the following questions.

Directed by Joseph Ruben and starring the stunning Julia Roberts as Laura and Patrick Bergin as her obsessive husband, *Sleeping with the Enemy* is a nerve-wracking thriller.

We first meet Laura at her seafront home where she is unhappily married to a rich handsome man who dominates and abuses her. She fakes death to escape her nightmarish marriage and adopts a new life in a small delightful midwest town, but inevitably her husband discovers the truth and begins to track her down.

Julia Roberts has the difficult task of being a passive victim but manages to come across as innocent and vulnerable. Her reawakening after years of torment is captured extremely sensitively. Patrick Bergin is frighteningly convincing as the psychopathic husband. He appears and disappears with economy of movement and sinister menace.

The story is quite similar to *Fatal Attraction*, but the characters are well observed and there are some imaginative moments. Although Ruben is a little too free with the fraudulent moments of suspense, the film jangles the nerves effectively with a series of shocks, which successfully disguises a rather weak plot.

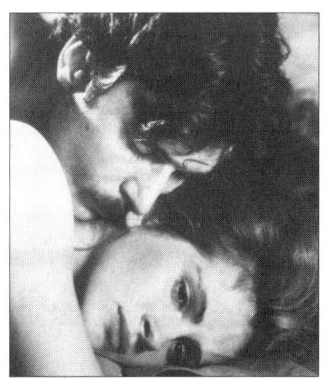

I would recommend this as an entertaining film for those who like to be kept on the edge of their seats.

---

1. In which paragraph does the reviewer talk about:
    (a) the plot
    (b) the performances
    (c) the background to the film?
2. Why is the review written in the present tense?
3. Make a list of the **adjectives** and **adverbs** used to describe the Julia Roberts character, Laura, her husband and the film in general.

WATCH YOUR LANGUAGE!

4. (a) Choose a film, TV programme, book or play and decide on the adjectives and adverbs you would use to describe the **characters** and the **story**.

    Example   exciting, hilarious, terrifying (adjectives)
    successfully, frighteningly, convincingly (adverbs)

    (b) Write a similar review to the one you've just read. You may use adjectives and adverbs from the above review, as well as those you exercised in Units 3 and 4.

    (c) Be aware of the excellent **verbs** used in the film review also, for example directed, starring, dominates, fakes, escapes. **Use** them — and others from Units 5 and 6 — in your review.

Exercise 29

Vocabulary — hyphenated words. Personal writing.

Study the photograph below. Then write your reaction to it in the form of an essay **or** a poem, using some of the hyphenated words below, and the words 'New Life' as your title.

Peace at last . . . as the finishing touches are put to a mural on the Shankill Road in Belfast.

1. Anglo-Irish
2. anti-climax
3. anti-social
4. by-product
5. by-election
6. broad-minded
7. cine-camera
8. cold-blooded
9. cold-hearted
10. counter-attack
11. cross-section
12. go-between
13. hair-raising
14. head-on
15. law-abiding
16. long-reaching
17. narrow-minded
18. non-committal
19. non-existent
20. non-stop
21. North-South
22. old-fashioned
23. one-sided
24. pent-up
25. pig-headed
26. pigeon-hole
27. point-blank
28. self-assured
29. self-centred
30. self-confident
31. self-conscious
32. self-contained
33. sell-out
34. short-sighted
35. single-handed
36. single-minded
37. small-minded
38. three-dimensional
39. two-dimensional
40. warm-hearted
41. well-being
42. well-meaning

BRINGING IT ALL TOGETHER: GRAMMAR, SPELLING, VOCABULARY

Exercise 30

Vocabulary and spelling — confusing words

And finally . . . the last instalment of 'The World According to Student Bloopers'! When you read it, you will see that it doesn't **always** make sense! Can you **rewrite** it so that it reads as a clear (if rather sketchy) version of these periods of history? Correct any spelling errors as you go. Have fun!

> Meanwhile in Europe, the enlightenment was a reasonable time. Voltare invented electricity and also wrote a book called Candy. Gravity was invented by Isaac Walton. It is chiefly noticeable in the Autumn, when the apples are falling off the trees.
>
> Bach was the most famous composer in the world and so was Handel. Handel was half German, half Italian, and half English. He was very large. Bach died from 1750 to the present. Beethoven wrote music even though he was deaf. He was deaf so he wrote loud music. He took long walks in the forest even when everyone was calling for him. Beethoven expired in 1827 and later died for this.
>
> France was in a very serious state. The French Revolution was accomplished before it happened. The Marseillaise was the theme song of the French Revolution, and it catapulted into Napoleon. During the Napoleonic Wars, the crowned heads of Europe were trembling in their shoes. Then the Spanish gorillas camed down from the hills and nipped at Napoleon's flanks. Napoleon became ill with bladder problems and was very tense and unrestrained. He wanted an heir to inherit his power, but since Josephine was a baroness, she couldn't bear children.
>
> The sun never set on the British Empire because the British Empire is in the East and the sun sets in the West. Queen Victoria was the longest queen. She sat on a thorn for 63 years. Her reclining years and finally the end of her life were exemplatory of a great personality. Her death was the final event which ended her reign.
>
> The nineteenth century was a time of many great inventions and thoughts. The invention of the steam boat caused a network of rivers to spring up. Cyrus McCormick invented the McCormick raper, which did the work of a hundred men. Samuel Morse invented a code of telepathy. Louis Pasteur discovered a cure for rabbis. Charles Darwin was a naturalist who wrote the Organ of the Species. Madman Curie discovered radium. And Karl Marx became one of the Marx brothers.
>
> The First World War, caused by the assignation of the Arch-Duck by a surf, ushered in a new error in the anals of human history.

WATCH YOUR LANGUAGE!

EXAM HINTS

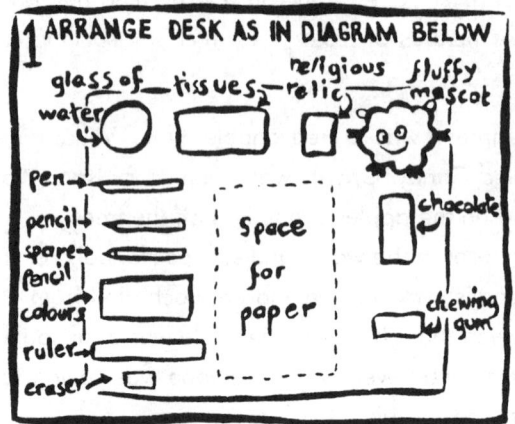

1. ARRANGE DESK AS IN DIAGRAM BELOW
- glass of water
- tissues
- religious relic
- fluffy mascot
- pen
- pencil
- spare pencil
- colours
- ruler
- eraser
- chocolate
- chewing gum
- Space for paper

2. SAY THANK YOU AND SMILE AT SUPERVISOR WHEN GIVEN PAPER
THANK YOU

3. MAKE FUNNY FACES AT FRIENDS TO SHOW IGNORANCE OF SUBJECT

4. READ ALL THE QUESTIONS

5. DO QUESTIONS ONE, FIVE AND SEVEN.

6. ASK TO BE EXCUSED AND READ NOTES (HIDDEN IN EAR)
may I be excused?

7. TELL EVERYONE YOU DID VERY BADLY
I don't care! / I KNOW I failed! / Sure I did NO study!

Spellbound